IMAGES
of America

PRINCETON

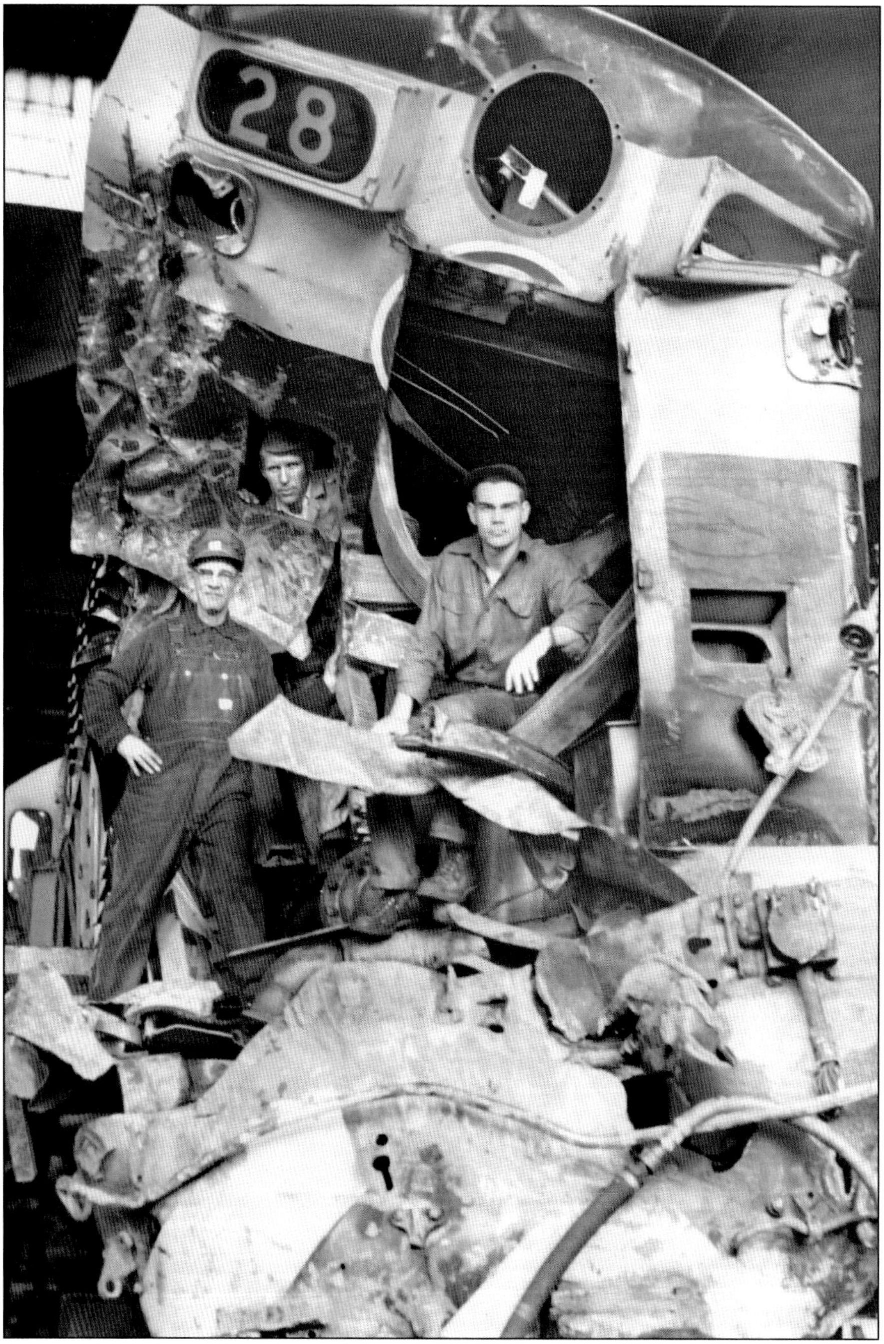

WRECK OF THE OLD 28. Workers of the Virginian Railroad Princeton Car Shops are shown here posing for a photograph by Virginian photograph chronicler Ernest "E. R." Belcher. Morris Smith (left) and Buck Hatcher (inside wreckage) are shown here with an unidentified apprentice. (Courtesy of Randolph Belcher.)

ON THE COVER: Alfred Lucas, Princeton chief of police, is shown on Mercer Street. See page 78 for more information.

IMAGES
of America

PRINCETON

William R. "Bill" Archer

ARCADIA
PUBLISHING

ISBN 978-0-7385-4251-5

Published by Arcadia Publishing
Charleston, South Carolina

Printed in the United States of America

Library of Congress Catalog Card Number: 2005938869

For all general information contact Arcadia Publishing at:
Telephone 843-853-2070
Fax 843-853-0044
E-mail sales@arcadiapublishing.com
For customer service and orders:
Toll-Free 1-888-313-2665

Visit us on the Internet at www.arcadiapublishing.com

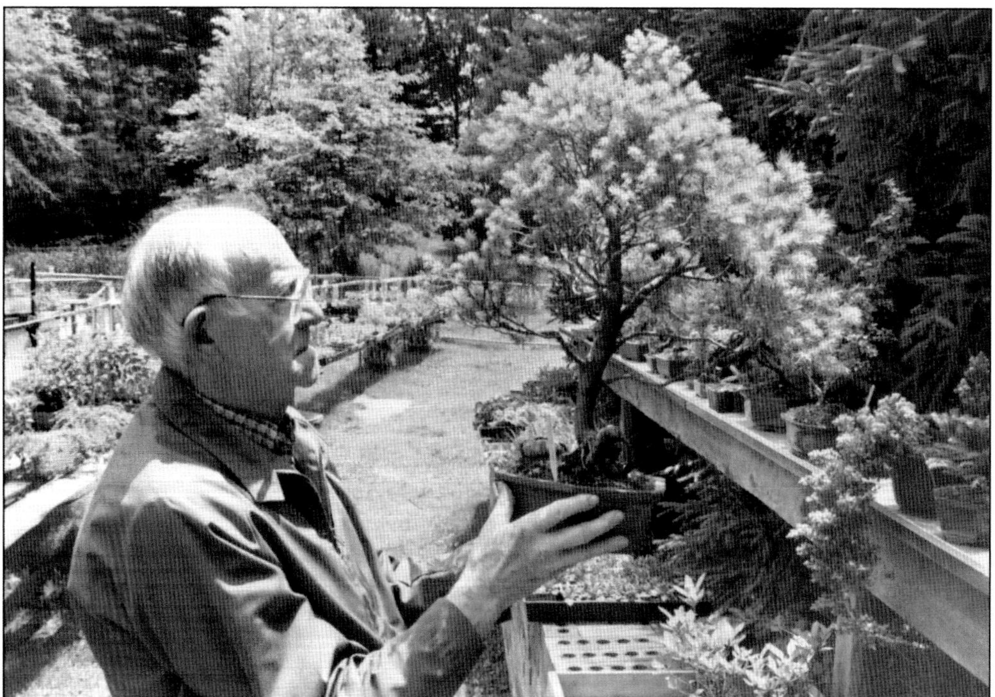

POWER IN DETAIL. Paul Broyles Sr. is shown here examining a bonsai plant at Broyles Gardens. The Broyles family has brought beauty to Princeton and the surrounding area for generations. Paul and his wife, Mary, opened Broyles Gardens in 1945. The nursery is still operated by Paul II and Rebecca Broyles. (Photograph by the author.)

Contents

INTRODUCTION

The city of Princeton can be defined by its resilience. The city grew from a very humble origin. Princeton was founded in 1837 to serve as the county seat of Mercer County, Virginia. At the time, the city's footprint was covered with brush, timber, and a scant few rustic residences. The nearest actual settlement was at Gladeville, about a mile from the courthouse on the New Hope Road. It was there that representatives of Giles, Tazewell, Logan, and Greenbrier Counties decided on the name Princeton. On March 17, 1837, the Virginia General Assembly named the county in honor of Revolutionary War general Hugh Mercer, who died as a result of wounds he received in the Battle of Princeton, New Jersey.

Development was slow in the early days, and the county seat was still sparsely settled at the start of the American Civil War. The majority of Mercer County residents supported the Confederate cause even though Mercer would be one of the 55 counties of western Virginia that split from the Old Dominion to form West Virginia in 1863. Confederates occupied Princeton until early May 1862, when a Union army moved south from Charleston, West Virginia, on its way to destroy the Virginia and Tennessee Railroad.

Confederate colonel W. H. Jennifer, commander of the 8th Virginia Cavalry, was in Mercer County at the time of the advance. He ordered Princeton burned to prevent the advancing Yankees from using its supplies and houses. The Union soldiers helped Princeton residents battle the structure fires and managed to save two residences, the McNutt home on North Walker Street and the David Hall residence, known as Aspenwold, on Douglas Street. Lt. Col. Rutherford B. Hayes, commander of the 23rd Ohio Infantry, characterized Princeton in a dispatch to Brig. Gen. Jacob D. Cox as "a lovely spot, a fine, clean village; most beautiful and romantic surrounding country, polite and educated sech people."

The Confederate forces regrouped to the south, east, and west, advanced on Princeton on May 16, 1862, and occupied the high hill to the south of the courthouse overlooking the town—a place called Pigeon Roost. The following day, Union reinforcements arrived and enabled the soldiers under Cox's command to establish a defensive position at Flat Top, 25 miles north of Princeton. Cox's losses in the engagement at Pigeon Roost included 23 dead, 64 wounded, and 21 missing, while Brig. Gen. Humphrey Marshall, commander of the Confederate defenders, reported 4 killed, 20 wounded, and 1 missing. The Union dead were buried near the intersection of North Walker and Douglas Streets but were later moved to Arlington. The Confederate dead were buried in Princeton's Oakwood Cemetery on West Main Street, where they remain.

The devastation of the war had a profound impact on Princeton. With a few exceptions, most of the city's leaders had been staunch supporters of the Confederacy. The "test oath"—a required statement of allegiance to the federal government—of the Reconstruction period that followed the war prohibited many pre-war civic leaders who served in the Confederate army from voting or participating in post-war public affairs. During the persistent troubles that prevailed during the post-war period, the town of Athens gained county control from Princeton, but on February 26, 1867, the state legislature made Princeton the permanent county seat.

The West Virginia State Legislature finally restored voting rights to former Confederate soldiers in 1870, and by then, Collis P. Huntington had pushed his Chesapeake and Ohio Railway (C&O) into the New River coalfields, providing jobs for willing workers. Ten years later, the Norfolk and Western Railroad (N&W) pushed through to Bluefield in 1882, luring additional Mercer County residents to rail and coal jobs in that part of the county.

Perhaps the most noteworthy event in Princeton from the end of the Civil War until the dawn of the 20th century remains the long-held myth that Frank James, one of the notorious James Gang members, visited Princeton in 1882 and spent the night at the home of Judge David E. Johnston, who was the attorney for the Princeton Bank and Trust (PB&T) at the time. Longtime *Princeton Times* editor Kyle McCormick debunked the story, but others, including prominent Princeton businessman and civic leader H. W. Straley, claimed that James passed up the opportunity to rob the PB&T because of its insignificant and dilapidated appearance and because Johnston—like Frank and his brother, Jesse James—served in the Confederate army.

Just as things were looking bleak for Princeton, one of the nation's most successful financial visionaries put his stamp on the city by making it part of the greatest single accomplishment of his illustrious career. Henry Huttleston Rogers was an inventor and a seasoned oil man who built a successful oil refinery in New York. In the mid-1870s, John D. Rockefeller acquired Rogers's company and made it part of his Standard Oil empire. Rogers stayed with Rockefeller and moved up the corporate ladder to the position of vice president in 1890. Of course, Rogers had other industrial interests including Consolidated Gas and the National Transit Company—a pipeline company to transport oil great distances.

Princeton figured prominently in Rogers's creation of the Virginian Railway, a railroad that occupied the middle ground between the C&O (now CSX) to the north and the N&W (now Norfolk Southern) to the south. Shrouded in secrecy that included a February 1904 survey team comprised of 125 engineers who claimed to be fishermen, Rogers personally financed the $40 million necessary to build the railroad, then stamped it with his personal commitment to power and efficiency. From Deepwater, West Virginia, through Princeton and on to Sewalls Point, Virginia, the Virginian Railway represented the best track bed and most powerful equipment known to man in the first decade of the 20th century. Rogers located the Virginian's car shops in Princeton and challenged the workers to use power to get West Virginia coal to foreign and domestic markets.

Rogers, who also served as Mark Twain's (Samuel L. Clemens) manager in the last years of the great author's life, started planning the Virginian in 1902. Tragically Rogers only lived long enough to take one inspection tour of the road on April 6, 1909. He was stricken with paralysis the following month and died at age 69 on May 19, 1909. Twain made some highly publicized visits to Rogers's railroad prior to its completion. The Virginian carried West Virginia coal to domestic and foreign customers until December 1959, when Norfolk Southern acquired the line. The Princeton Car Shop remained in action for several years but was downsized and finally closed in the early 1980s. The culture of power and efficiency created by Rogers still remains as his legacy to generations steeped in the Virginian tradition.

Even before the decline of passenger service on the Virginian and the N&W, Princeton benefited as the southern terminus of the 88-mile long West Virginia Turnpike when it opened November 8, 1954. It would take another 20 years until Interstate 77 would be completed south to Columbia, South Carolina, with the December 20, 1974, opening of the H. Edward Steele Memorial Tunnel, but with improvements to U.S. Route 460, the main east-west highway in the region, Princeton found itself at the nexus of a major highway crossroads.

Other businesses and industry flourished in Princeton during the apex of the Virginian's power. The Dean Company, a high-end wood veneering company, enjoyed several years of industry leadership, and New York–based Maidenform Inc., a bra manufacturer, established its first plant outside of New York at Princeton in 1943 during World War II, employing as many as 500 people at one point in its long run. North American Rockwell, a producer of electrical components, operated a facility in Princeton for several years. The 58-bed Memorial Hospital, which served the community for many years, gave way to the modern Princeton Community Hospital.

At the dawn of the new millennium, Princeton has embarked on a new era of re-invention. The community has embarked on a restoration and rejuvenation effort including restoring the old Virginian passenger station and the East Mercer Streetscape project. At the same time, the Chuck Mathena Center for the Arts is rapidly rising to take its place on the Princeton skyline. Princeton has always been a hub of commerce, and new businesses are continuing that tradition. Modern motels and restaurants just outside city limits serve the local trade and the traveling public.

Princeton is not easily defined, but the community continues to demonstrate its resilience by meeting its challenges head on and positioning itself for future growth. The "lovely spot" that Rutherford B. Hayes wrote of 15 years before he was elected president of the United States in 1877 continues to survive and thrive in the first decade of the 21st century.

One

MAKINGS OF A CITY

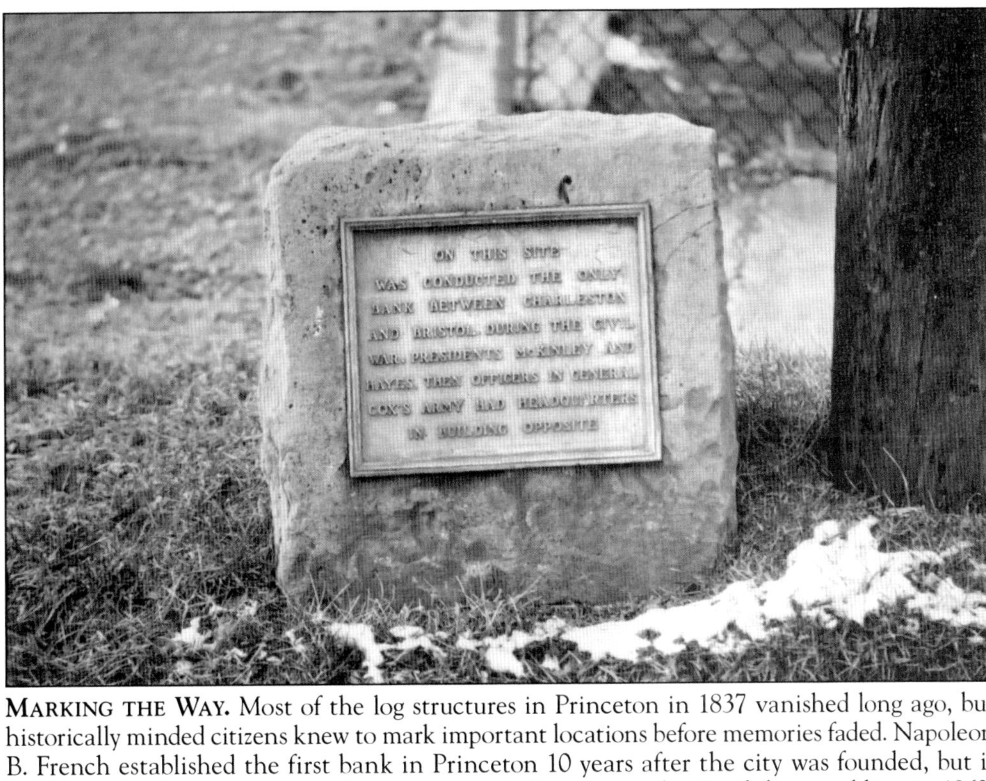

MARKING THE WAY. Most of the log structures in Princeton in 1837 vanished long ago, but historically minded citizens knew to mark important locations before memories faded. Napoleon B. French established the first bank in Princeton 10 years after the city was founded, but it was burned—along with most other structures in Princeton—by Confederate soldiers in 1862. (Photograph by the author.)

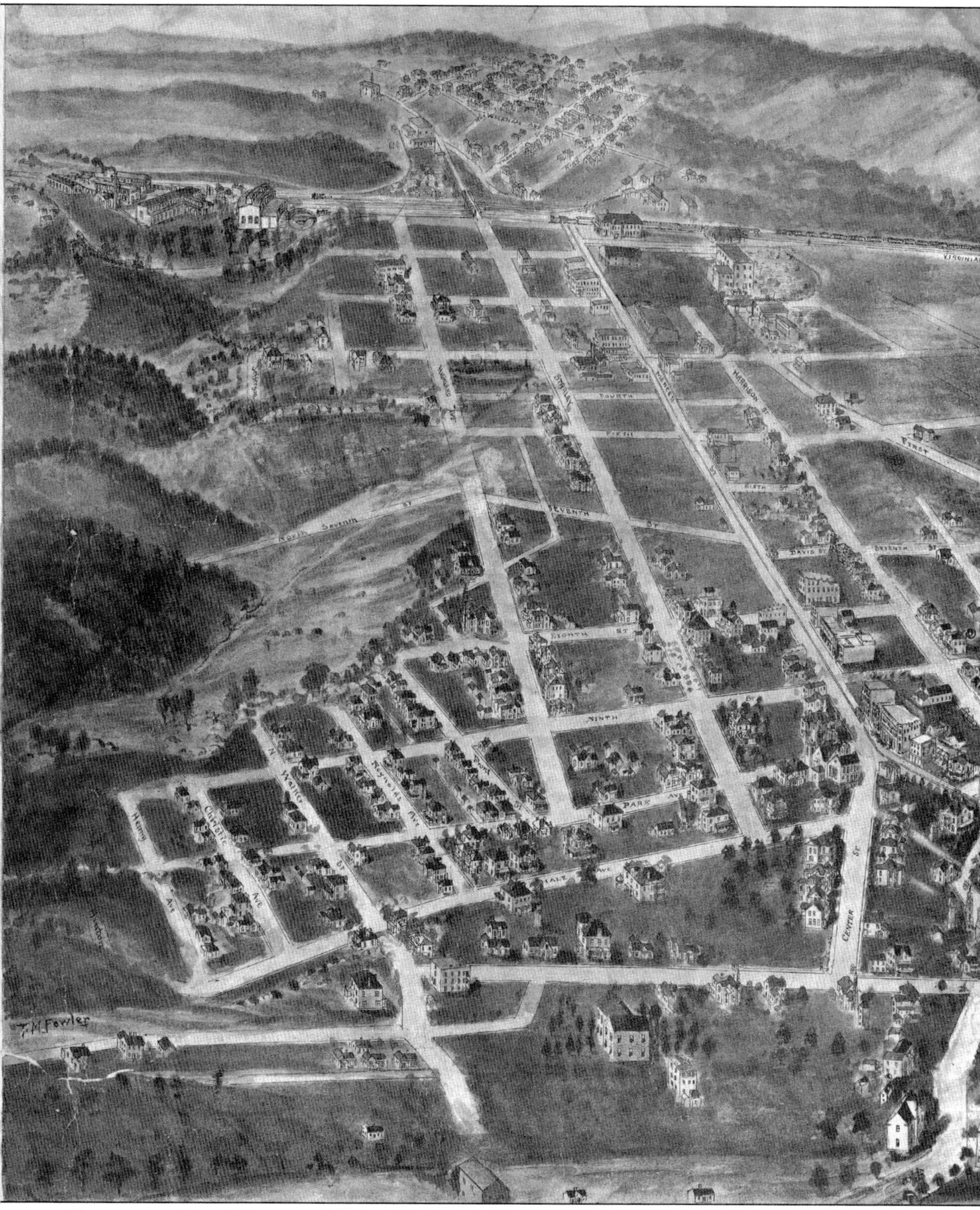

THIS IS THE CITY. This incredible map of Princeton in 1911 drawn by T. M. Fowler of Flemington, New Jersey, was initially in the possession of the Pioneer Coal Company but eventually came to the late W. G. "Grady" Carper. His son, William G. "Bill" Carper gave it to a well-known Princeton-based architect, Todd Boggess. The map has incredible detail, including the Tri-City Traction trolley line, the budding Virginian Railway Princeton Car Shops, the Mercer County

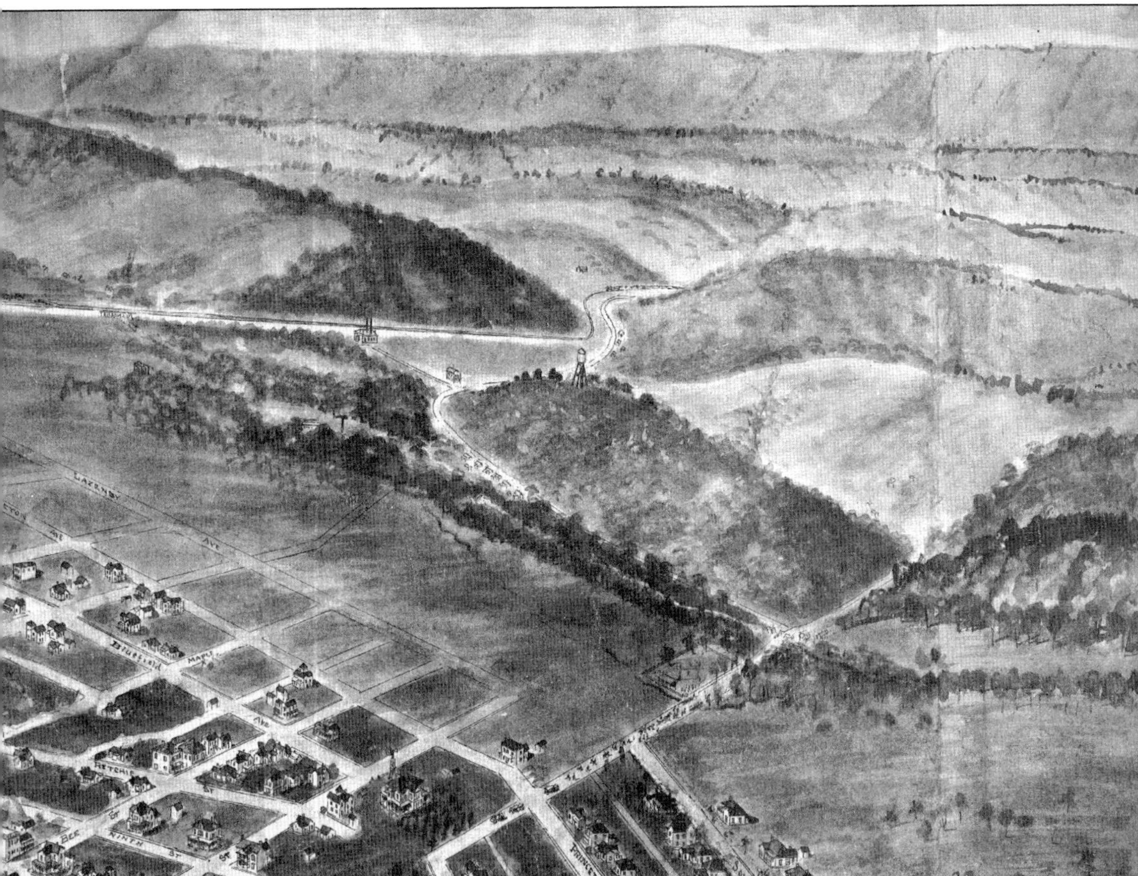

Courthouse, and other landmarks of great historical significance. It's interesting to note that M. W. Christie was city recorder; the Stag Clothiers and Haberdashers, managed by G. C. Bowling, was on Mercer Street; the J. H. Lilly and A. T. Caperton real estate offices were both promoting timber lands; and C. Mosrie and Company had a grocery store on Walker Street. (Courtesy of Todd Boggess.)

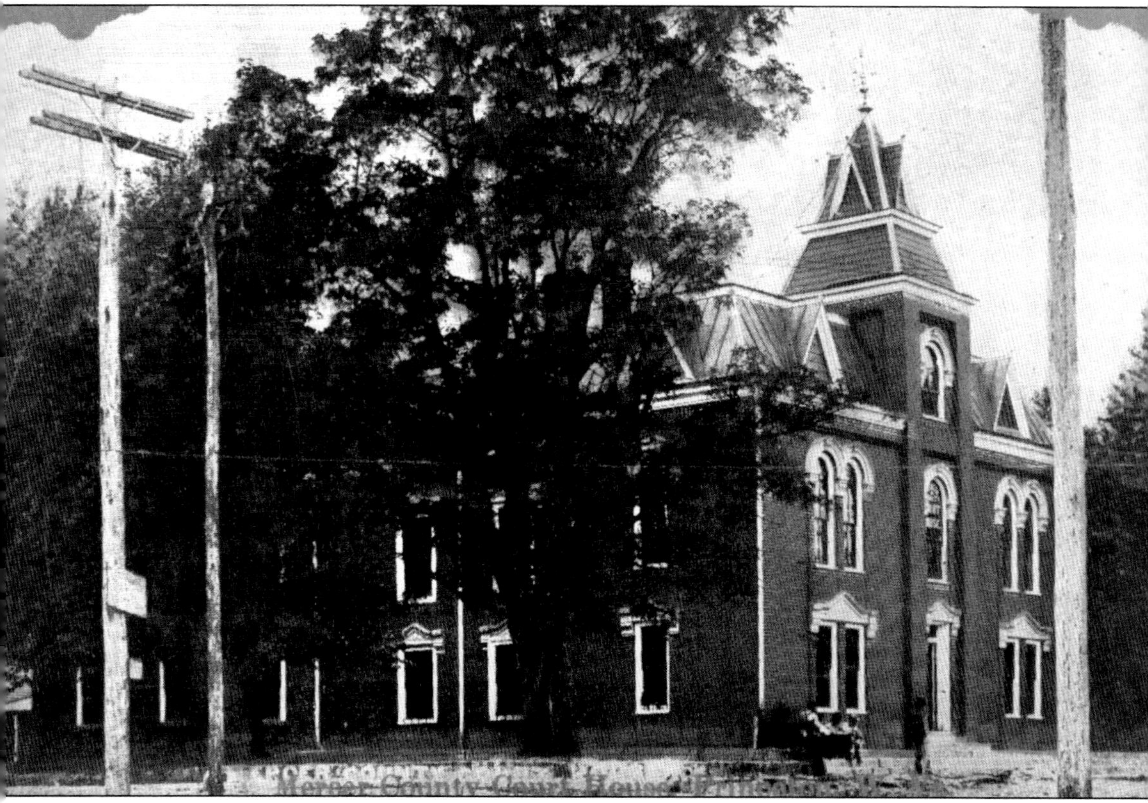

ORDER IN THE COURT. Princeton was established as the county seat of Mercer County, which was created on March 17, 1837, out of portions of Giles, Tazewell, Greenbrier, and Logan Counties by the Virginia General Assembly. Confederate soldiers set the original courthouse on fire and destroyed it in 1862 to prevent an advancing Union army from occupying it. (Courtesy of Mel Grubb.)

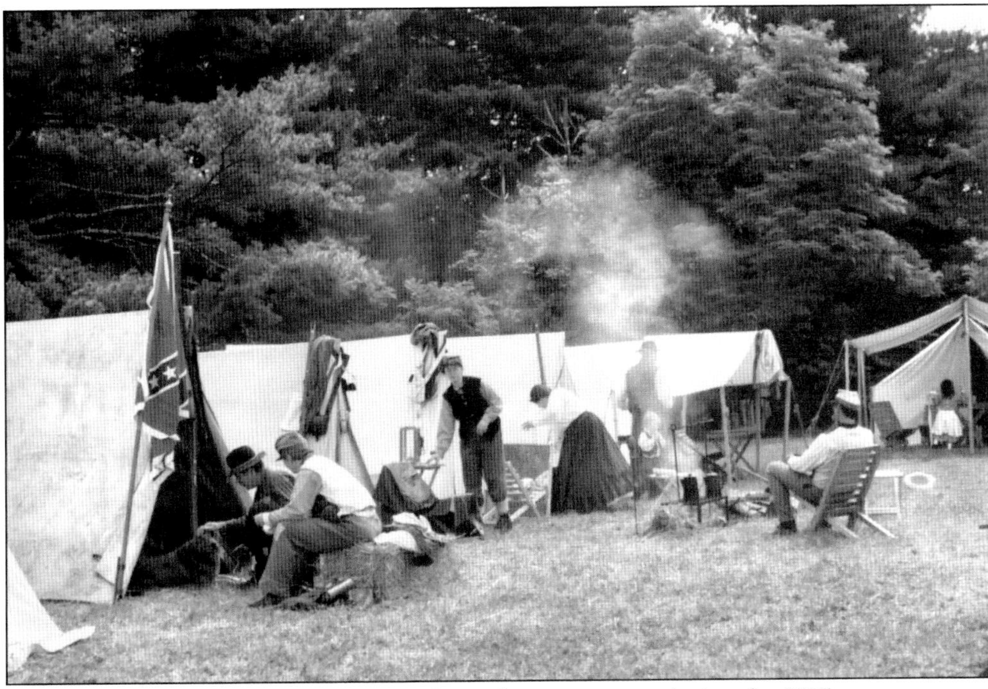

REBEL CAMP. Civil War reenactors are shown here at a camp during the 1995 reenactment of the May 17, 1862, Battle of Pigeon Roost. The late Carlton Smith and his wife, Shirley Smith, thoroughly researched the battle prior to the event. (Courtesy of Shirley Smith.)

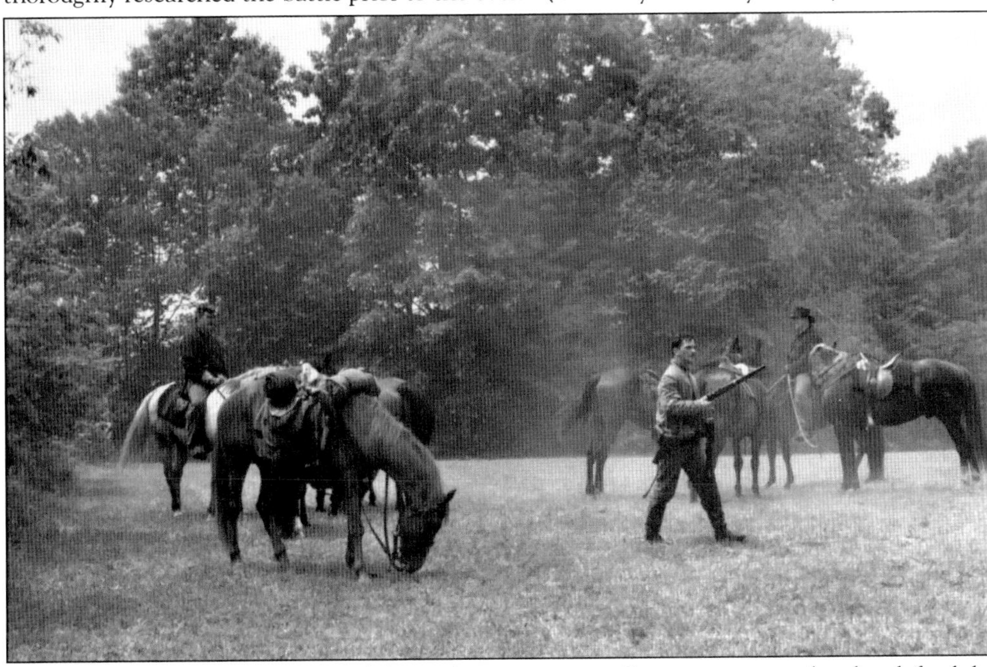

DEFEND THE RAILROAD. The Confederate forces occupying Princeton were ordered to defend the Virginia and Tennessee Railroad from an advancing Union army. Two men who would become U.S. presidents were among the Union occupiers of Princeton—Lt. Col. Rutherford B. Hayes and Lt. William McKinley, both of the 23rd Ohio Infantry. (Courtesy of Shirley Smith.)

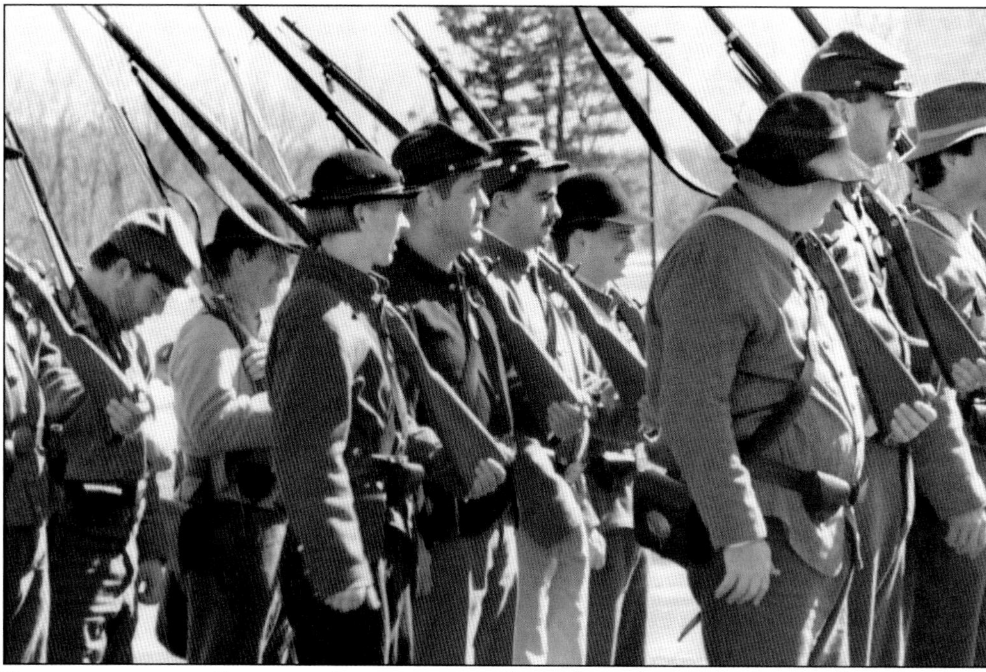

Brother against Brother. Reenactors are shown here during the Battle of Pigeon Roost reenactment in 1995. Mercer County was galvanized in its support of the South and sent 10 companies into Confederate service during the war. (Courtesy of Shirley Smith.)

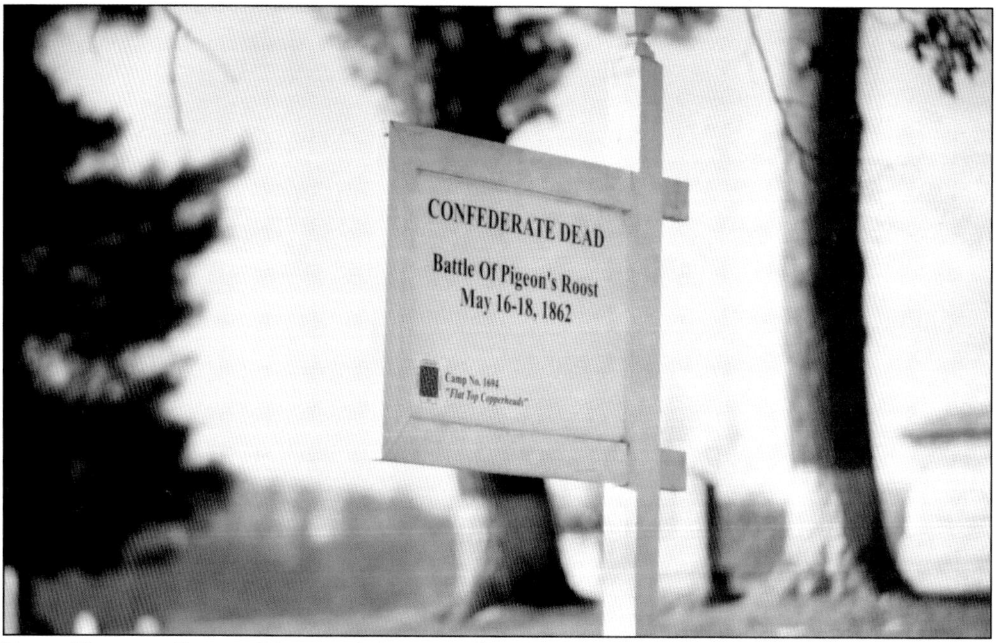

Final Resting Place. The Confederates suffered 4 soldiers killed in action during the Battle of Pigeon Roost, and 23 Union soldiers were killed in action. The Confederate soldiers were buried at Oakwood Cemetery, and the Union soldiers were buried at the corner of North Walker Street at Douglas Street but were later removed and reburied at Arlington National Cemetery. (Photograph by the author.)

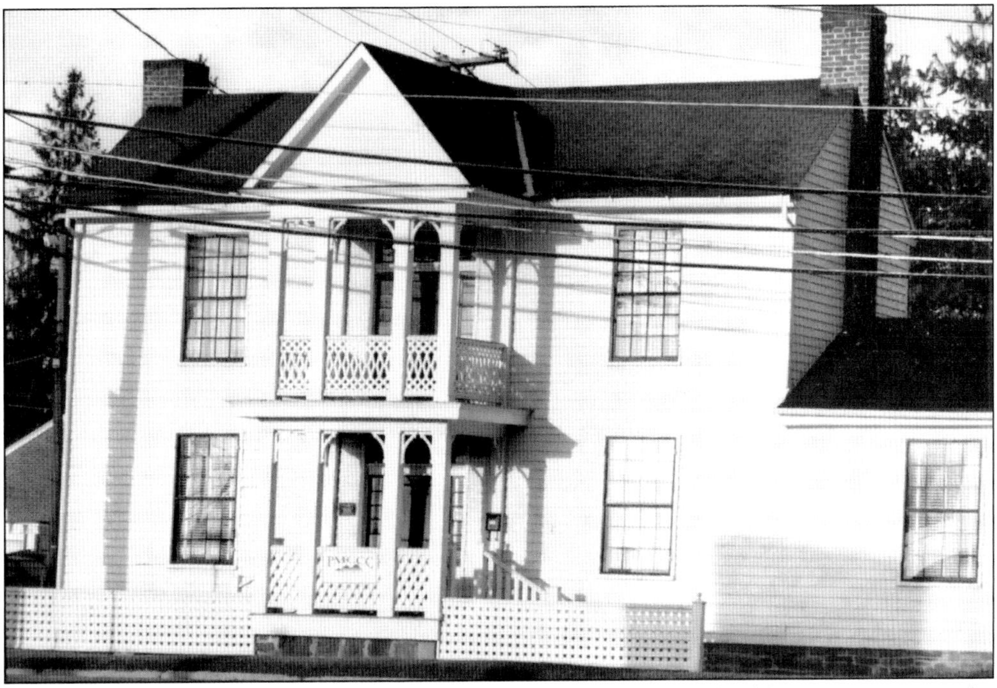

McNutt Home. The withdrawing Confederates burned all but two buildings in Princeton: the McNutt home, shown here, and the David Hall residence, called Aspenwold. The McNutt home was recently transformed into offices for the Princeton–Mercer County Chamber of Commerce. (Photograph by the author.)

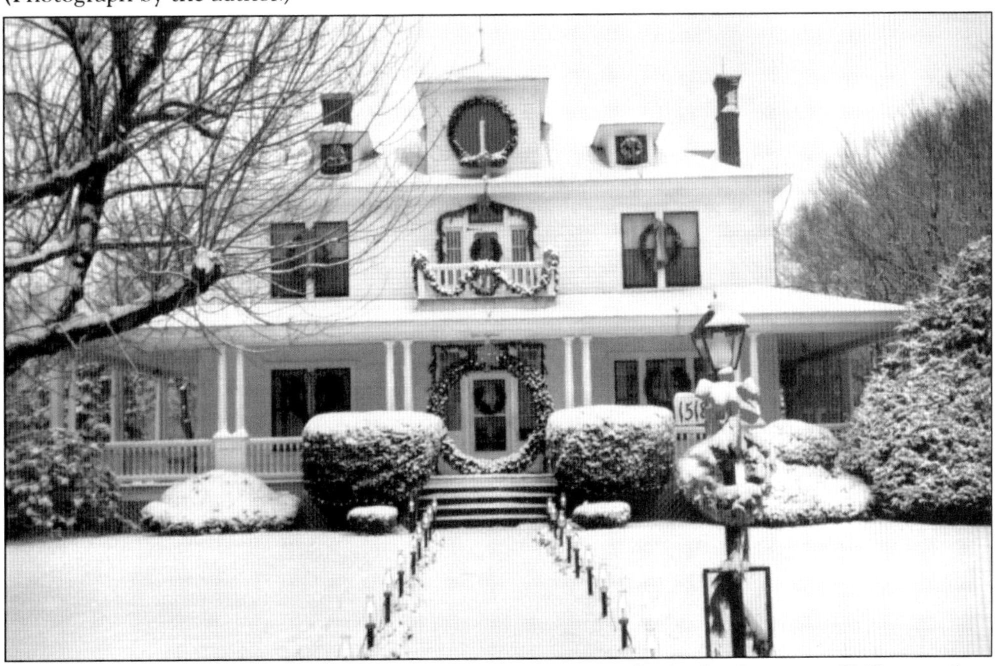

The Princeton Inn. A son of Dr. Robert Blaine McNutt built this house in 1903 next door to the original McNutt home. It is now the home of Jo Anna and Ott Fredeking. (Courtesy of Jo Anna Fredeking.)

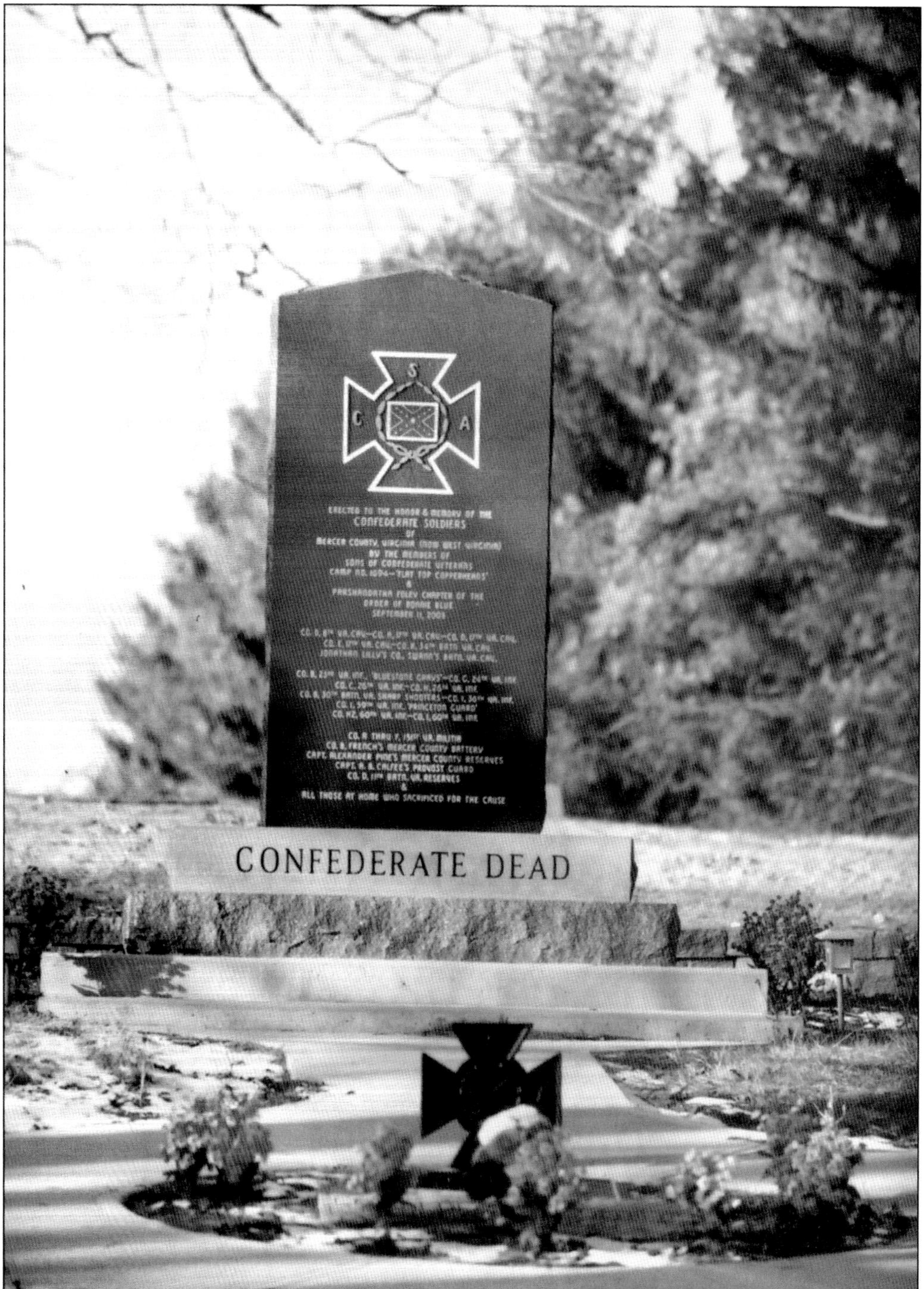

HONORED DEAD. The Mercer County chapter of the Sons of Confederate Veterans, Camp 1694, "Flat Top Copperheads," and the Parshandatha Foley Chapter of the Order of the Bonnie Blue dedicated this monument in memory of the Confederate veterans buried in Oakwood Cemetery on September 11, 2003. (Photograph by the author.)

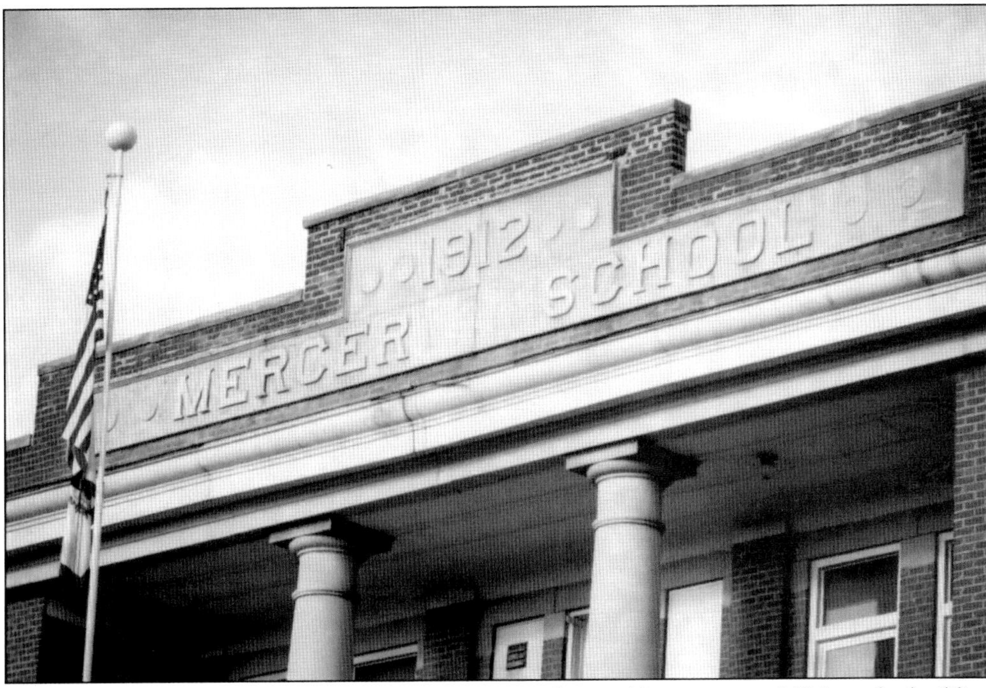

OLD SCHOOL. Mercer School continues to serve students of Princeton in 2006, as the building itself draws closer to its centennial. The school has been serving as an elementary school for the past several years. (Photograph by the author.)

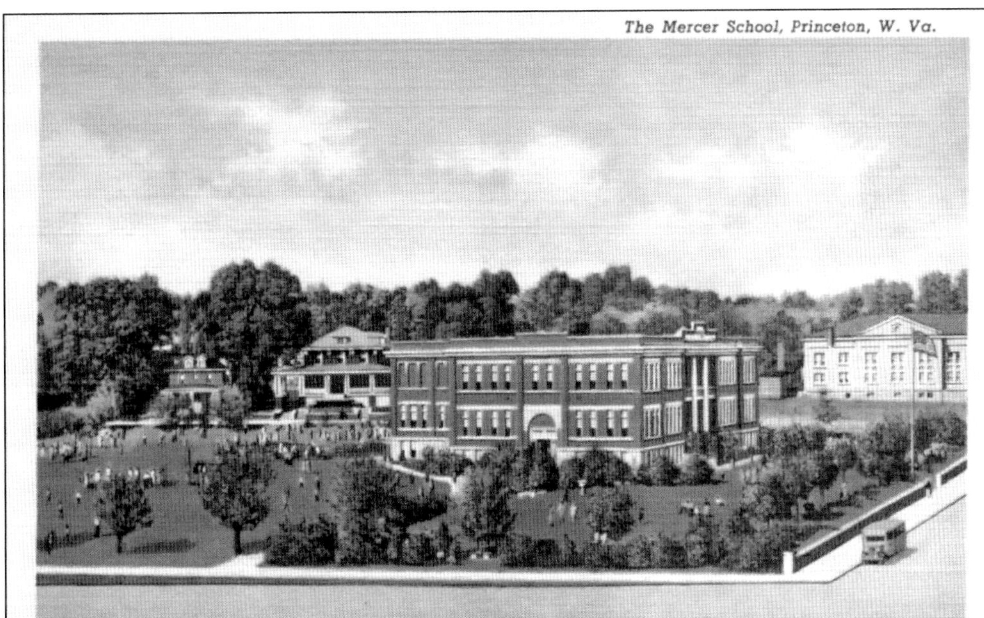

READING, WRITING, AND RIGHT PRETTY. Despite a constantly changing environment, Mercer School remains as one of the region's most beautiful settings for education in Mercer County. (Courtesy of Winfrey Shrewsbury.)

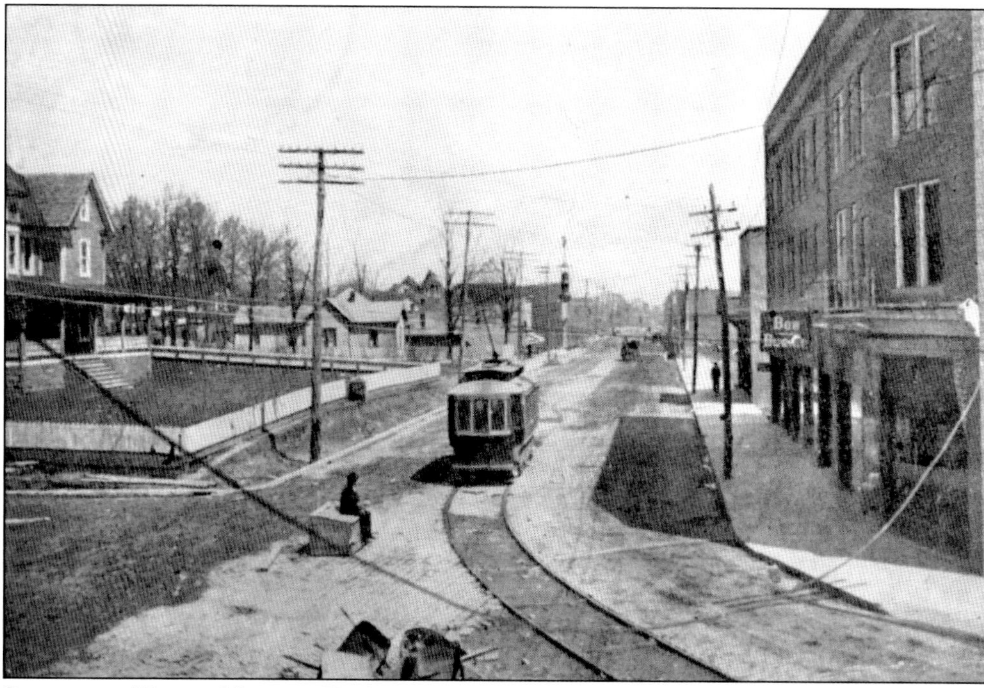

STREETCAR NAMED MERCER. Tri-City Traction operated passenger service between Princeton and Bluefield, West Virginia, and Graham, Virginia, starting near the end of the first decade of the 20th century. The lines served the communities until the late 1920s and early 1930s. (Courtesy of Vernon Fields.)

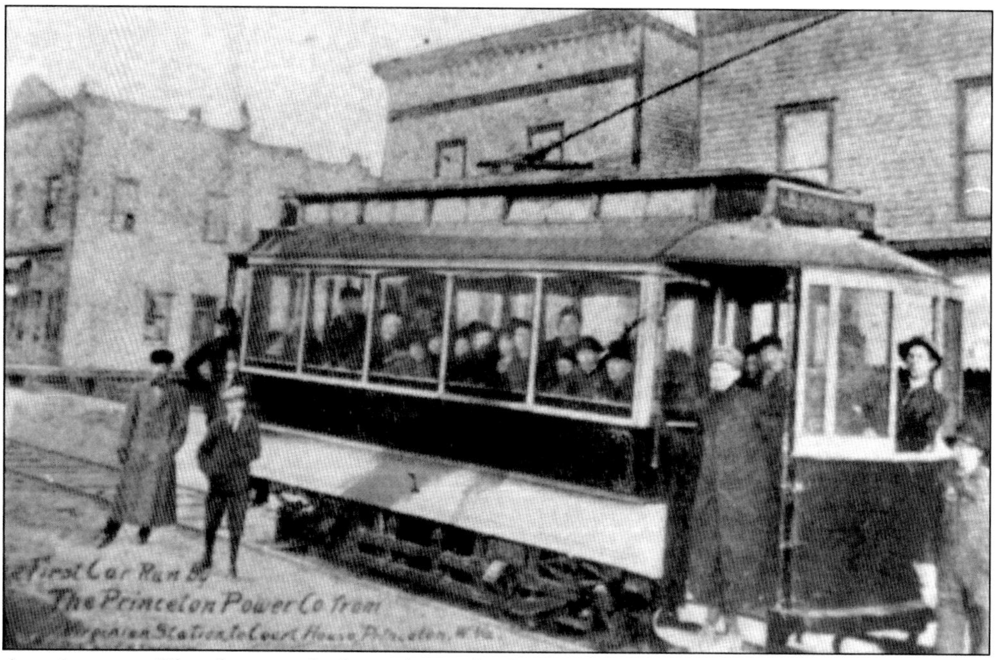

ALL ABOARD. The photograph above shows the first streetcar for Princeton Power Company to provide service from the Virginian railway station on East Mercer Street to the county courthouse. (Courtesy of Mercer County Historical Society.)

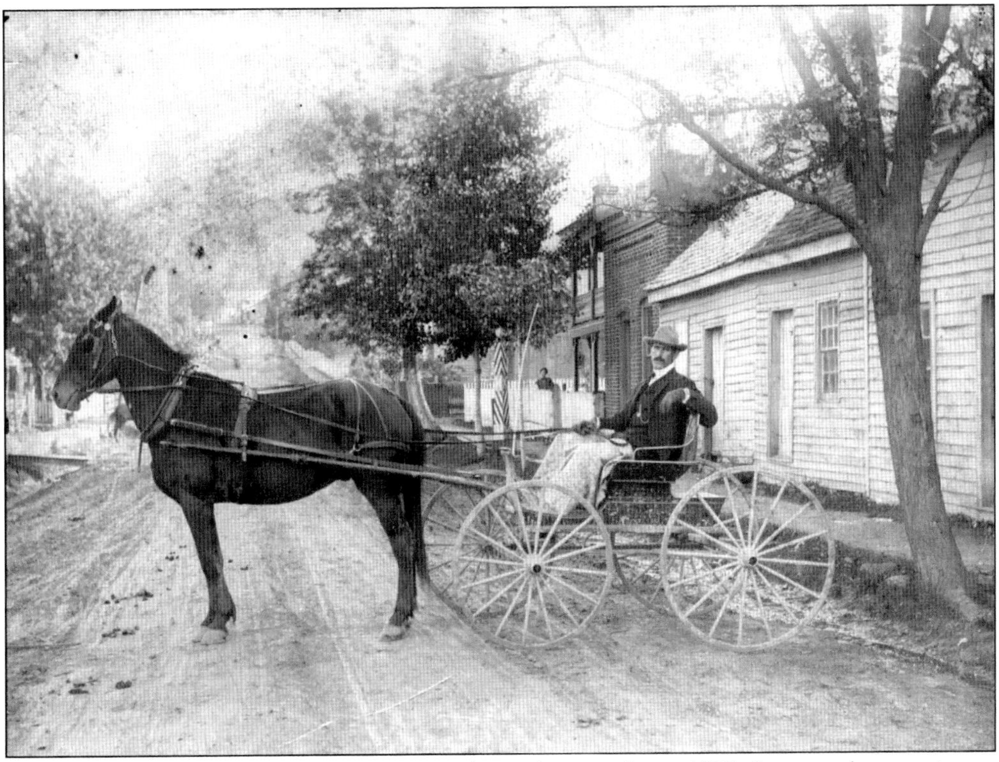

OUT ON THE TOWN. William N. Looney is shown here in this *c.* 1905 photograph preparing to take a ride down Straley Avenue. (Courtesy of Bill Looney.)

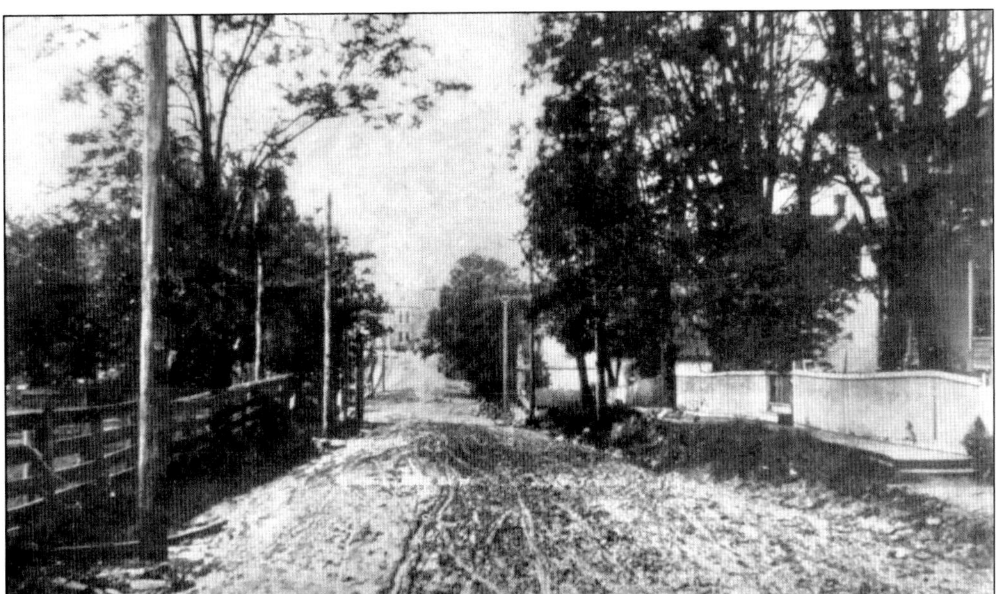

BEFORE PAVING. This Walker Street scene shows a city street in Princeton before streets of the city were paved. (Courtesy of the Mercer County Historical Society.)

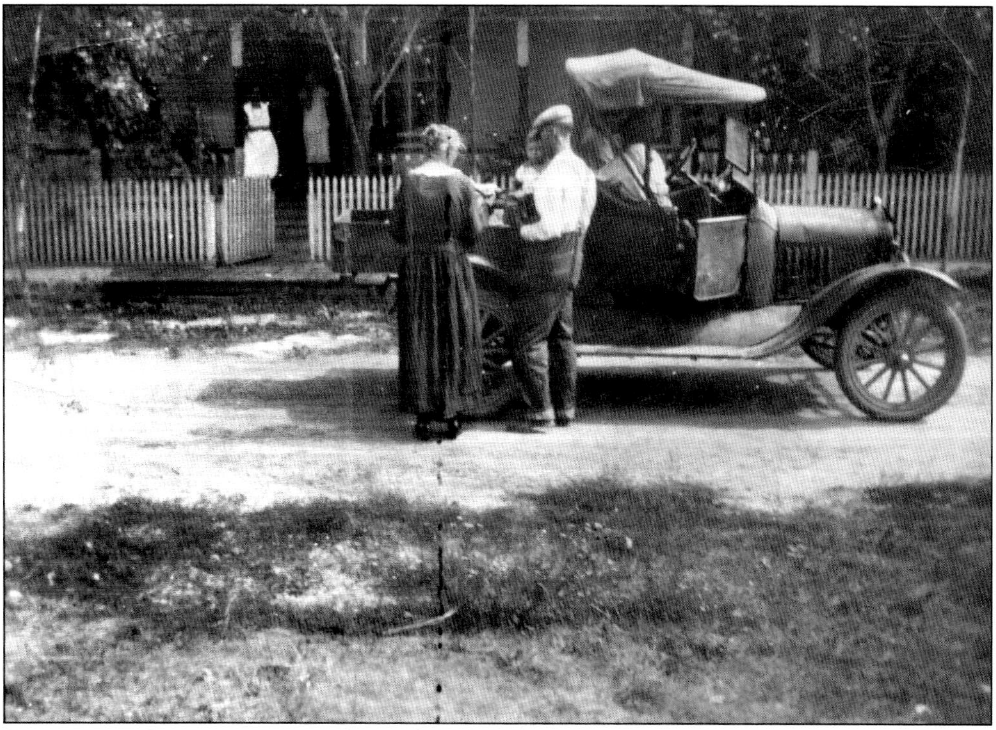

STREET-SIDE SHOPPING. Mrs. John B. (Elizabeth) Day is shown here in front of her Bluefield Avenue home on September 3, 1925, shopping for meats from a peddler known in the community as Mr. Weaver. (Courtesy of Sheila Shorter.)

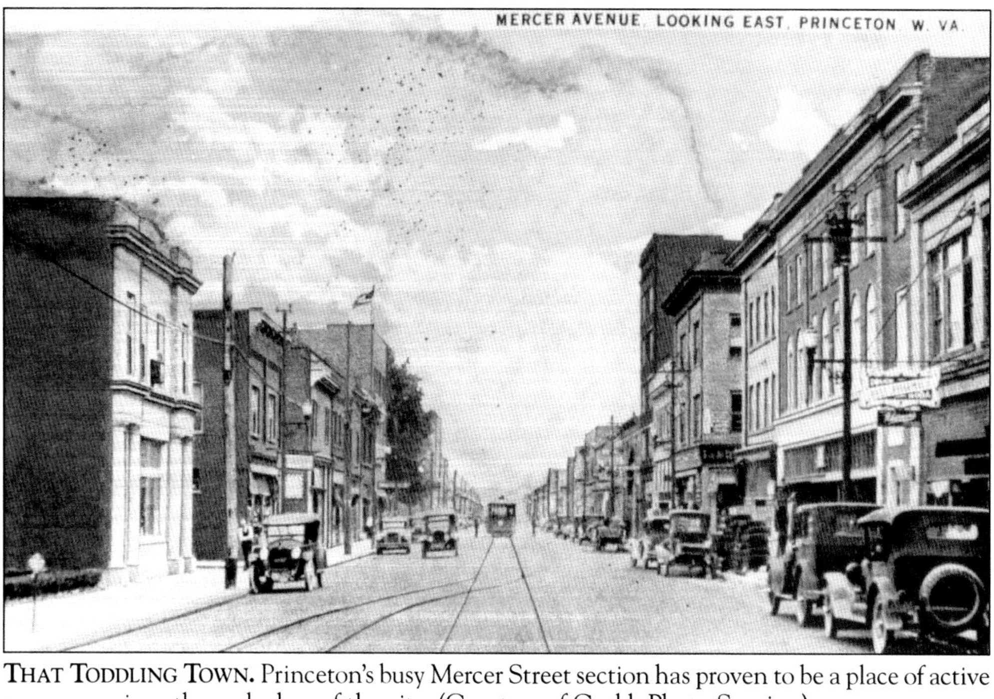

THAT TODDLING TOWN. Princeton's busy Mercer Street section has proven to be a place of active commerce since the early days of the city. (Courtesy of Grubb Photo Service.)

Two

THE VIRGINIAN

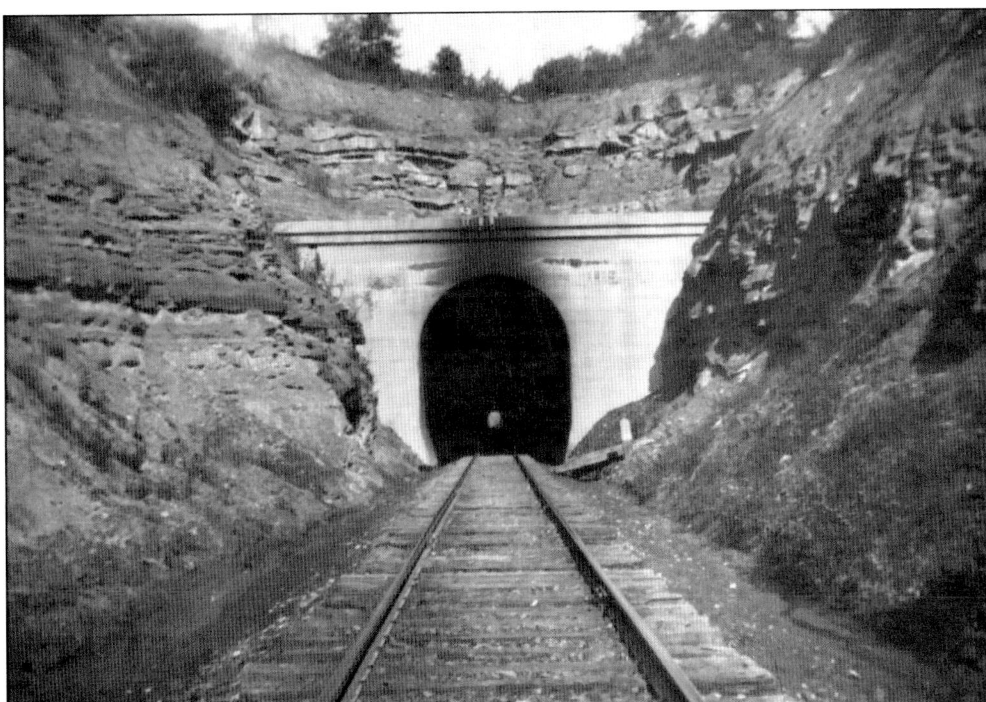

ONEY GAP TUNNEL. The Oney Gap Tunnel on the Virginian mainline served as a point of entrance into Princeton for thousands of passengers of the Virginian Railway. In 1917, a 14-year-old Princeton boy, Watson Chambers, was accidentally shot and killed here by West Virginia National Guard soldiers who were stationed at the tunnel to defend it against possible sabotage. Soldiers of the National Guard protected tunnels and bridges on the Virginian line during World War I. (Courtesy of Randolph Belcher.)

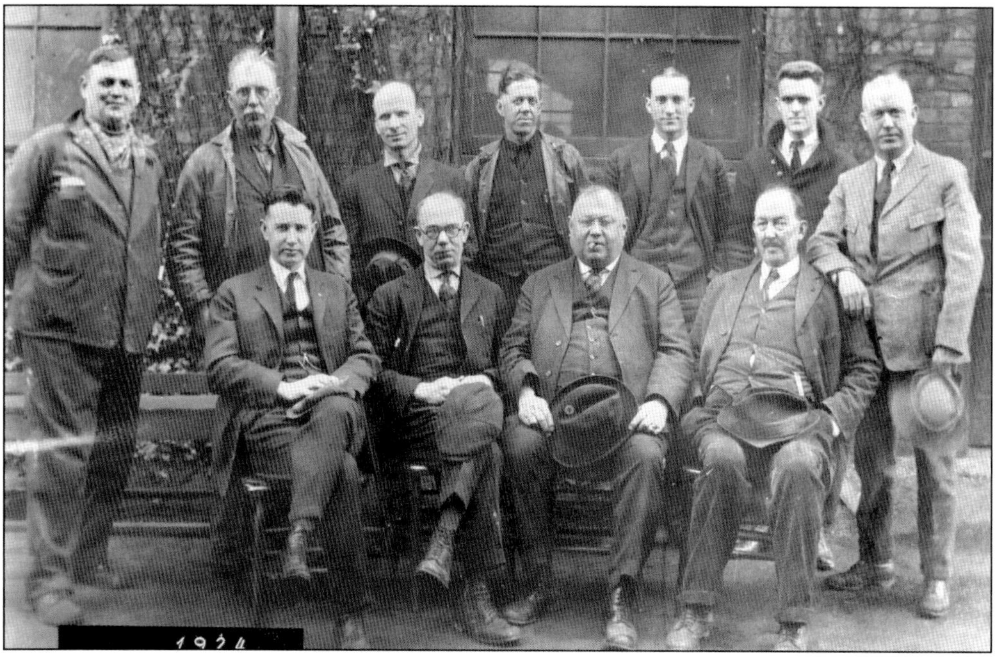

VIRGINIAN STAFF. Members of the Princeton shop staff are shown in this 1924 photograph by E. R. Belcher. Standing from left to right are R. H. Carsten, boilermaker; C. W. Bingham, labor; T. M. Johnson, machine shop; C. M. Thomason, pipe and tin; R. B. Johnson and H. G. Stafford, timekeepers; and E. A. Hutchens, blacksmith. Seated from left to right are J. H. Evans, clerk shop superintendent; F. S. Tender, erecting; F. Welboan, shop superintendent; and H. C. Roney, rod and wheel. (Courtesy of Randolph Belcher.)

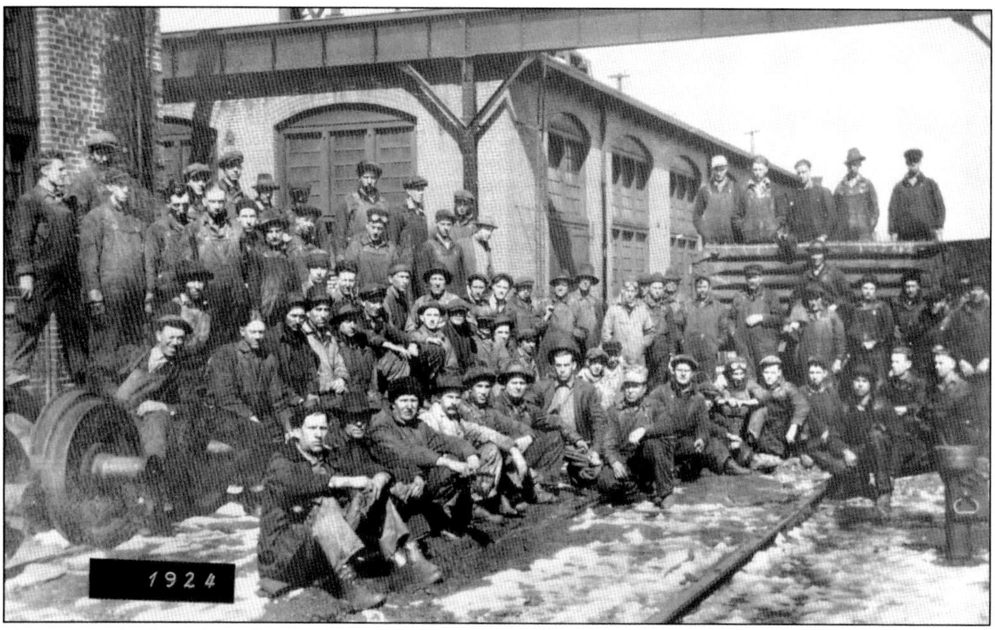

CARMEN. Railroad workers organized as the Brotherhood of Carmen. The Carmen of the Princeton shops are shown here in this 1924 photograph by E. R. Belcher. (Courtesy of Randolph Belcher.)

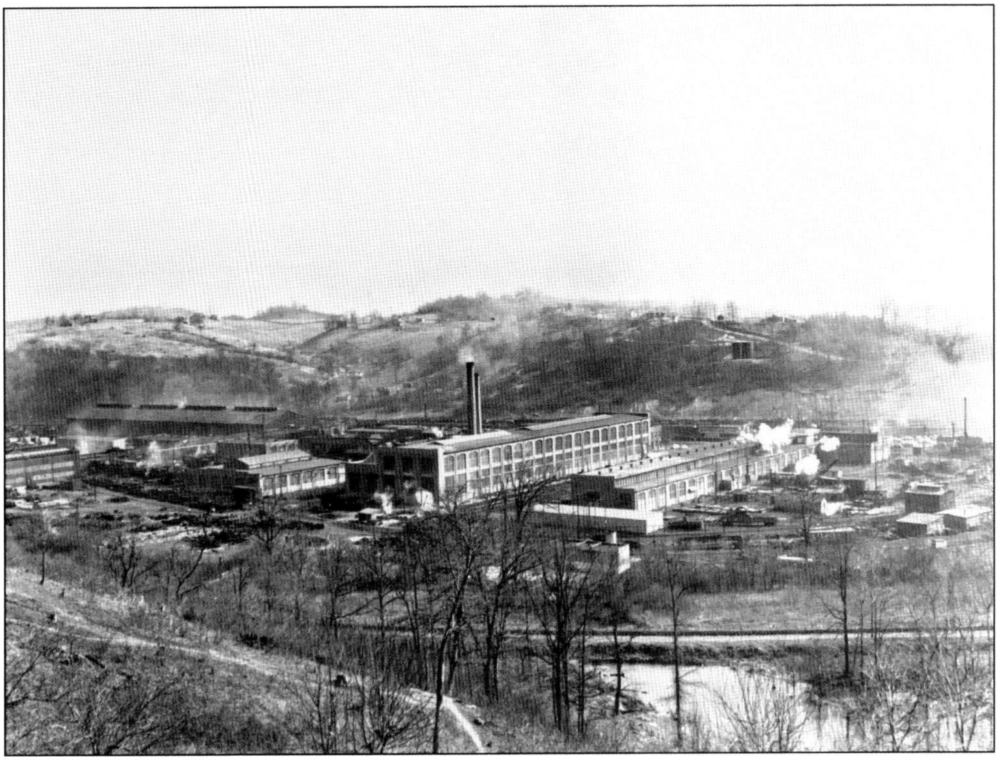

PRINCETON CAR SHOPS. The Virginian Railway Princeton Car Shops represented one of the major places of employment for turn-of-the-century residents. Although the ranks of the workers fluctuated through the years, at times the work force swelled to almost 1,000 workers. (Courtesy of Grubb Photo Service.)

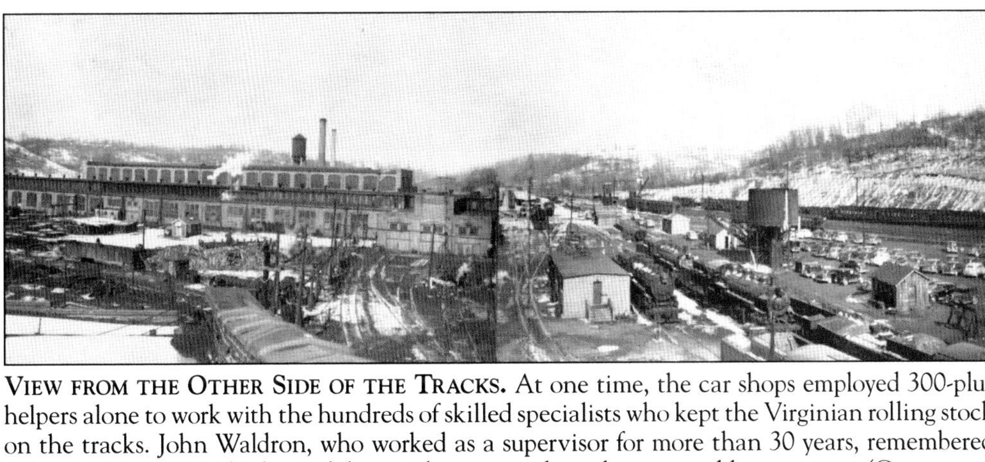

VIEW FROM THE OTHER SIDE OF THE TRACKS. At one time, the car shops employed 300-plus helpers alone to work with the hundreds of skilled specialists who kept the Virginian rolling stock on the tracks. John Waldron, who worked as a supervisor for more than 30 years, remembered that the employees rebuilt gondola cars, hoppers, cabs, cabooses, and locomotives. (Courtesy of Randolph Belcher.)

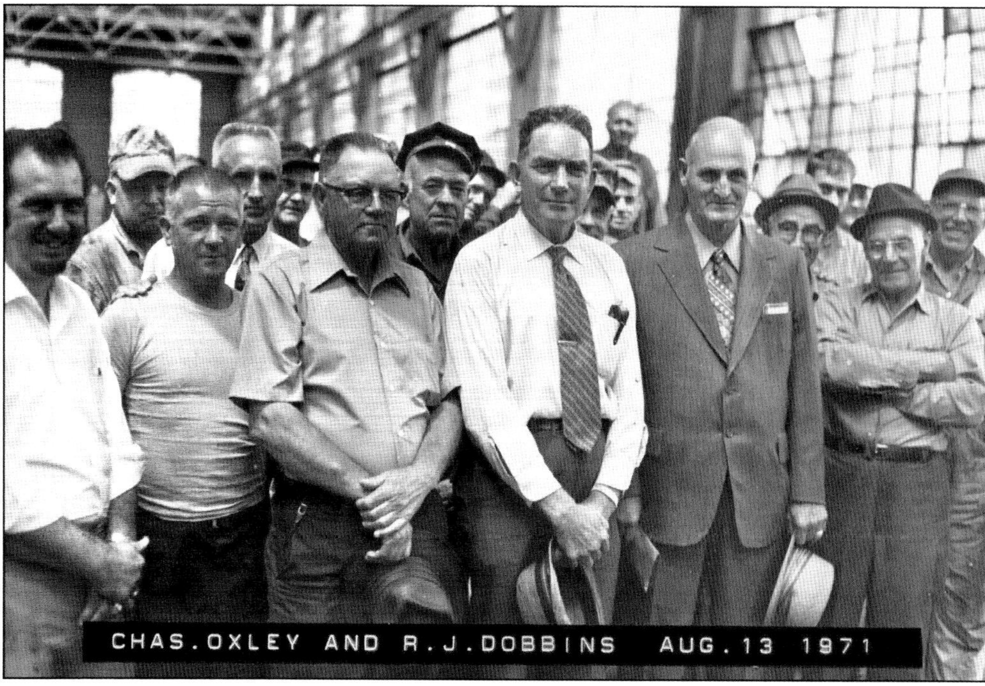

HUMBLE SERVICE. The pride on the Virginian Railway workers' faces shines through in this photograph of the August 13, 1971, retirement of Chas Oxley and R. J. Dobbins by E. R. Belcher. (Courtesy of Randolph Belcher.)

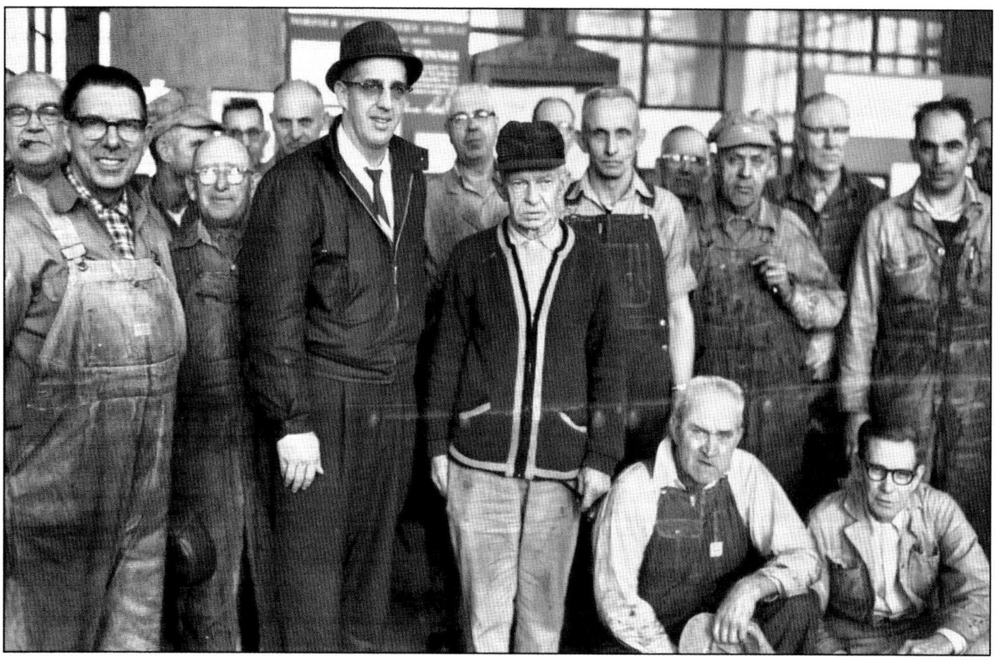

MADE IT. Clyde Taylor (white shirt and tie) is shown here at the December 1, 1965, retirement celebration for R. W. Dowdy. E. R. Belcher learned to become a top-notch photographer by capturing the images of scores of Virginian Railway retirement celebrations. (Courtesy of Randolph Belcher.)

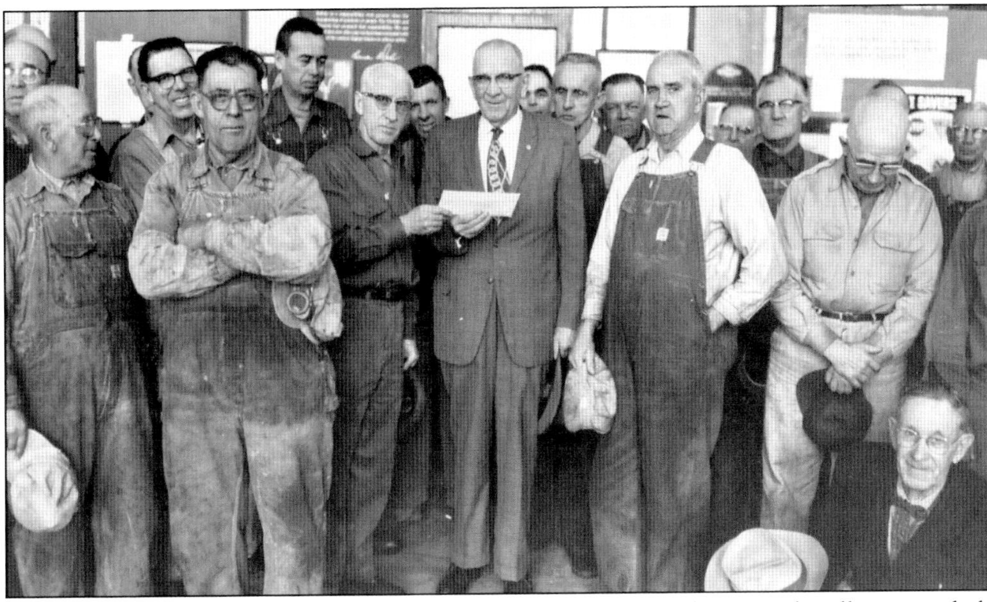

Presentation. The workers at the Princeton shops routinely took up a cash collection to help retirees as they left employment at the car shops. G. W. St. Clair is shown here at his retirement celebration on Nov. 1, 1965, receiving a check. Some retirees received large envelopes containing cash, and others received gift boxes with money inside. (Courtesy of Randolph Belcher.)

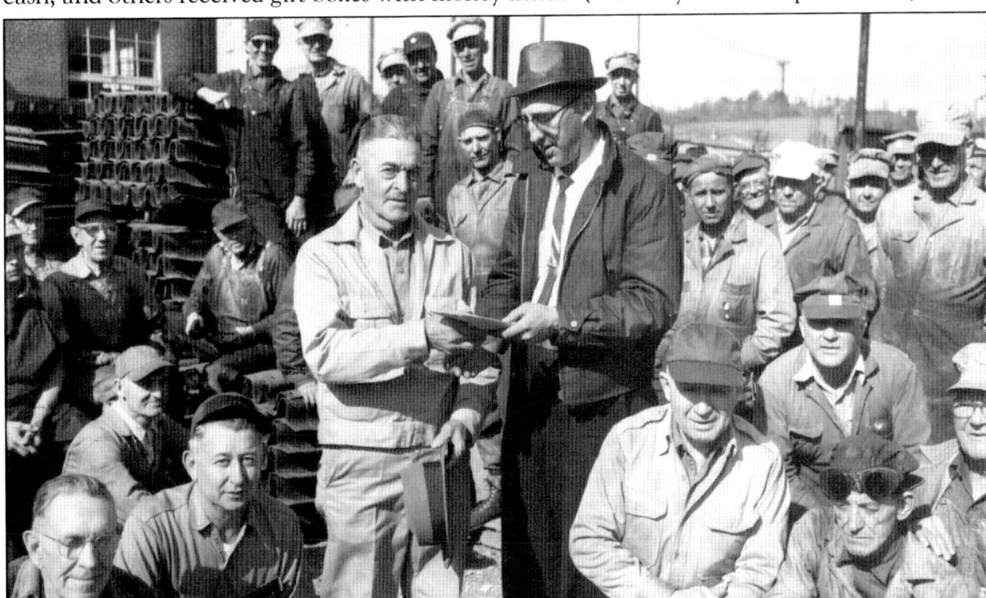

Hat in Hand. Ulysses Clemons is shown here receiving an envelope of cash from Clyde Taylor (standing right of Clemons in a hat and tie) at his November 5, 1965, retirement. Some of the workers also shown include G. W. "Bill" Linkenhoker (kneeling at left of Clemons), Albert Hill and Jack French (far left), Charles E. Miller, Robert Lewis Thomas, John Clemons, Henry Hill, Paul Brown, Ray E. Bailey, Ted Malcolm, Blake Ferrell, James David White (kneeling to right of Clyde Taylor), Albert Long, Lee Goodykoontz, Hugh Swim, Lloyd Griffith, Clyde Cooper, Grover White, Leonard Richardson, and Carl Belcher. (Courtesy of the author's collection.)

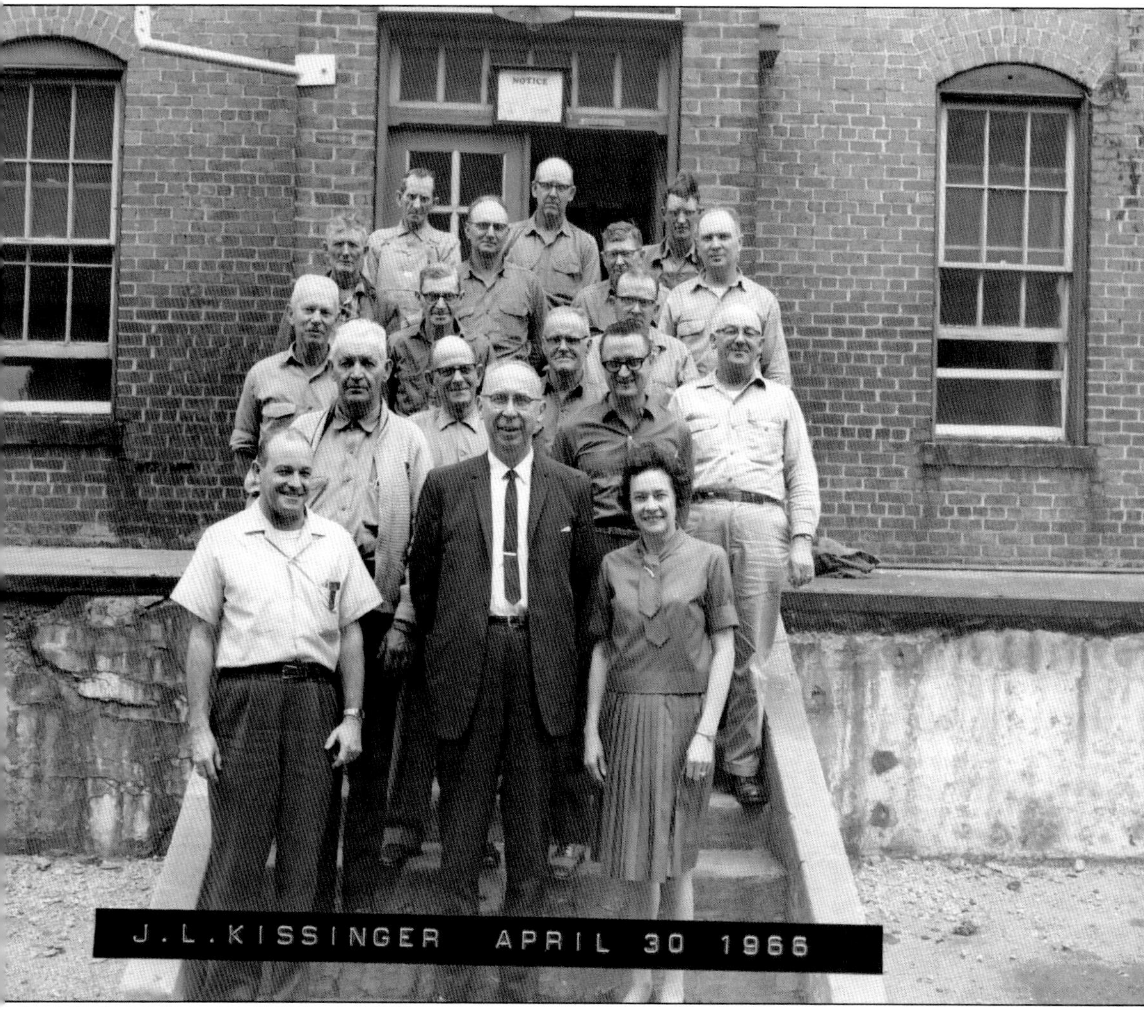

OFFICE CREW. J. L. Kissinger is shown here at his April 30, 1966, retirement celebration surrounded by members of the Virginian Princeton Car Shops store department. Tony Swim and several others are shown in this E. R. Belcher photograph. (Courtesy of Randolph Belcher.)

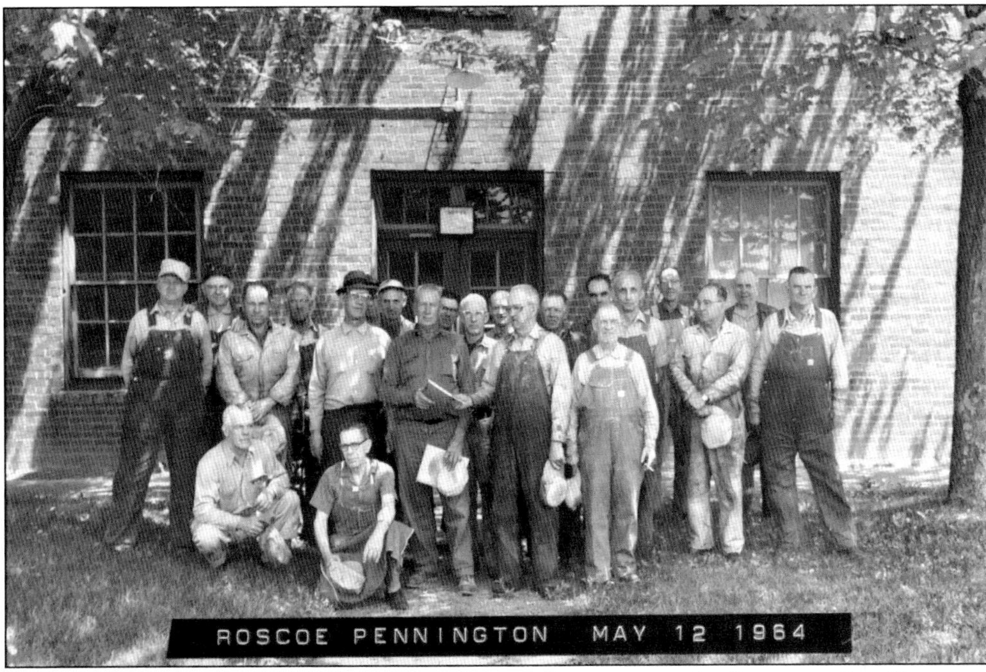

HONORING RETIREES. E. R. Belcher worked as an electrician at the Princeton Car Shops and took up photography as a hobby. He shared retirement photographs with Virginian retirees and their families. Roscoe Pennington is shown here at his May 12, 1964, retirement celebration. (Courtesy of Randolph Belcher.)

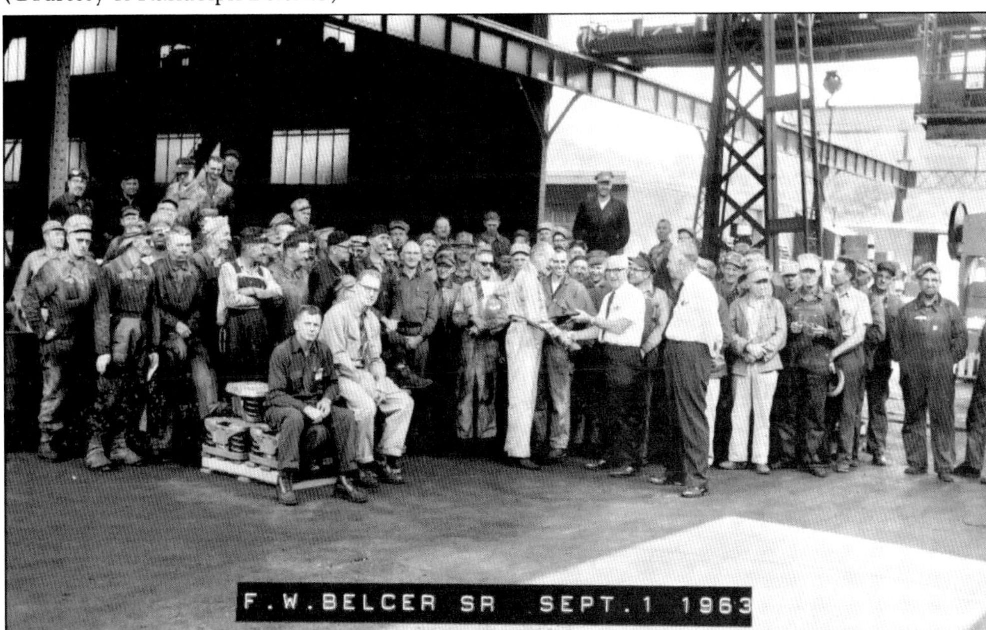

THE BIG AND LITTLE PICTURE. E. R. Belcher compiled several books of retirement presentation photographs. He recorded the date of the event on the front of the photograph and usually took two pictures, including a close-up of the presentation and an overview of the gathering like this picture of F. W. Belcer Sr. at his September 1, 1963, retirement. (Courtesy of Randolph Belcher.)

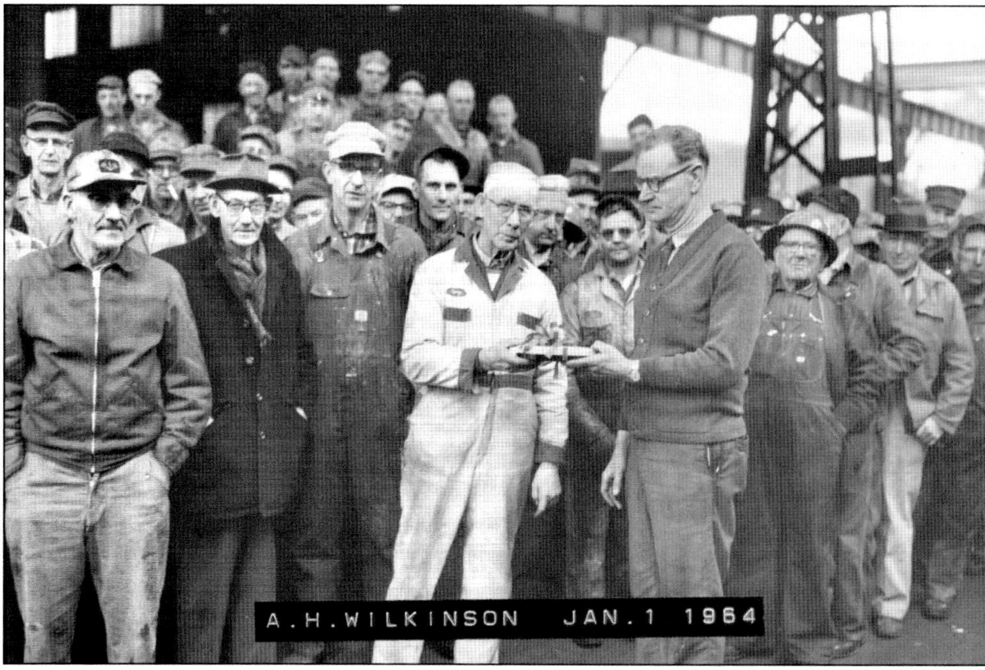

PRESENTATION. A. H. Wilkinson (center, holding gift) is shown receiving his retirement gift from Milton "Red" Brookman (right). E. R. Belcher's photographic genius is evident in the pictures he left as a legacy to his service with the Virginian Railway. (Courtesy of Randolph Belcher.)

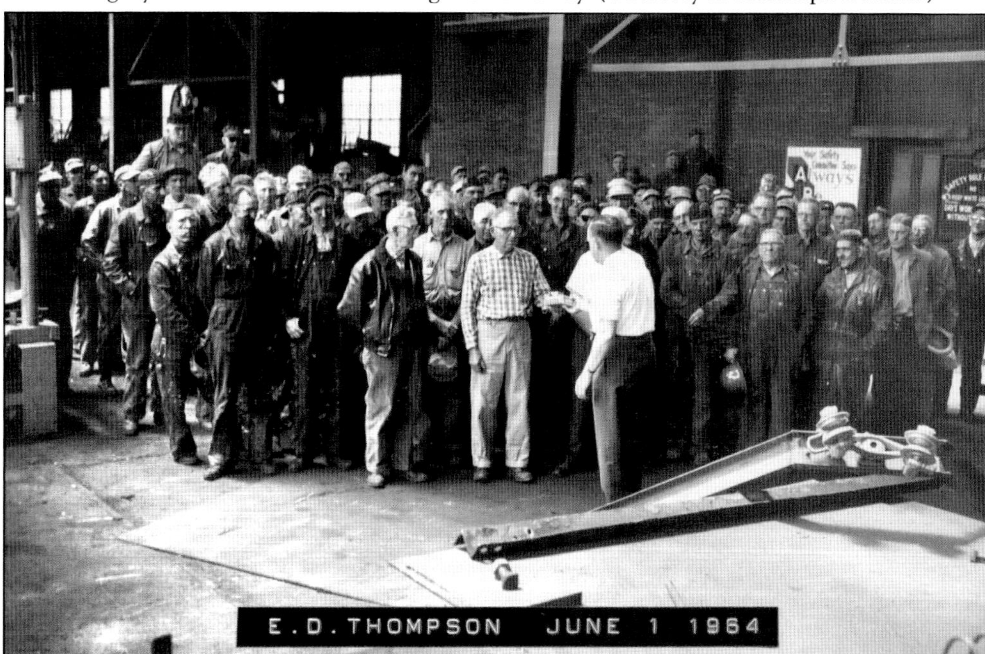

RETIREMENT. E. D. Thompson is shown receiving his retirement gift in this June 1, 1964, photograph by E. R. Belcher. Although the Princeton Car Shops had an estimated 1,000 workers covering three shifts at its high point, the employees of each department treated each other like family. (Courtesy of Randolph Belcher.)

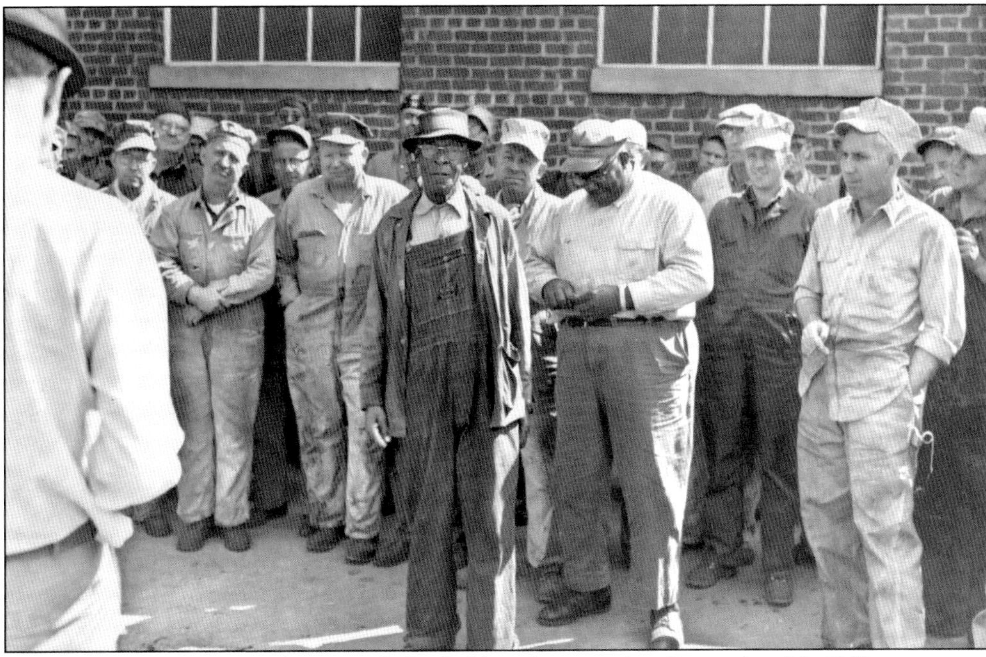

VIRGINIAN DIVERSITY. Chapman Oaks (left) is shown at his September 30, 1968, retirement celebration. While there were not a great many African American workers at the Princeton Car Shops, both Randolph Belcher and John Waldron said that Virginian workers respected all of their fellow workers, white or black. Another black shop worker, Bill Henry, is shown to the right of Oaks. (Courtesy of Randolph Belcher.)

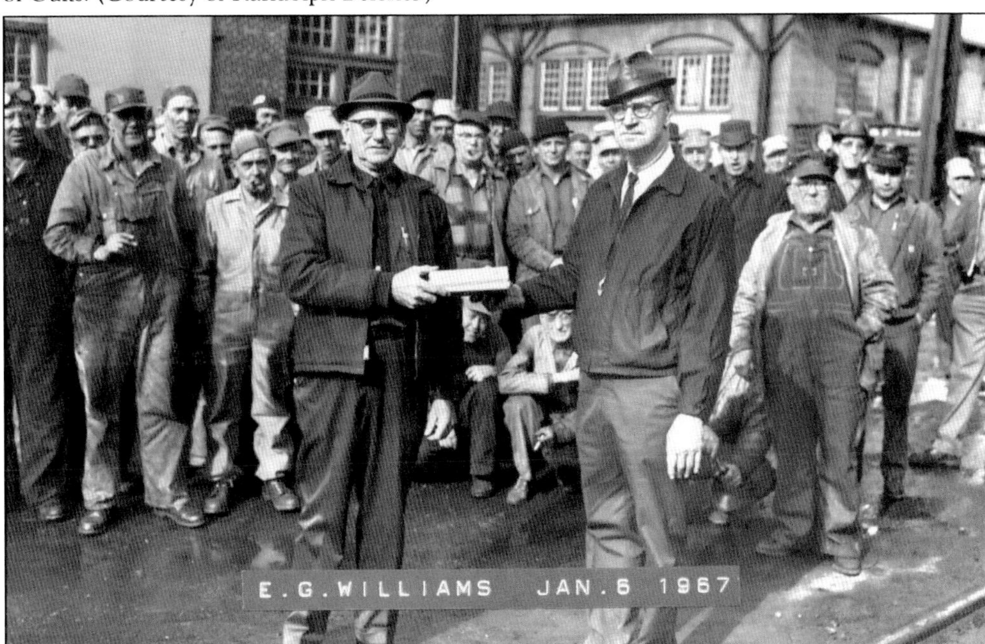

IN THE GENES. E. G. "Gene" Williams (left) is shown receiving his retirement gift from Milton "Red" Brookman (right) in this January 6, 1967, E. R. Belcher photograph. Shorty Six and John Waldron (with arms folded) are shown to the right of Brookman. (Courtesy of Randolph Belcher.)

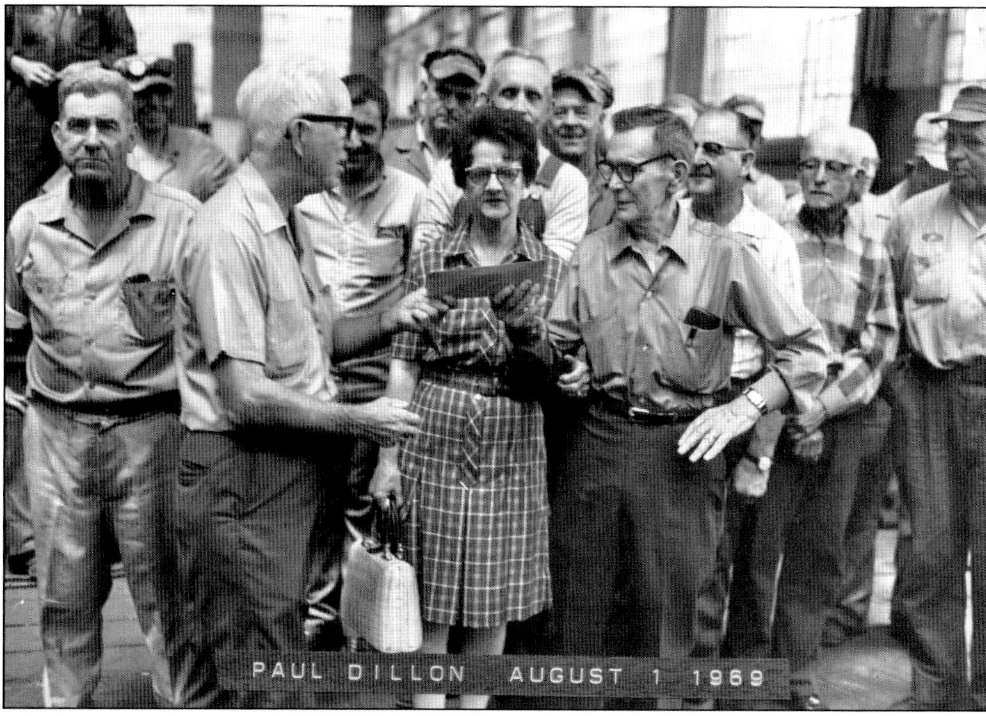

FAMILY MATTERS. Paul Dillon is shown receiving a retirement gift from his fellow employees in this August 1, 1969, E. R. Belcher photograph. (Courtesy of Randolph Belcher.)

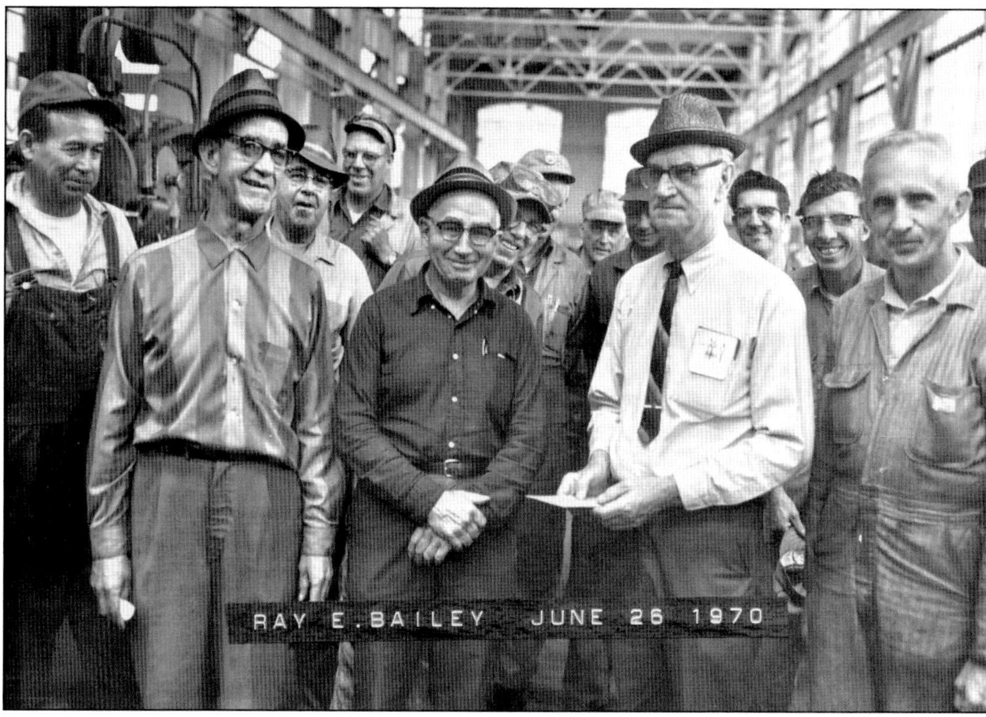

POWERFUL MOMENT. Ray E. Bailey and his fellow workers appear extremely happy at Bailey's June 26, 1970, retirement. (Courtesy of Randolph Belcher.)

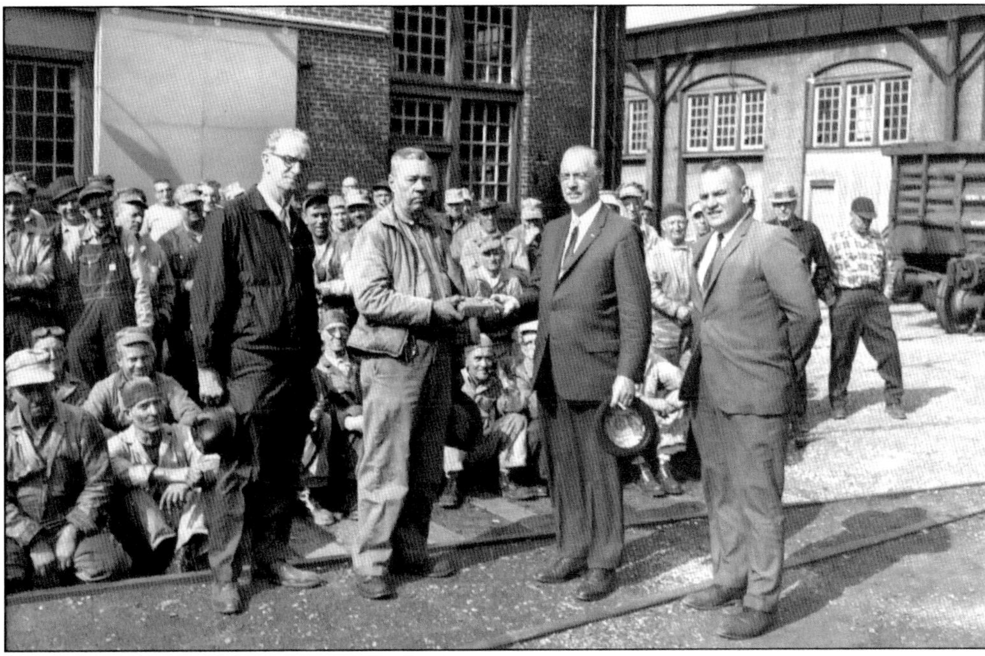

Forty-six Years of Service. John R. Bridges, standing second from left, is shown here receiving a gift from master mechanic G. T. Strong Jr., at his October 31, 1966, retirement celebration. M. E. "Red" Brookman, general foreman, is shown to the left of Bridges, and David C. Foster, assistant master mechanic, is shown to the right of Strong. Bridges retired from the N&W Railway after 46 years of service. (Courtesy of Randolph Belcher.)

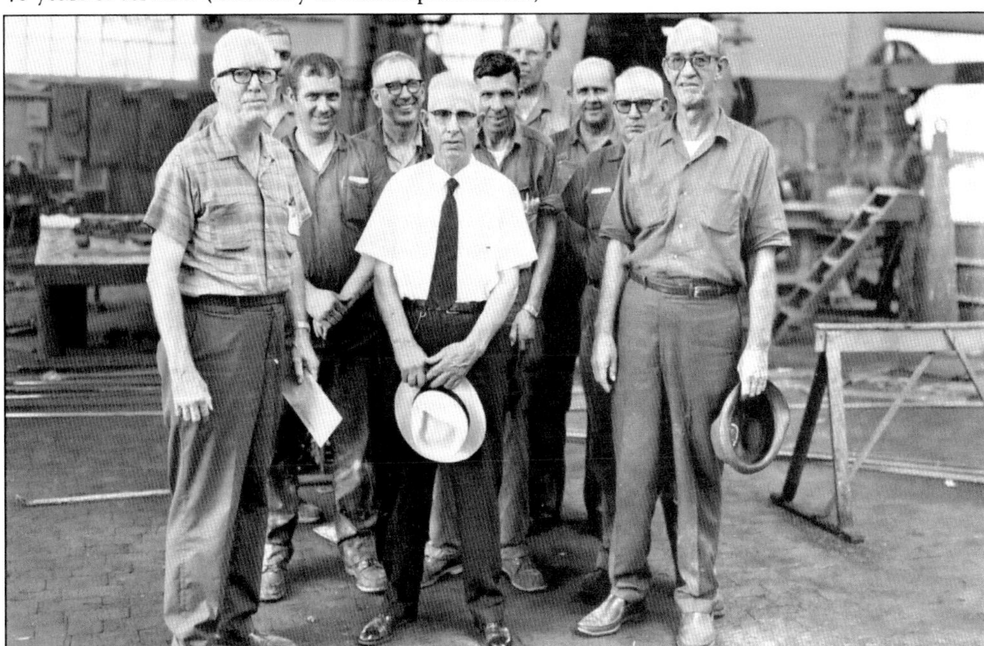

Boiler Room. L. W. Dennis is shown here with the Virginian Princeton Car Shops "boiler gang" at his June 27, 1969, retirement. The boiler gang worked on the boilers in steam locomotives. (Courtesy of Randolph Belcher.)

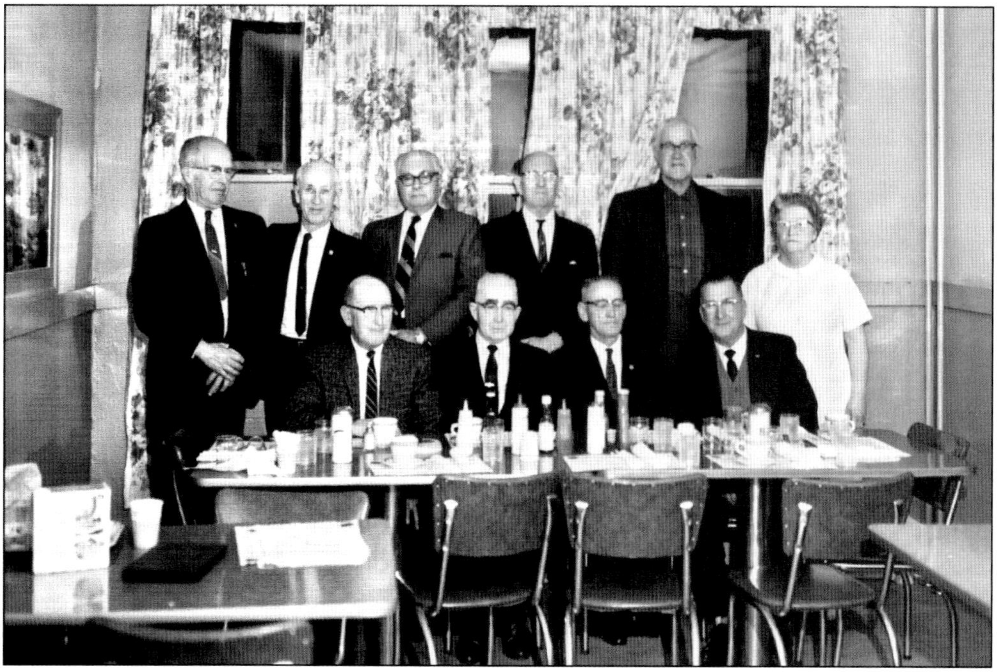

PHOTOGRAPHER'S TRICK. E. R. Belcher is shown standing at the left of this March 22, 1968, photograph taken in Jimmy's Restaurant in Princeton. As he got into his hobby, Belcher used a large-negative camera and set his shutter on a timer so he could get into the picture himself. (Courtesy of the author's collection.)

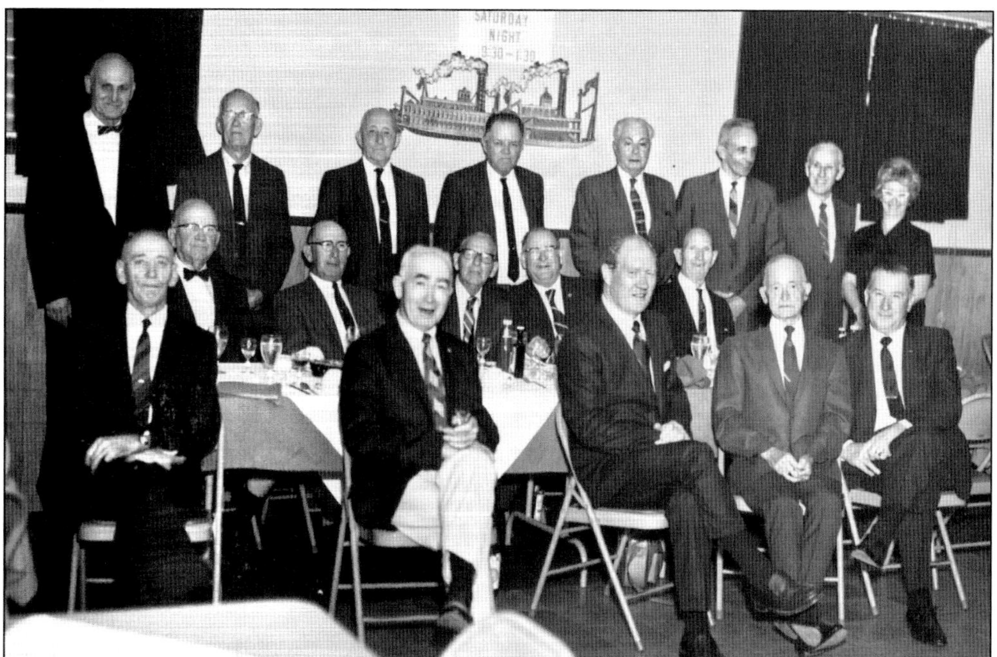

GOOD-LOOKING GROUP. Several Virginian railroaders are shown in this E. R. Belcher photograph taken on October 2, 1970, at the Dinner Bell Restaurant in Princeton. (Courtesy the author's collection.)

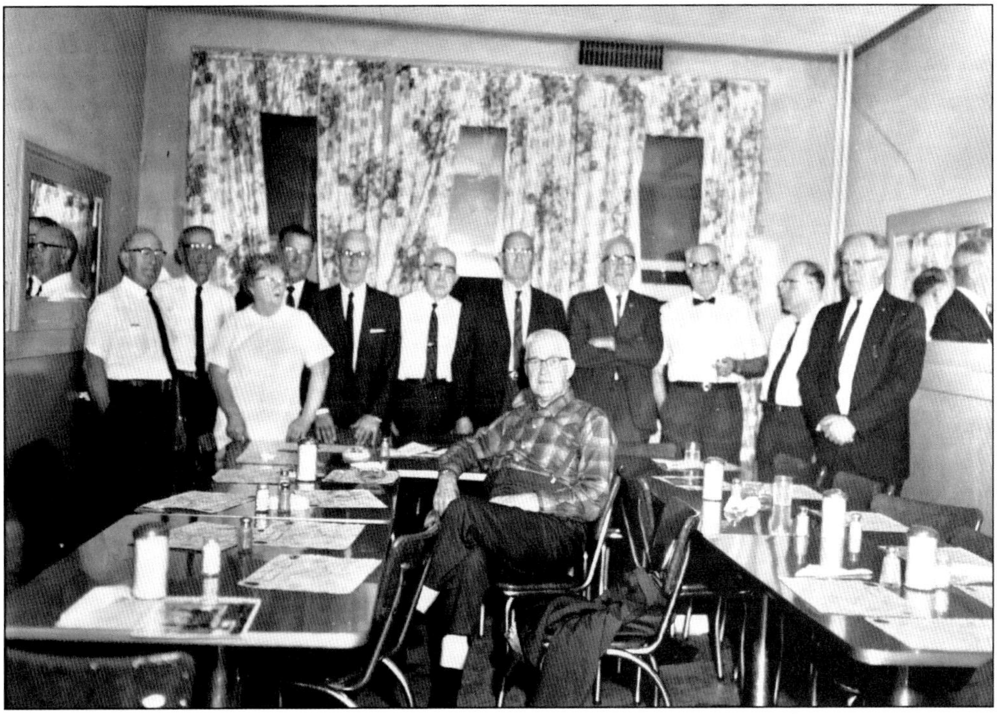

BACK AT JIMMY'S. E. R. Belcher took his own photograph again in this September 20, 1968, picture at Jimmy's Restaurant. That's Belcher on the far right. (Courtesy of the author's collection.)

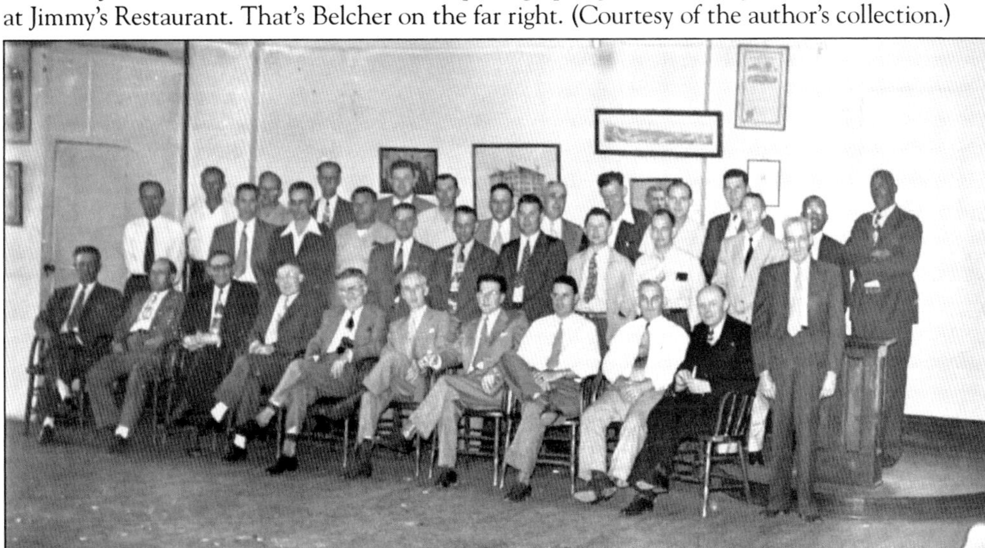

MEETING. Virginian railroaders are shown at this System Federation No. 40 Convention on June 21, 1955, in Princeton. Pictured here from left to right are (first row) N. A. Craft, W. M. Sarver, C. A. Welch, W. C. Nutter, C. J. McClosky, J. W. Munsey, W. J. Bailey, H. C. Pennington, F. E. Huff, A. C. Ludwick, and H. P. Pritchett; (second row) V. L. Danley, W. J. Clay, C. J. Hylton, H. G. Powers, R. H. Swim, E. D. Thompson, E. L. Clark, G. W. Linkenhoker, A. R. Hearn, and C. E. Tiller; (third row) G. H. Saunders, V. W. Miller, C. E. Rumburg, J. W. Moore, E. L Martin, J. H. Altic, D. W. Christian, E. C. Barr, W. E. Pedneau, J. H. Moore, Thomas Wallace, and J. H. Brown. (Courtesy of the author's collection.)

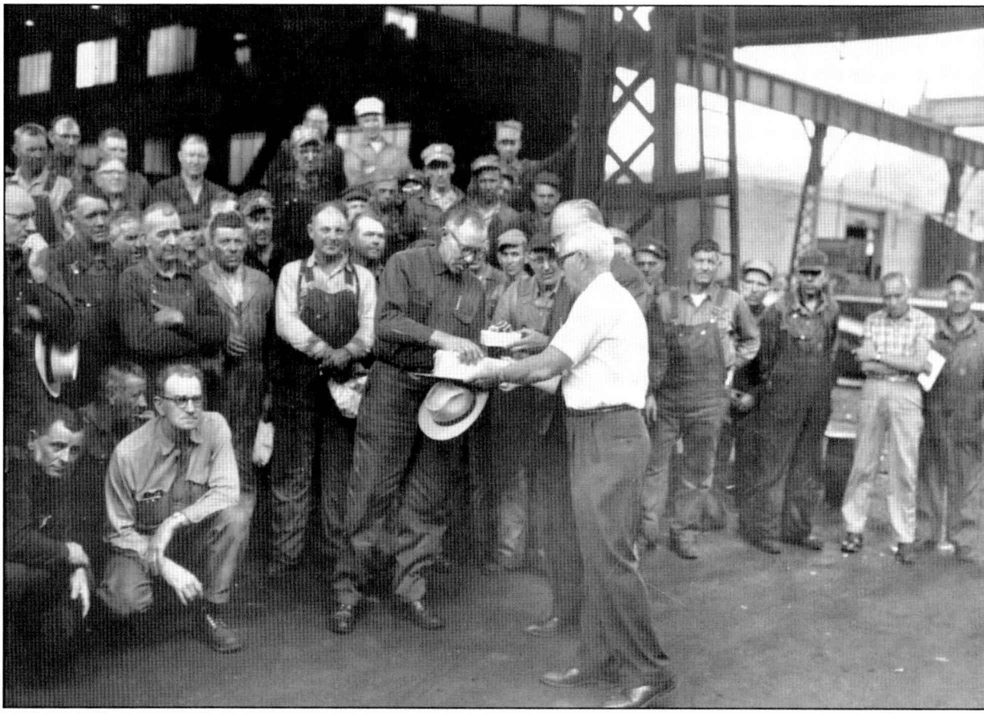

EXPRESSION. Bowen Repass, foreman, is shown receiving a gift from John Frederick, general foreman, at Repass's retirement on June 8, 1963. (Courtesy of the author's collection.)

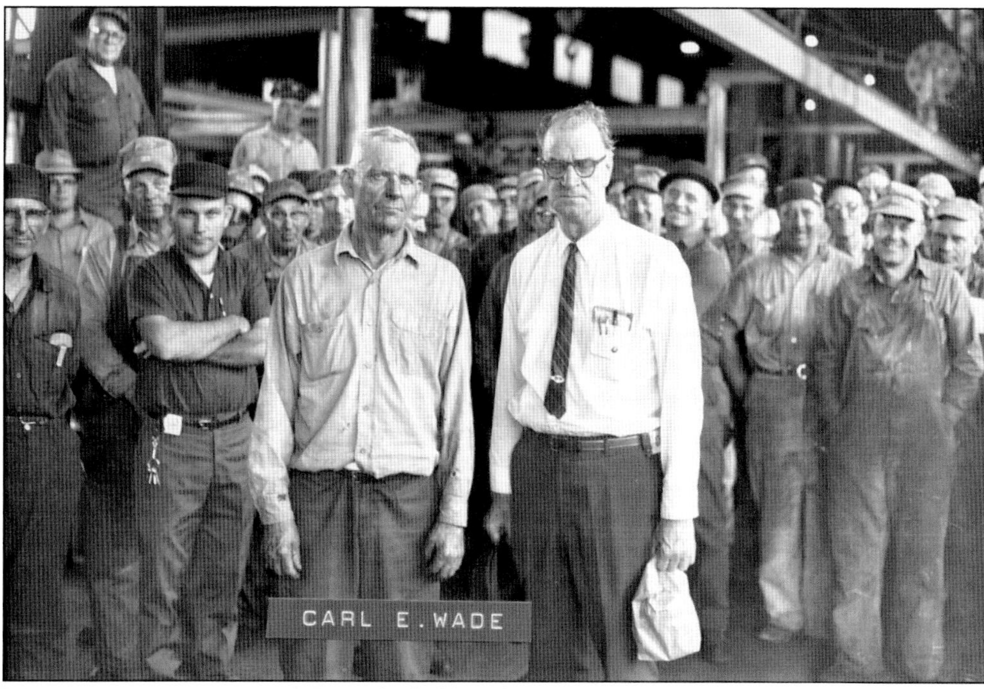

MEMORABLE MOMENT. Carl E. Wade (left) is shown with Milton "Red" Brookman (right) at Wade's retirement celebration on June 23, 1967, at the Princeton Car Shops. E. R. Belcher's photographic talent is on display in this photograph. (Courtesy of Randolph Belcher.)

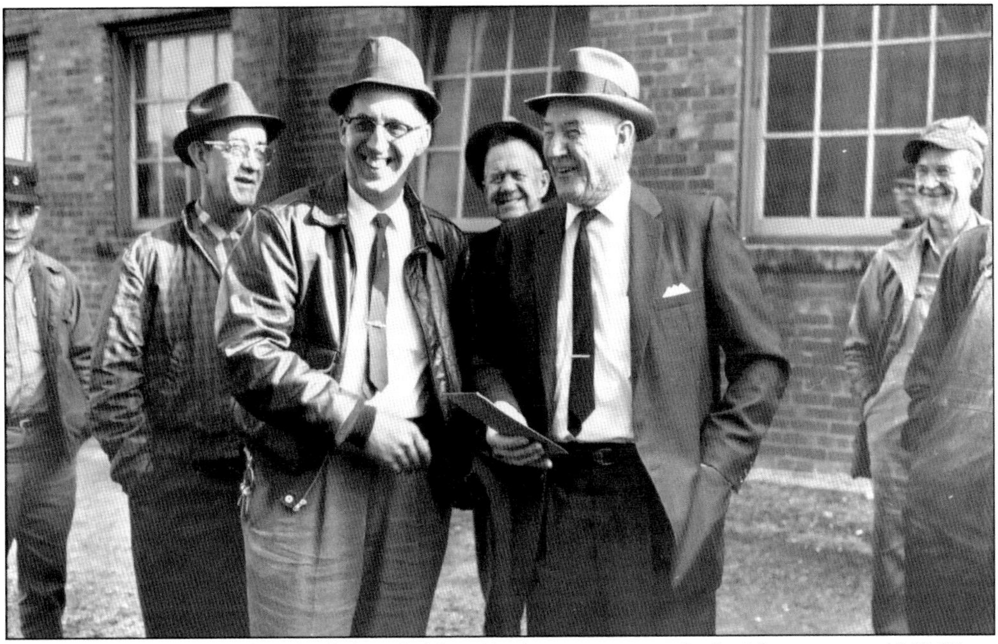

LONG RUN. Fred J. Bushee (right) ended his 38-plus-year run with the Virginian and N&W on December 31, 1964. He joined the Virginian as a machinist on May 6, 1926, and became motor car supervisor in 1957. Bushee never had a reportable injury during his 38 years and seven months of service. Bushee is pictured receiving a present from Clyde Taylor, general foreman (left). Clyde Thomason and W. V. Lovern are in the background. (Courtesy of Randolph Belcher.)

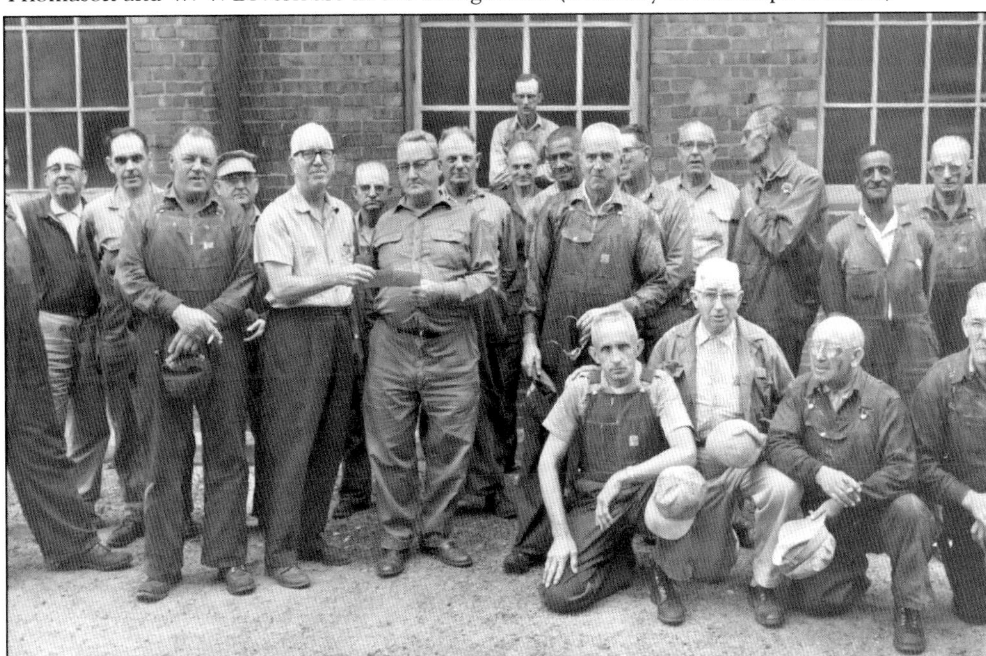

A JOB WELL DONE. G. V. Evans is shown at his August 25, 1966, retirement. E. R. Belcher's mastery of photography enabled him to take pictures in various lighting conditions. (Courtesy of Randolph Belcher.)

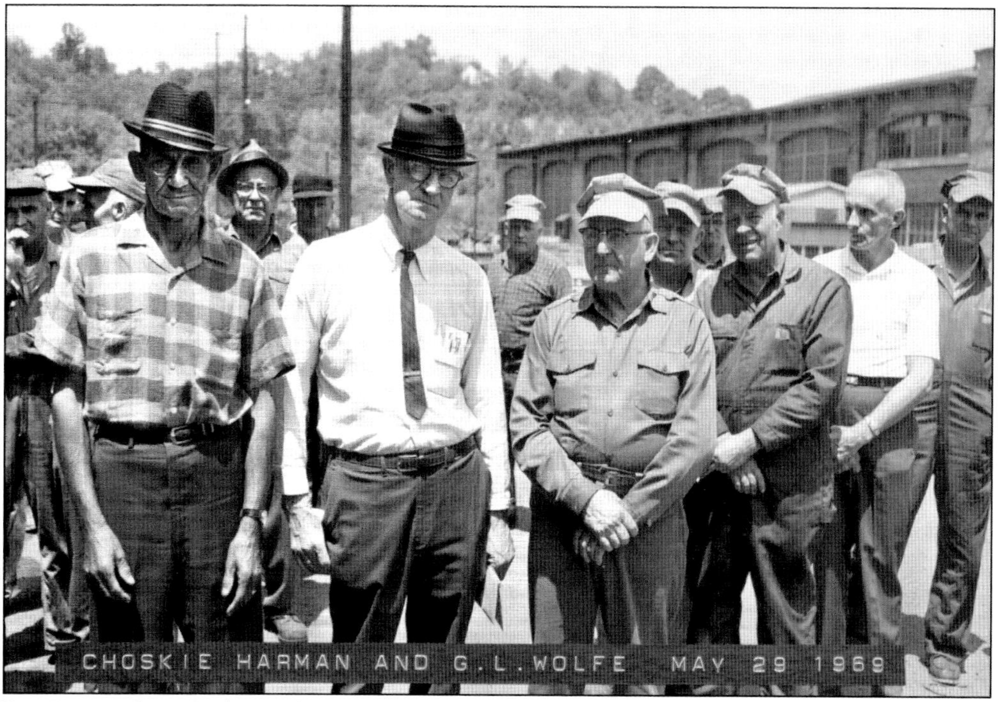

BIG DAY. Milton "Red" Brookman (in hat and tie) is shown between Choskie Harman (left) and G. L. Wolfe at the joint retirement celebration for Harman and Wolfe on May 29, 1969. (Courtesy of Randolph Belcher.)

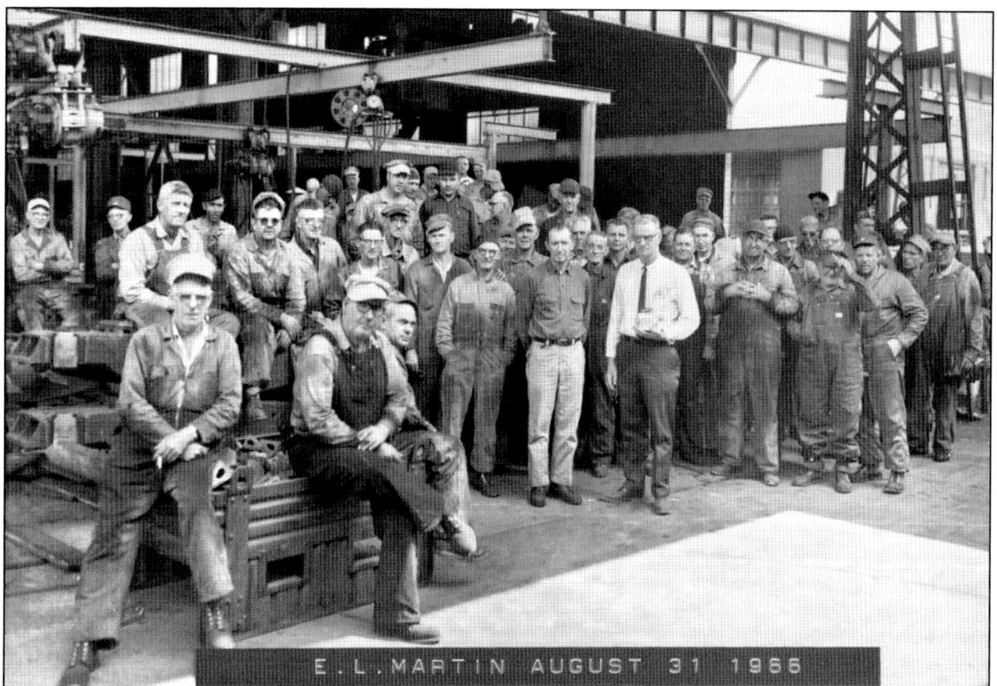

ONE OF THE WORKERS. E. L. Martin is just left of Milton "Red" Brookman (in white shirt and tie) at Martin's August 31, 1966, retirement celebration. (Courtesy of Randolph Belcher.)

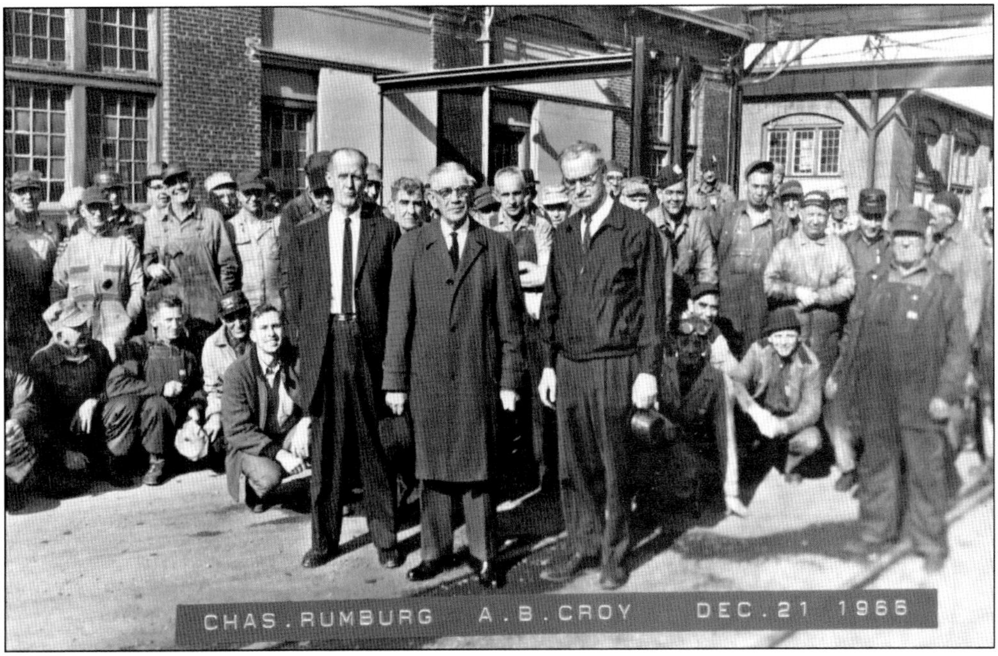

Retirees. Charles Rumburg (left) and A. B. Croy (center) are shown together at their joint retirement on December 21, 1966. Milton "Red" Brookman (right) is also shown. (Courtesy of Randolph Belcher.)

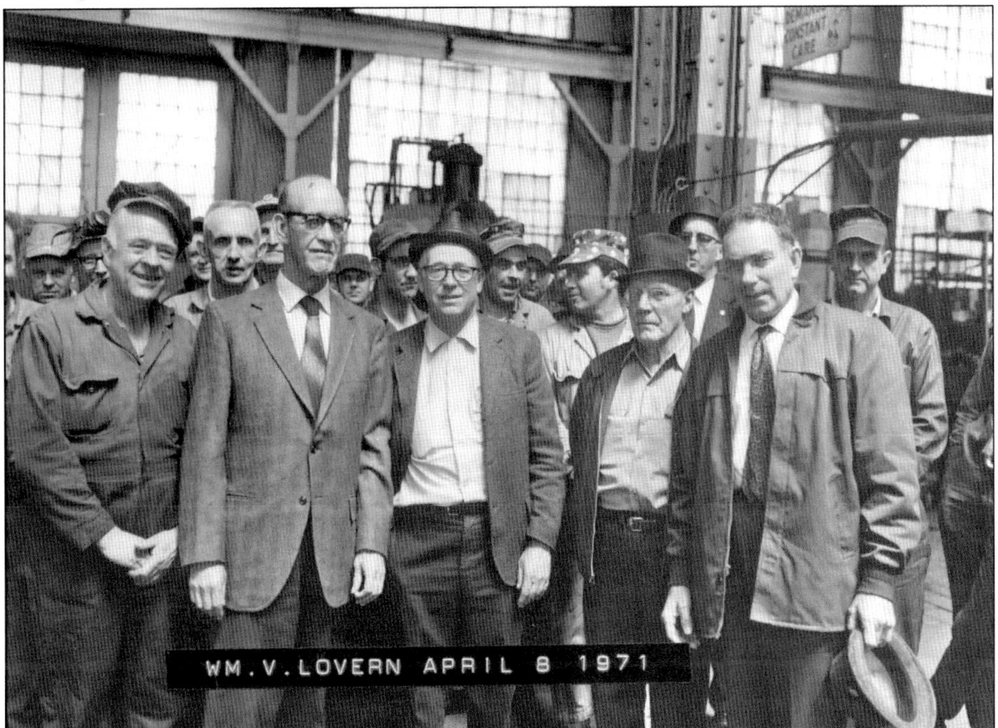

Good Friends. Virginian car shop employees gathered for the April 8, 1971, retirement of William V. Lovern. (Courtesy of Randolph Belcher.)

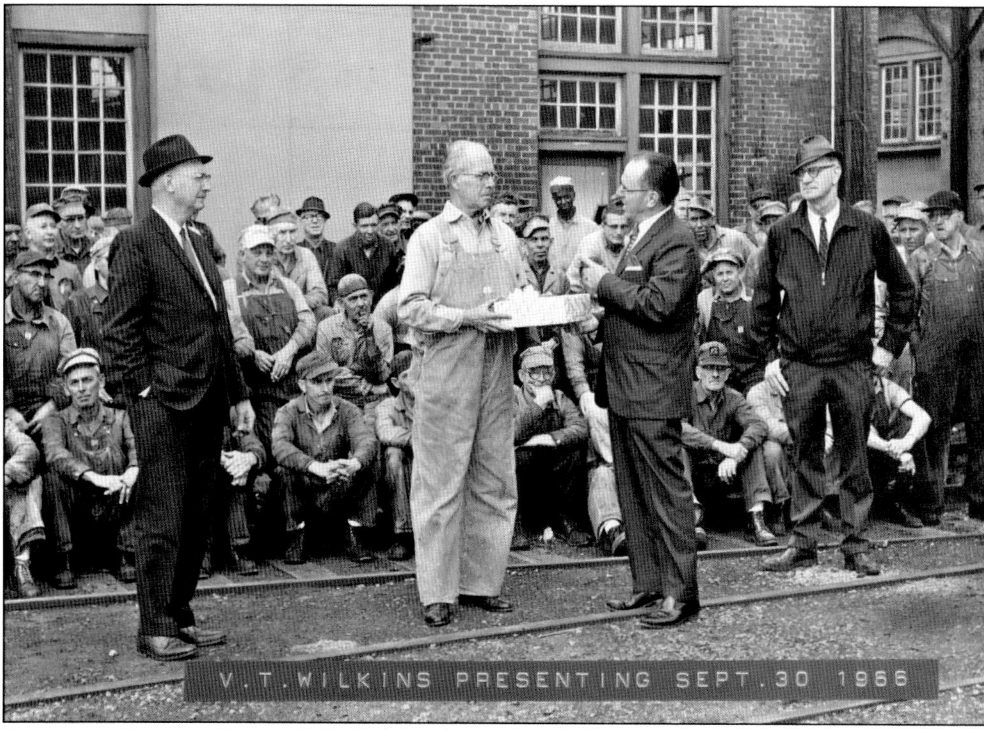

THROUGH ALL THE YEARS. E. R. Belcher (center) took his own picture with a camera that had a timer on the shutter at the presentation from V. T. Wilkins of Norfolk, Virginia, upon Belcher's retirement on September 30, 1966. Milton "Red" Brookman (standing at far right) looks on in approval. (Courtesy of Randolph Belcher.)

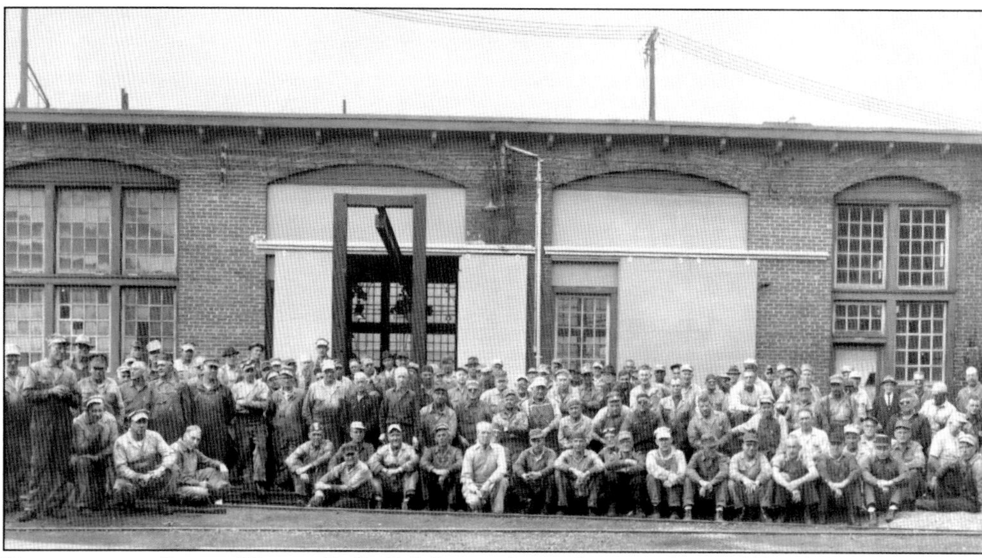

FORTH-EIGHT GREAT YEARS. E. R. Belcher is shown here in the middle of the crowd at his 1966 retirement celebration. G. T. Strong Jr. presented Belcher a gift from his fellow employees, and V. T. Wilkins presented an additional gift on behalf of the International Brotherhood of Electrical Workers (IBEW). Belcher was a member and officer of the IBEW for 32 years and served as general chairman and on the system council. (Courtesy of Randolph Belcher.)

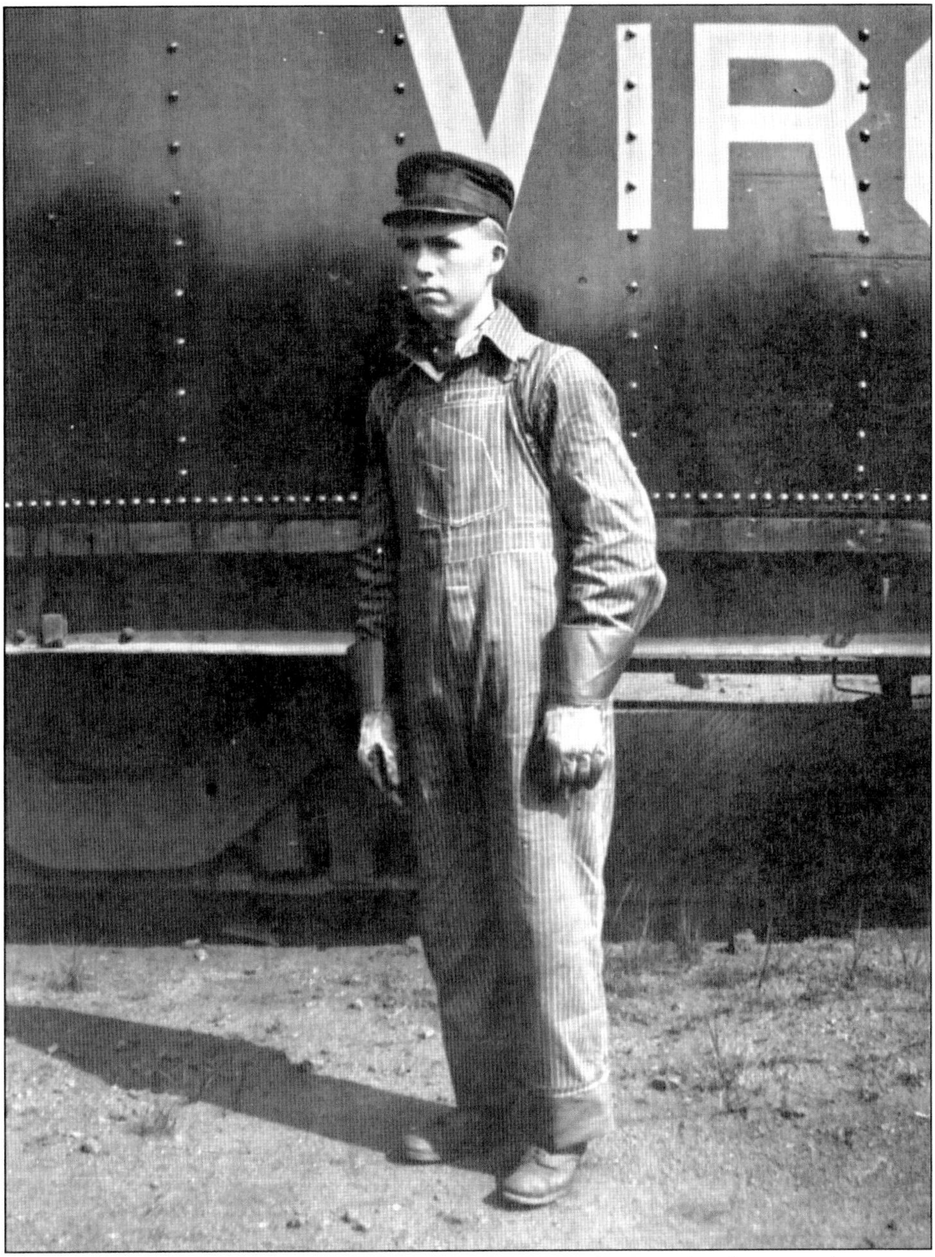

THE RIGHT TRACK. E. R. Belcher is shown in this 1918 photograph taken just three months after he went to work for the Virginian Railway. He used a speed graphic–style camera with external lighting to capture images of his fellow workers. He continued photographing retirees well after his retirement. He also enjoyed gardening at his home on the Old Ingleside Road. Ernest Belcher was 16 years old when he started working for the Virginian in 1918. He was born in 1902, the same year that Henry H. Rogers started planning the Virginian. His father, T. A. "Tobe" Belcher, started working for the Virginian before World War I and died in 1931. Belcher's son, R. A. "Randolph" Belcher, worked for the Virginian from 1942 until 1984. E. R. Belcher died in 1983, just one year after the Norfolk Southern Railway (NS) closed the Princeton Car Shops. (Courtesy of Randolph Belcher.)

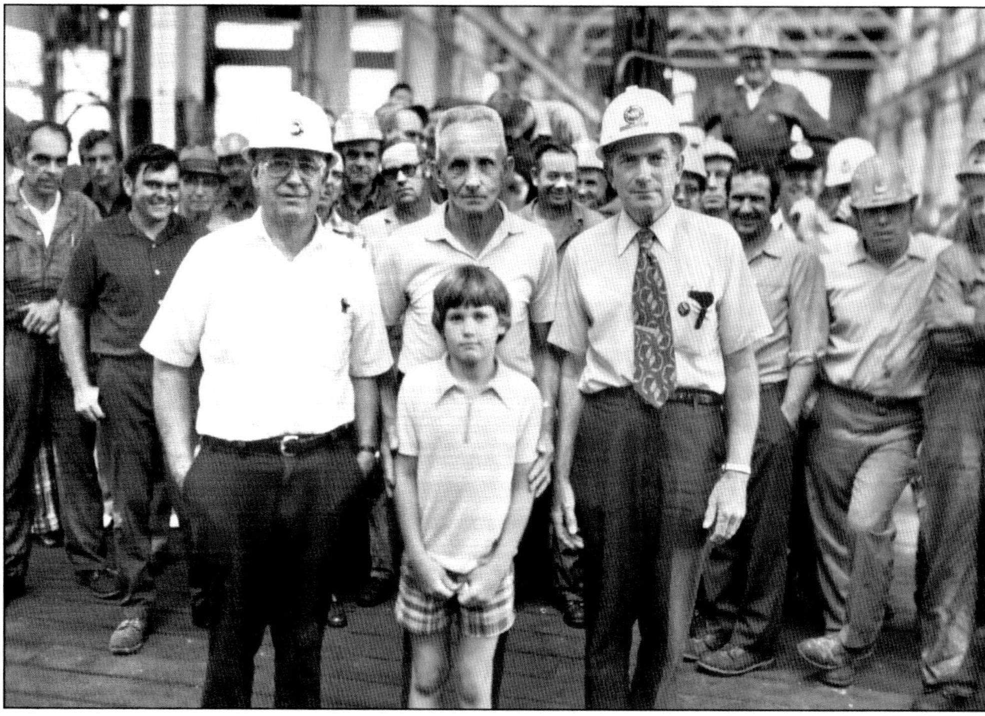

CENTER STAGE. C. J. Hylton is shown here at his August 10, 1973, retirement, flanked by two unidentified supervisory personnel and standing behind a child. E. R. Belcher's camera used slide film that had to be loaded for each exposure. (Courtesy of Randolph Belcher.)

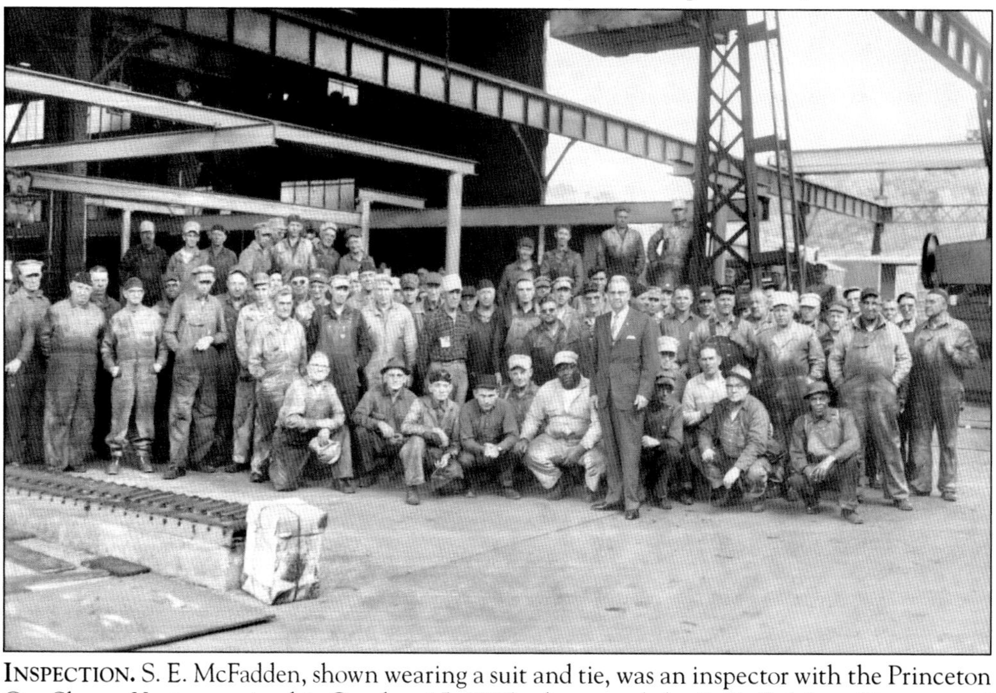

INSPECTION. S. E. McFadden, shown wearing a suit and tie, was an inspector with the Princeton Car Shops. He is seen in this October 15, 1965, photograph by E. R. Belcher. (Courtesy of John Waldron.)

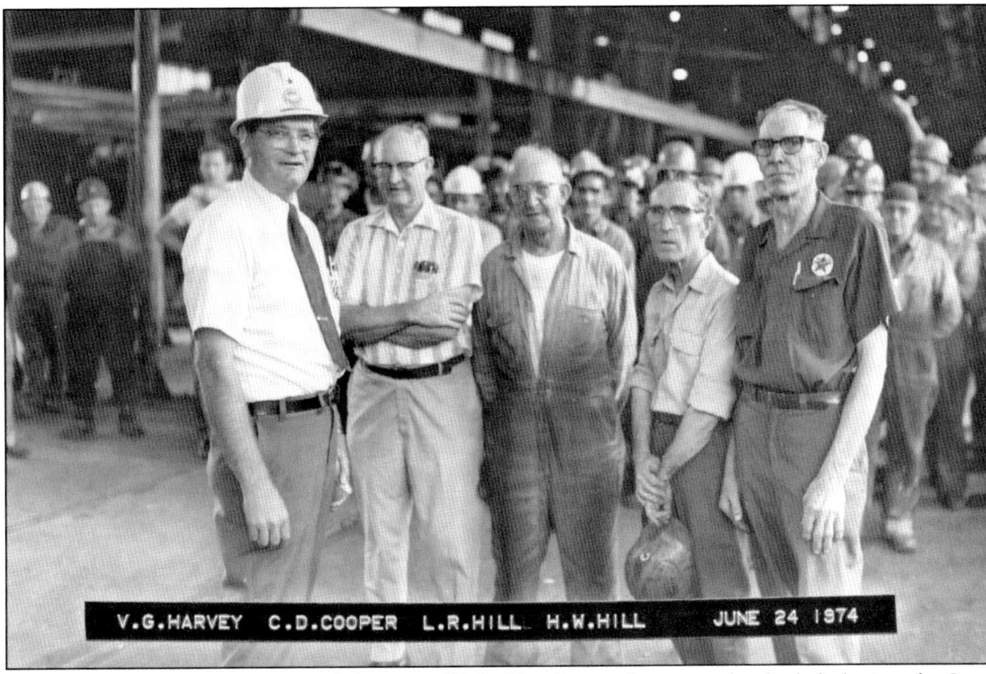

FOUR RETIRE. Assistant general foreman W. L. Hatcher is shown at the far left during the June 24, 1974, retirement celebration for (from left to right) V. G. Harvey (34 years of service), C. D. Cooper (34 years of service), L. R. Hill (32 years of service), and H. W. Hill (34 years of service). The four men retired after a combined service of 134 years. (Courtesy of Randolph Belcher.)

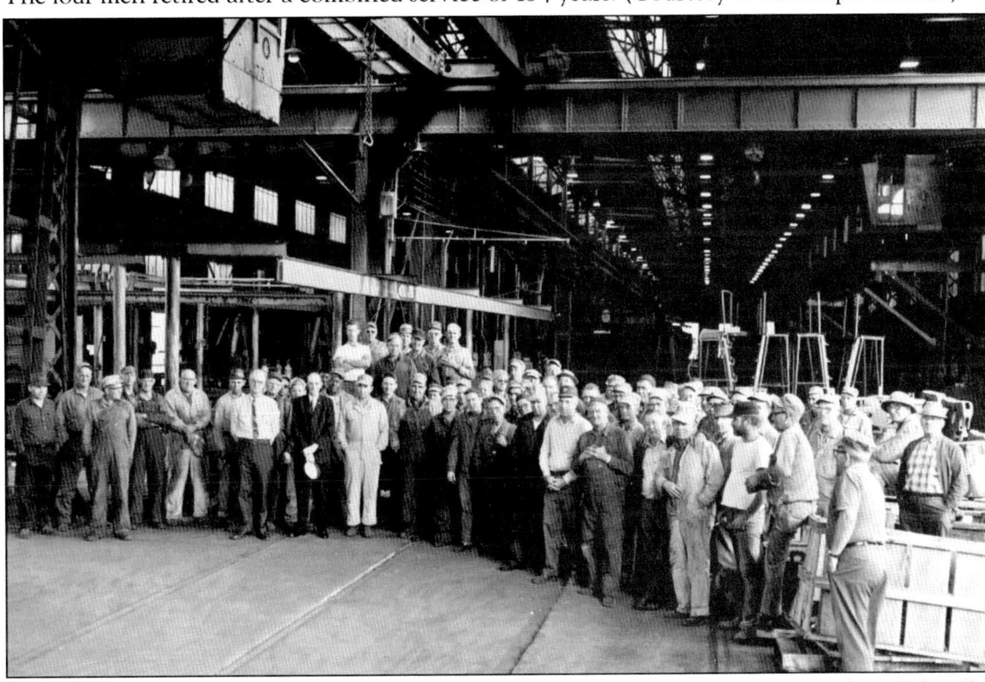

SHOP OF DISTINCTION. A group of Princeton Car Shop workers are gathered for the September 23, 1969, retirement of E. G. Pettrey in this E. R. Belcher photograph. (Courtesy of Randolph Belcher.)

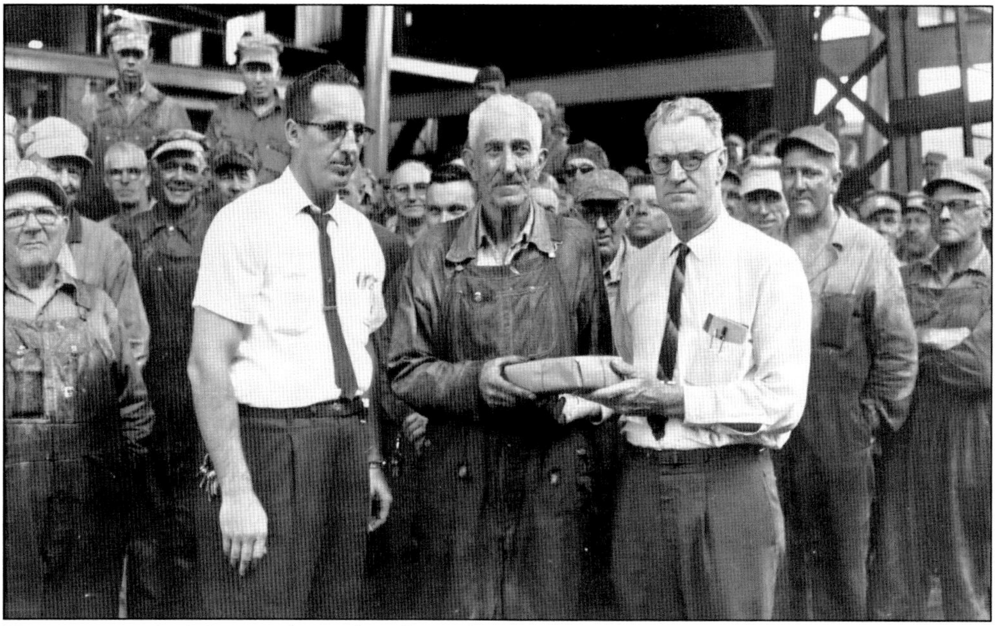

TRANSITION. Carl Stinson (center) is shown here receiving a gift from Milton "Red" Brookman (right) at Stinson's September 15, 1965, retirement celebration. Clyde Taylor, Brookman's replacement from the N&W, is to the left of Stinson. Others in the photograph include John Jones, to the right of Stinson's shoulder, and John Waldron to the left. (Courtesy of Randolph Belcher.)

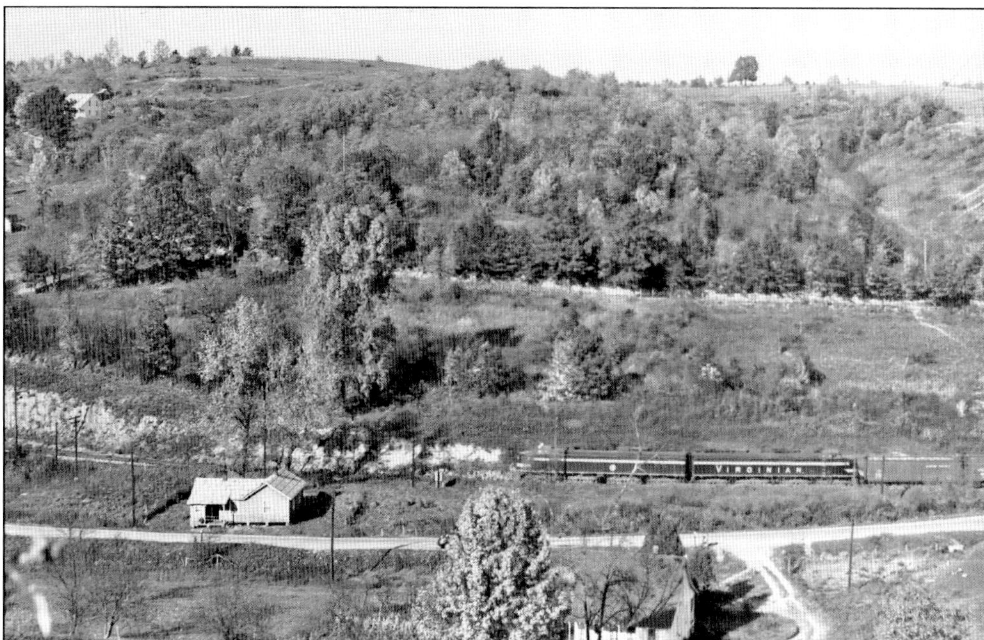

NO PLACE LIKE HOME. The E. R. Belcher home on 12 Mile Road just outside Princeton was located on the Virginian Railway mainline. Belcher worked the family farm shown here in addition to his demanding work in the Princeton Car Shops and still found time to amass an incredible collection of images documenting the history of the railroad's relationship with the city of Princeton. (Courtesy of Randolph Belcher.)

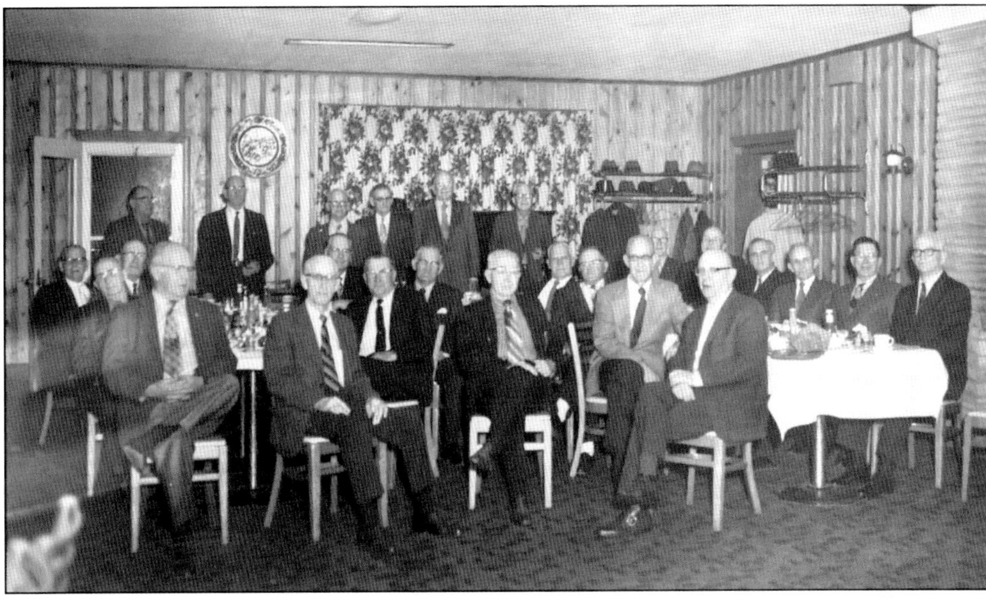

Out on the Town. Virginian employees are shown here at the Town-N-Country Restaurant gathered for an April 7, 1972, meeting. E. R. Belcher is seated on the front row at the left, Ray Bailey is in the middle, and Bill Miles is also pictured, according to John Waldron. (Courtesy of the author's collection.)

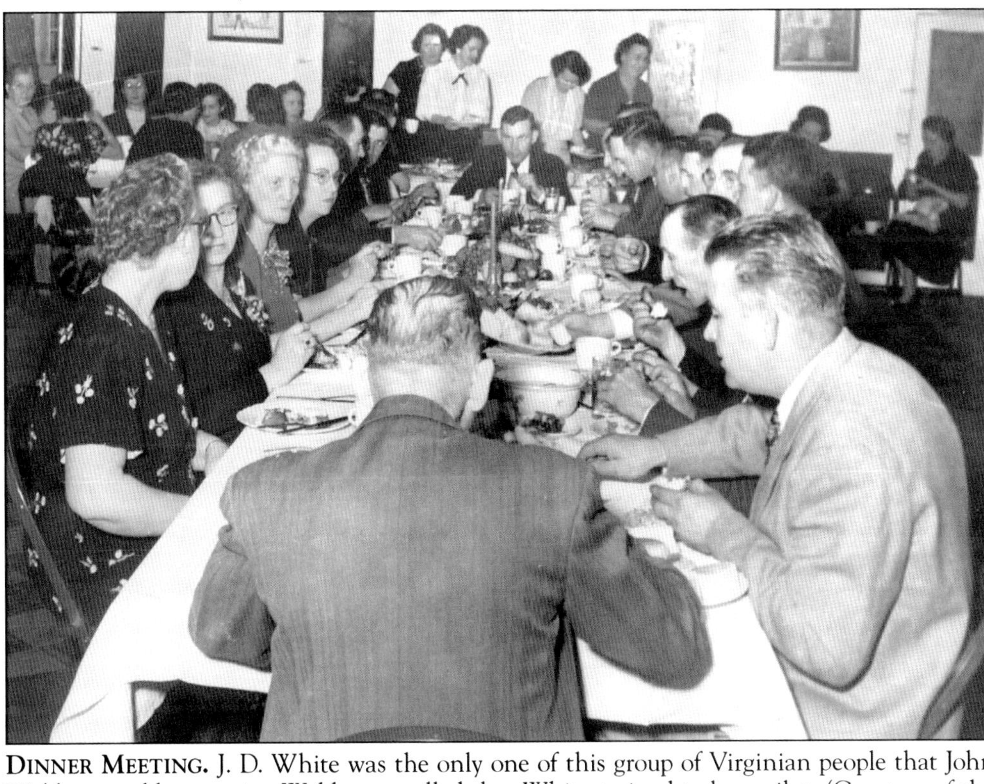

Dinner Meeting. J. D. White was the only one of this group of Virginian people that John Waldron could recognize. Waldron recalled that White trained to be a pilot. (Courtesy of the author's collection.)

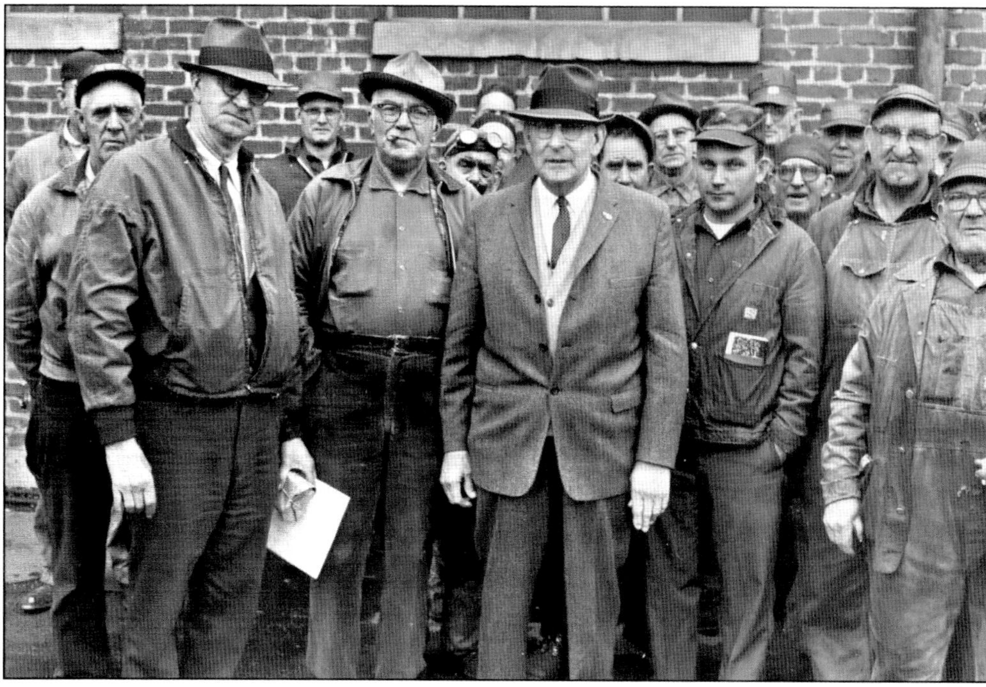

Looking Good. R. J. Boles is shown at his April 5, 1966, retirement. Milton "Red" Brookman is standing to the left of Boles, and John Waldron is to his immediate right. (Courtesy of Randolph Belcher.)

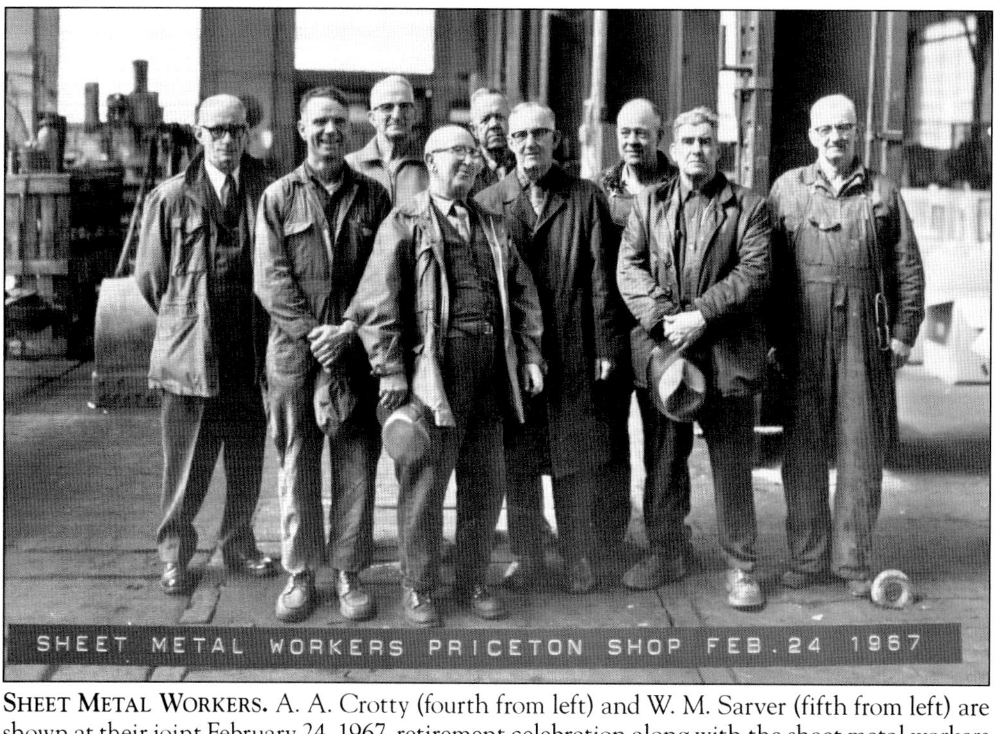

Sheet Metal Workers. A. A. Crotty (fourth from left) and W. M. Sarver (fifth from left) are shown at their joint February 24, 1967, retirement celebration along with the sheet metal workers of the Princeton Car Shops. (Courtesy of Randolph Belcher.)

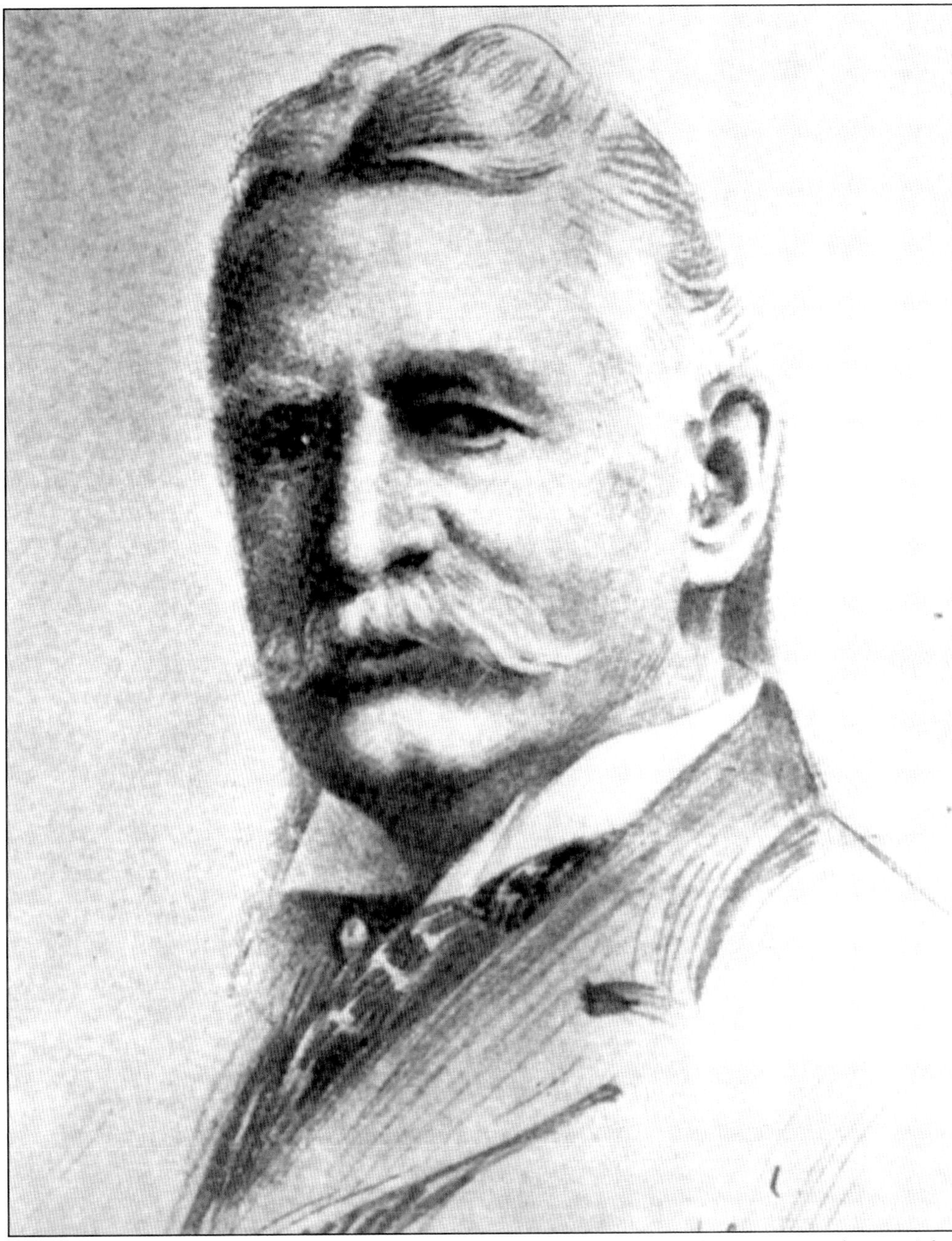

RAILROADING DREAM. Henry H. Rogers represented the very best of the American dream. After helping build the Standard Oil empire of the Rockefeller family, Rogers set out to open up the coalfields of southern West Virginia that weren't already being served by the C&O railroad to the north of Princeton and the N&W to the south. Rogers was more than an industrialist or a railroad man. He spent a considerable amount of effort trying to help the great American author Mark Twain (Samuel Clemens) to be comfortable in the twilight of his life. Rogers understood power, and he put that stamp on the Virginian Railway culture; that stamp endured through the history of the line. (Courtesy of Bill Carper.)

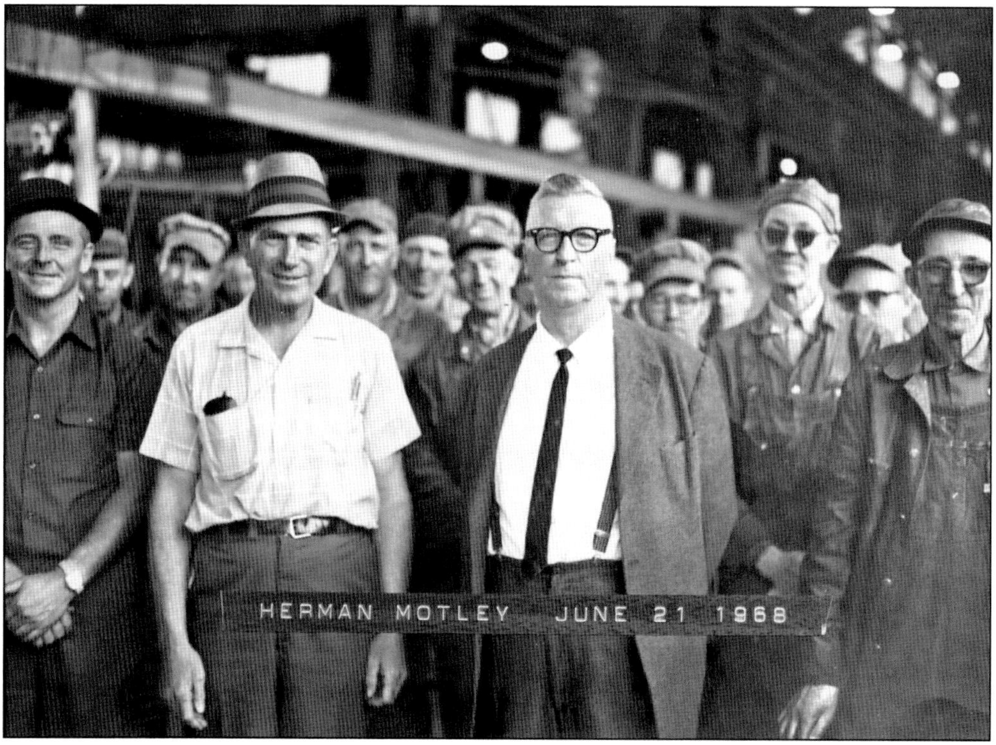

MOTLEY AND CREW. Herman Motley is shown at his June 21, 1968, retirement celebration. (Courtesy of Randolph Belcher.)

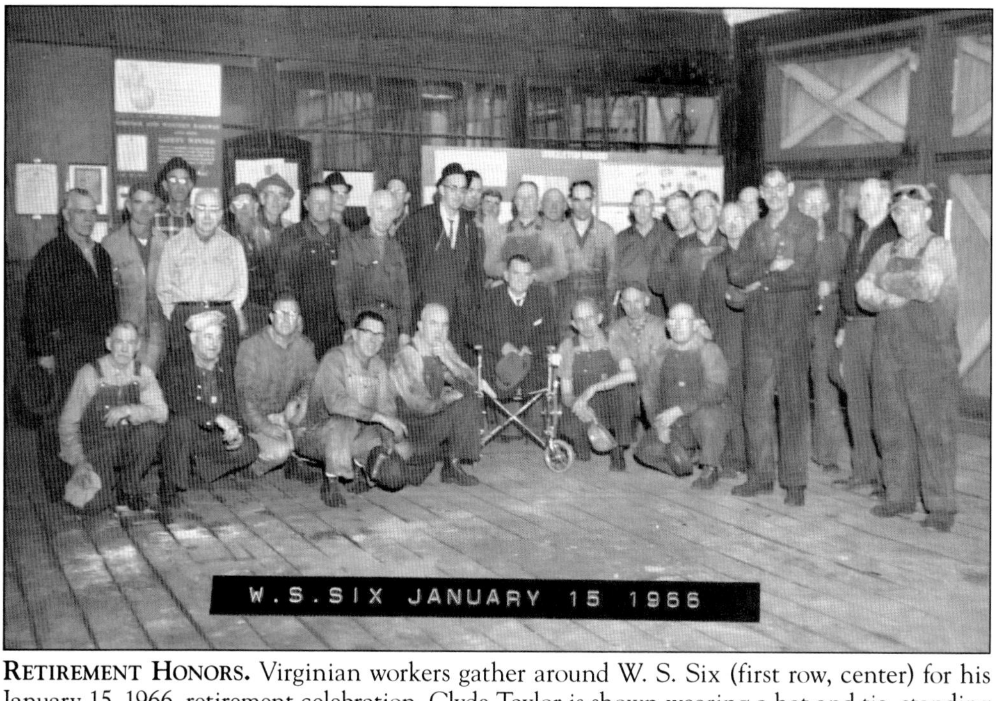

RETIREMENT HONORS. Virginian workers gather around W. S. Six (first row, center) for his January 15, 1966, retirement celebration. Clyde Taylor is shown wearing a hat and tie, standing in the second row to the left of Six. (Courtesy of Randolph Belcher.)

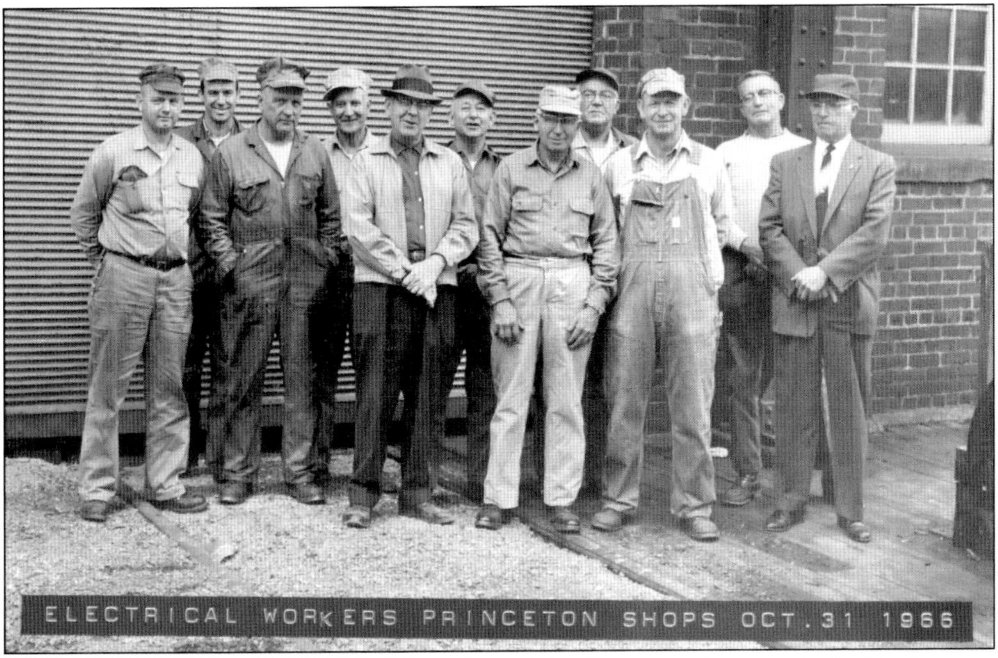

ELECTRICAL WORKERS. The electrical workers of the Princeton shops worked with the most powerful electrical motors ever built. Almost the entirety of the Virginian Railroad line was serviced by electric locomotives. This photograph is dated October 31, 1966. (Courtesy of Randolph Belcher.)

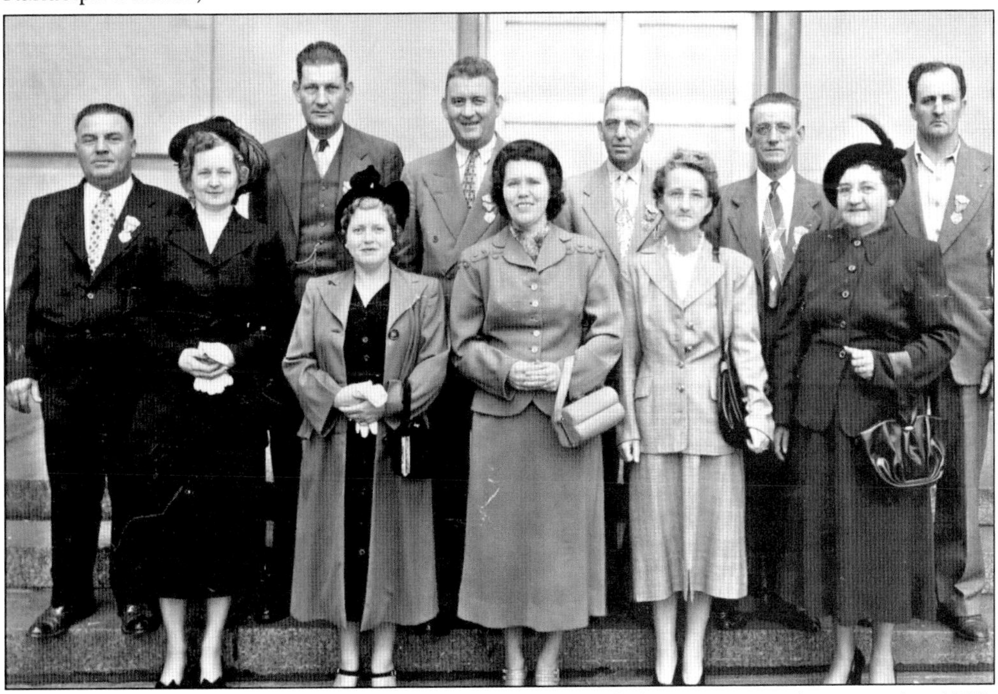

BETTER HALVES. Several Virginian Railway delegates and their wives are shown in this 1950s vintage photograph from Kansas City, Missouri. John Waldron could only recognize the second man from the right as Hugh Swim. (From the author's collection.)

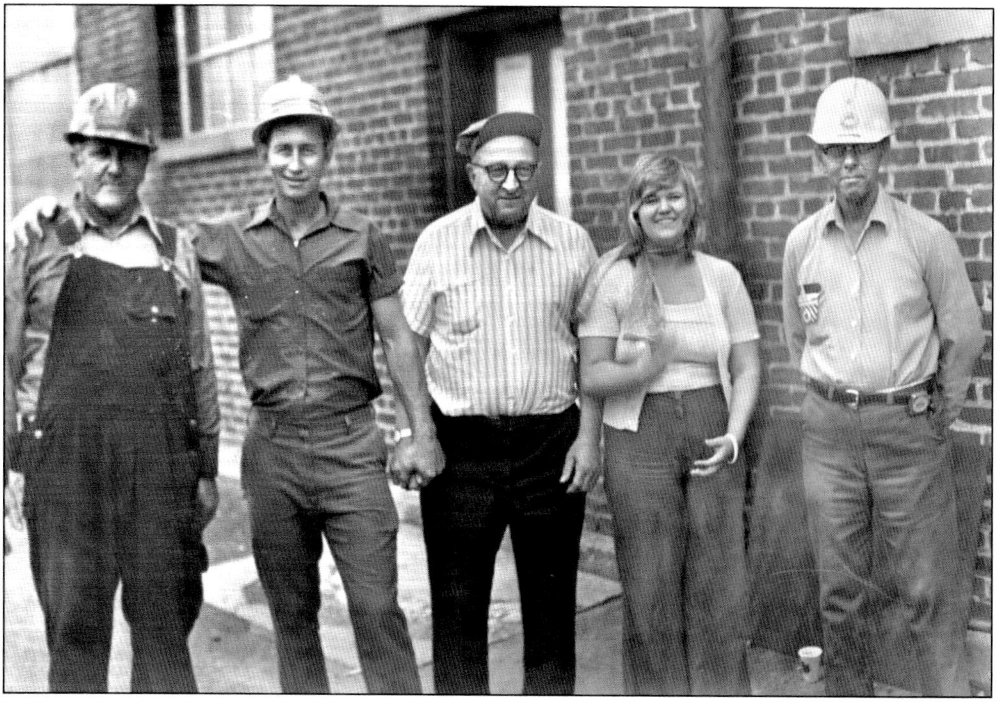

VIRGINIAN ROCKS. Roxanne Bourne (fourth from left) is shown in this photograph from July 1975. Bourne was hired by the N&W to work at the Princeton shops and remains with the NS, now in Bluefield. (Courtesy of Randolph Belcher.)

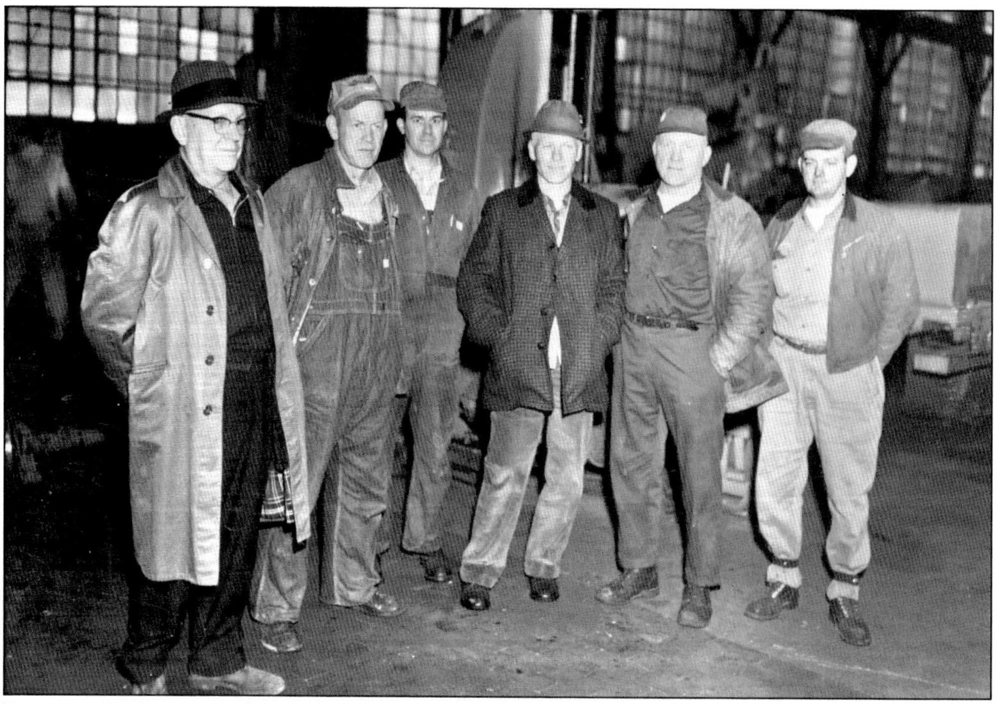

PLUGGED IN. Virginian electrical workers shown here from left to right include Bill Miller, Red Elmore, Buck Hatcher, Pete Belcher, Ted Malcolm, and Freddie White. (Courtesy of John Waldron.)

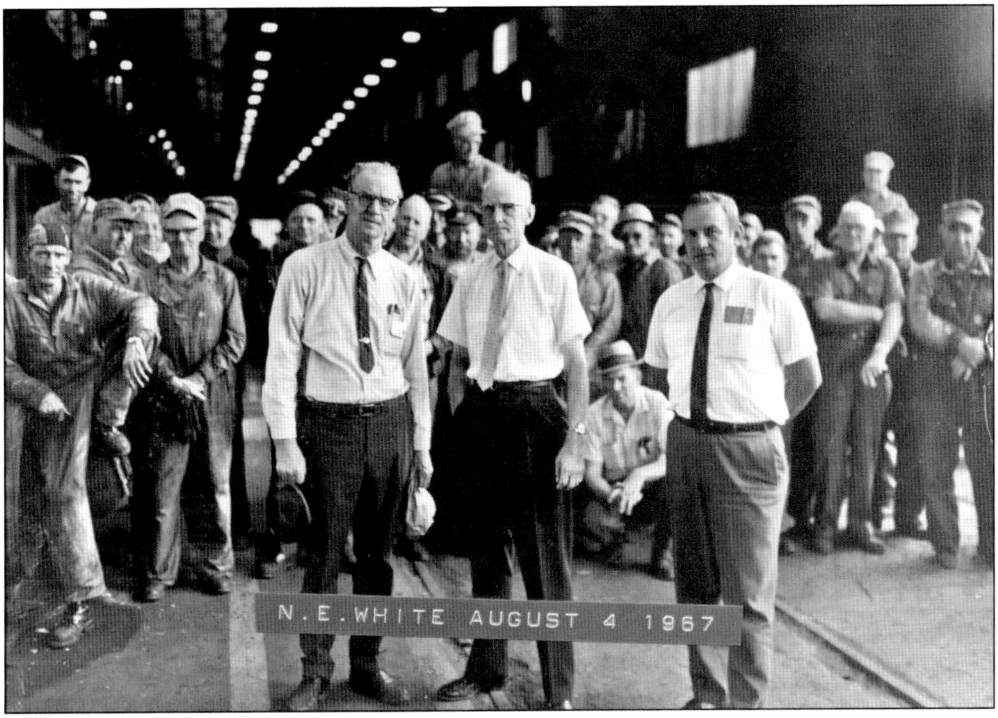

RED AND WHITE. N. E. White (center) is shown at his August 4, 1967, retirement celebration. Milton "Red" Brookman is shown to the left of White. (Courtesy of Randolph Belcher.)

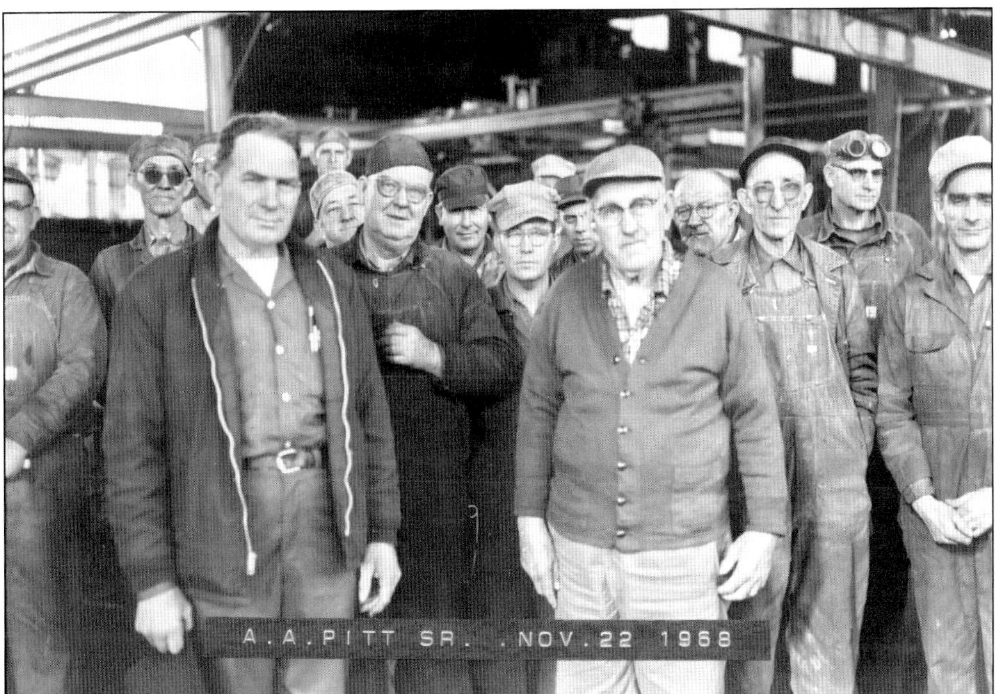

GO PITT. A. A. Pitt Sr. is shown here at his November 22, 1968, retirement celebration. (Courtesy of Randolph Belcher.)

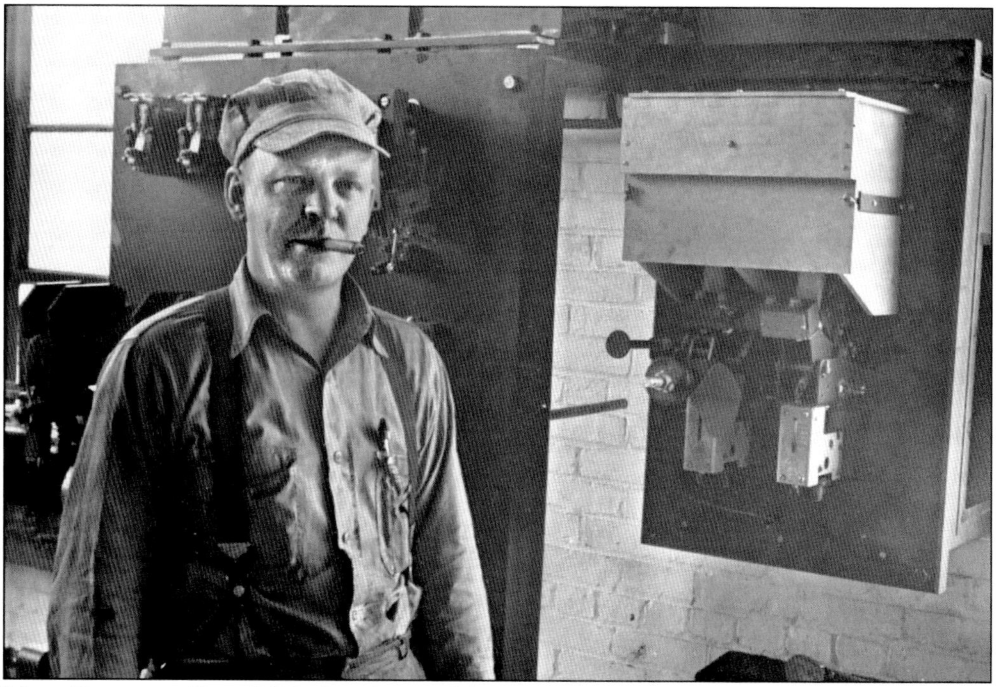

MORE POWER TO YOU. Bill Miles, electrical foreman at the Princeton Car Shops, is shown in a candid photograph taken by E. R. Belcher. (Courtesy of Randolph Belcher.)

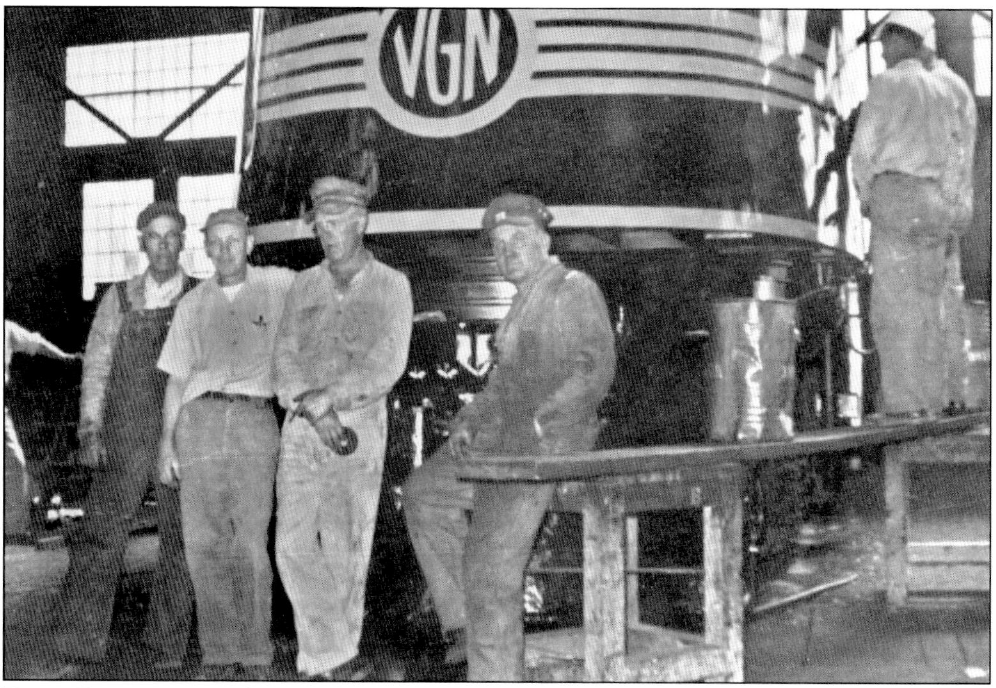

FRESH PAINT JOB. Workers are shown inside the Princeton shops putting the finishing touches on a Virginian locomotive. The third man from the left above is R. A. "Randolph" Belcher, benefactor of many of the incredible Virginian Railway photographs in this book. (Courtesy of Randolph Belcher.)

Three

A City of Fuel and Power

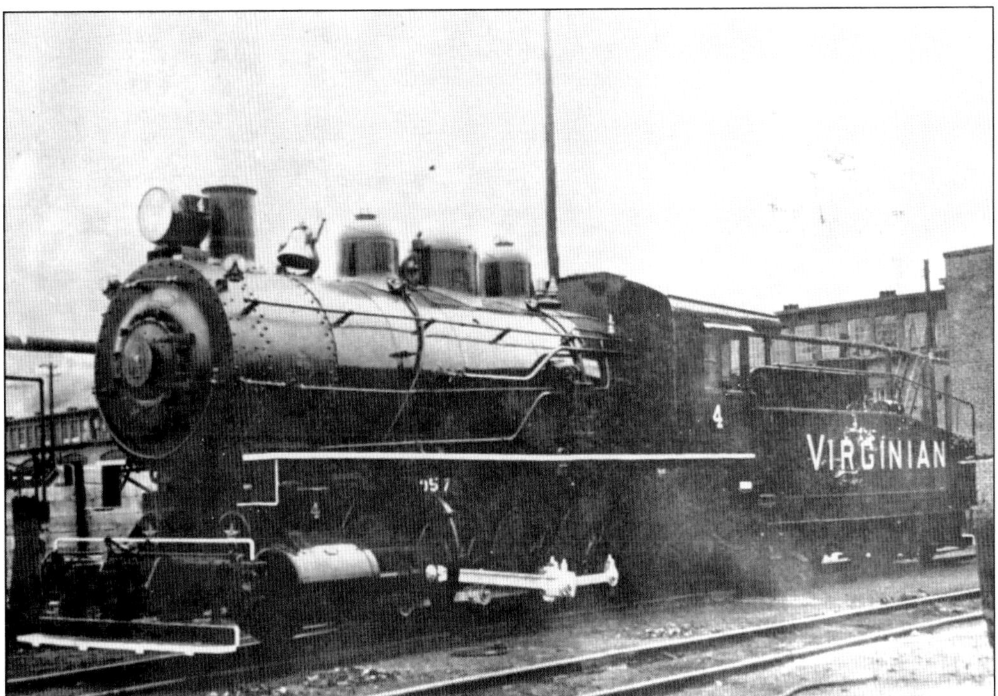

Four Spot. Workers at the Virginian's Princeton shops used the old "Four Spot" locomotive to move cars around the rail yard surrounding the repair shop. Randolph Belcher said workers took the Four Spot to Roanoke once to pick up some cars, but it never ran faster than 10 miles per hour on the whole trip. (Courtesy of Randolph Belcher.)

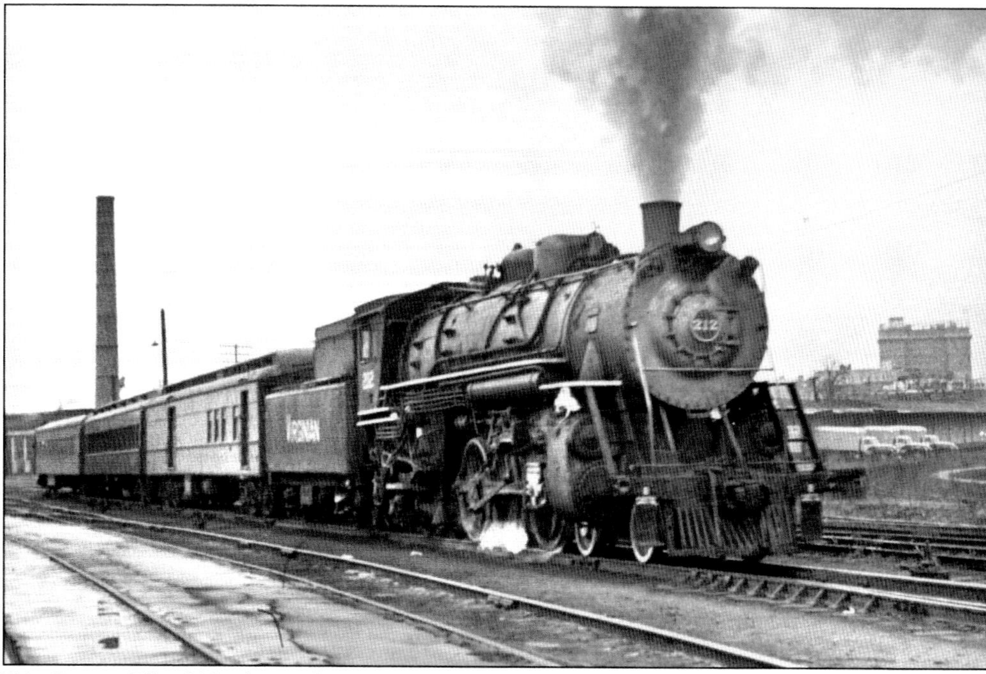

PA Class. The 212, shown here steaming up in Princeton, was one of the Virginian's PA class of steam locomotives that were acquired in 1920 to power passenger trains. The powerful PAs maintained fast freight and passenger schedules, pulling as many as 12 cars. (Courtesy of Randolph Belcher.)

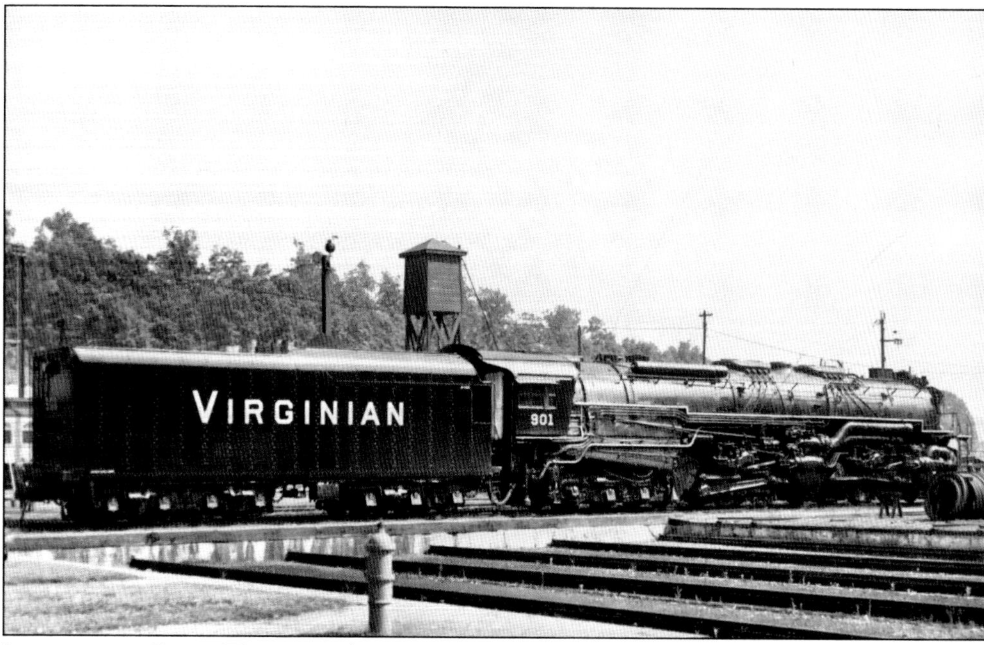

Last of the Line. The Lima class 901, shown here, was the last of the steam locomotives rebuilt in the Princeton shops. Although it was rebuilt to perfection, it never returned to regular mainline service. Its sister locomotive, the 900, was built in 1945 and sold in 1960. (Courtesy of Randolph Belcher.)

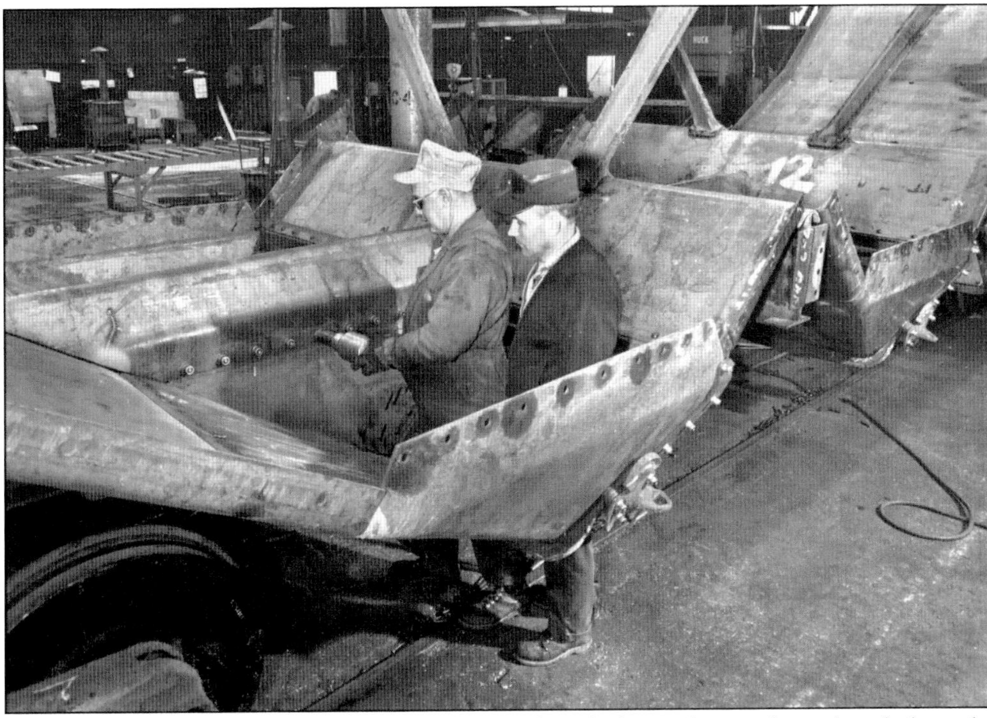

Hog Backs. J. D. "David" White (right) and an unidentified coworker are shown here bolting the shoots or "hog backs" of a gondola car in the Princeton Car Shops. (Photograph by Mel Grubb.)

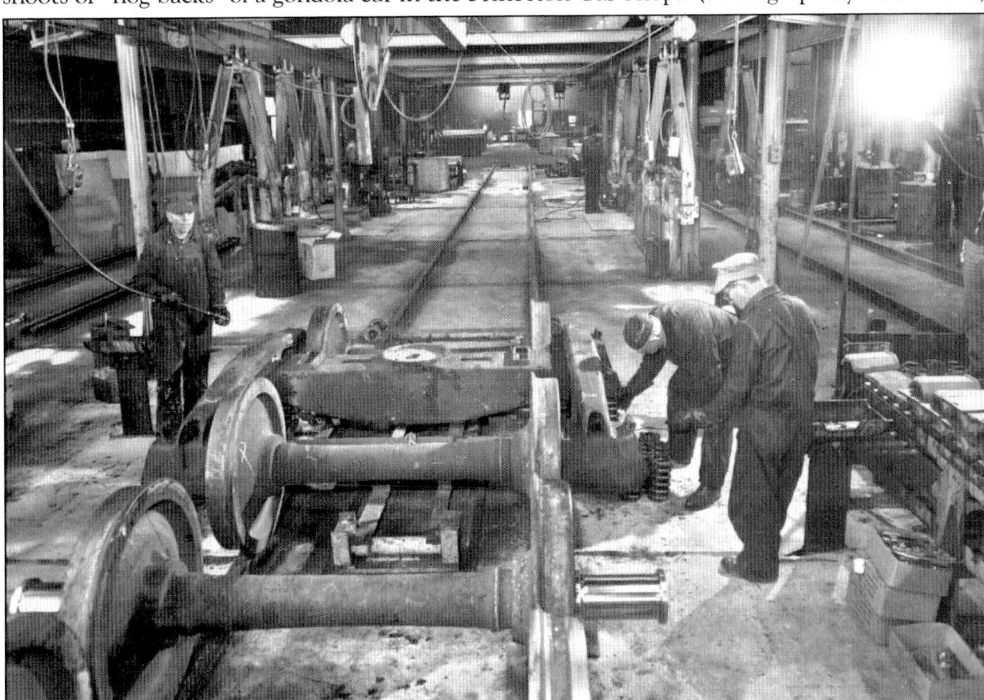

Keep on Truckin'. Willard Walters (left), Dave Gordon (center), and Lloyd Hill are shown here working on the trucks of a railroad car at the Princeton Car Shops. (Photograph by Mel Grubb.)

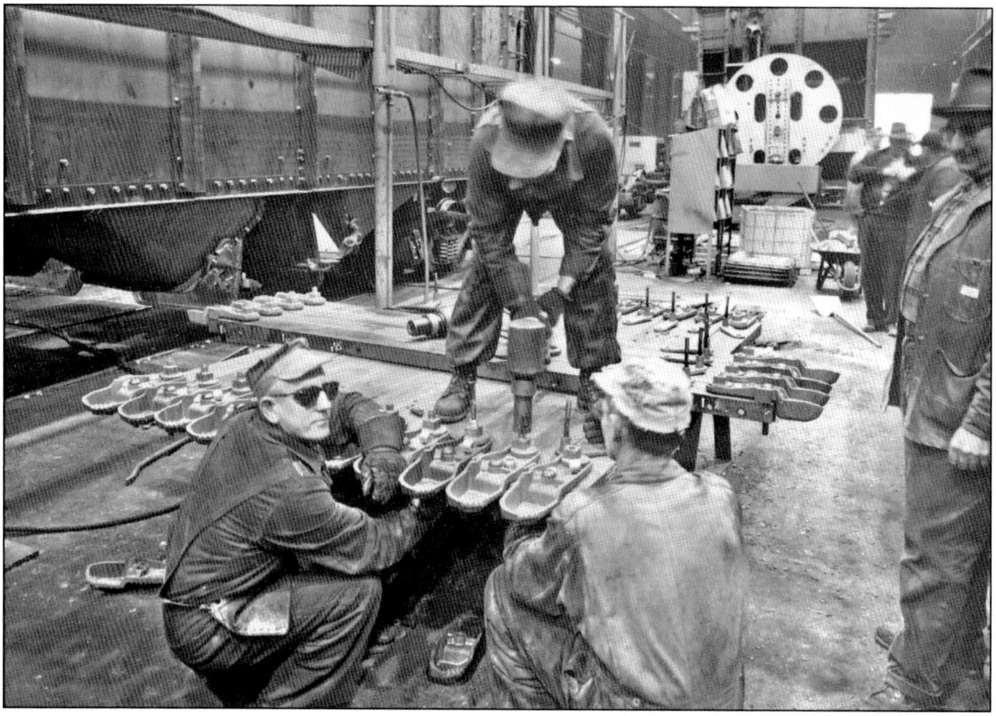

SPREADERS. O. D. Pendleton (kneeling at left) is installing door spreaders in a gondola car as Gene Williams (far right) looks on. (Photograph by Mel Grubb.)

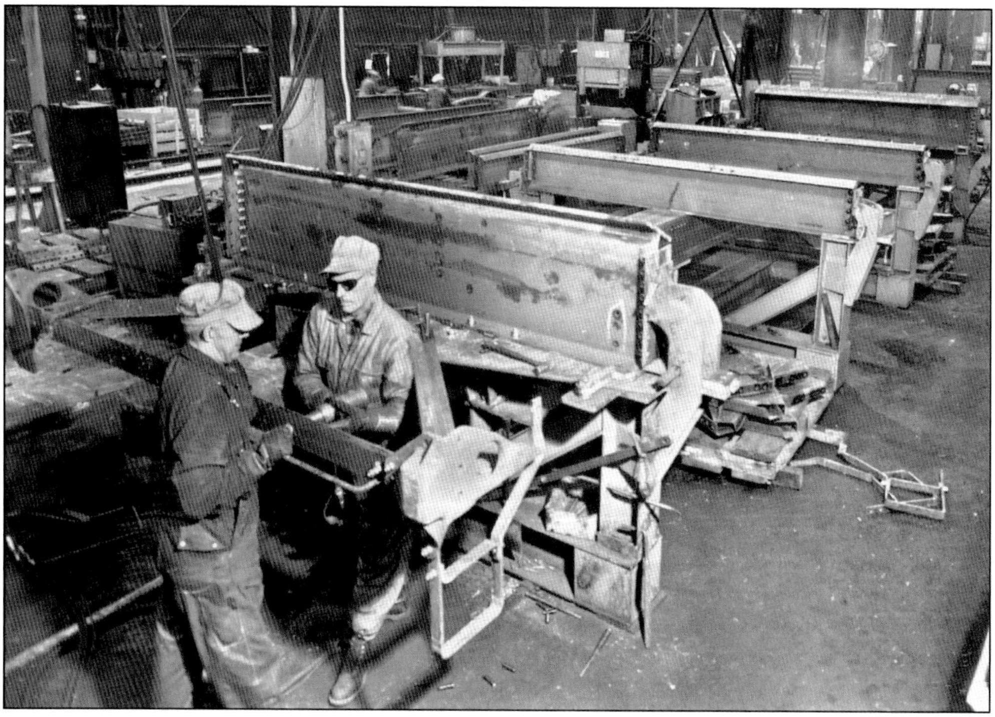

NUTS AND BOLTS. Jim Thornhill and Henry Hill are shown here bolting pieces of a railroad car together. (Photograph by Mel Grubb.)

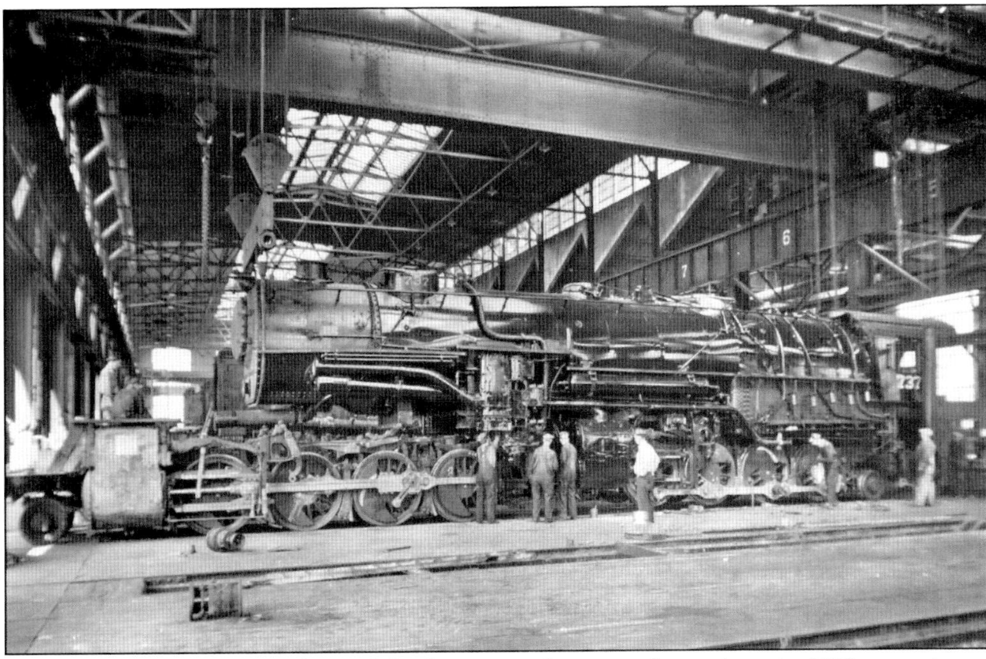

Rebuilding the 737. Workers of the Princeton shops are shown here in 1948 preparing to rebuild the U.S. E-Class 2-8-8-2 steam locomotive No. 737. The mallet-type locomotive was built to deliver maximum power for operating on the grades of the southern West Virginia coalfields. (Courtesy of Randolph Belcher.)

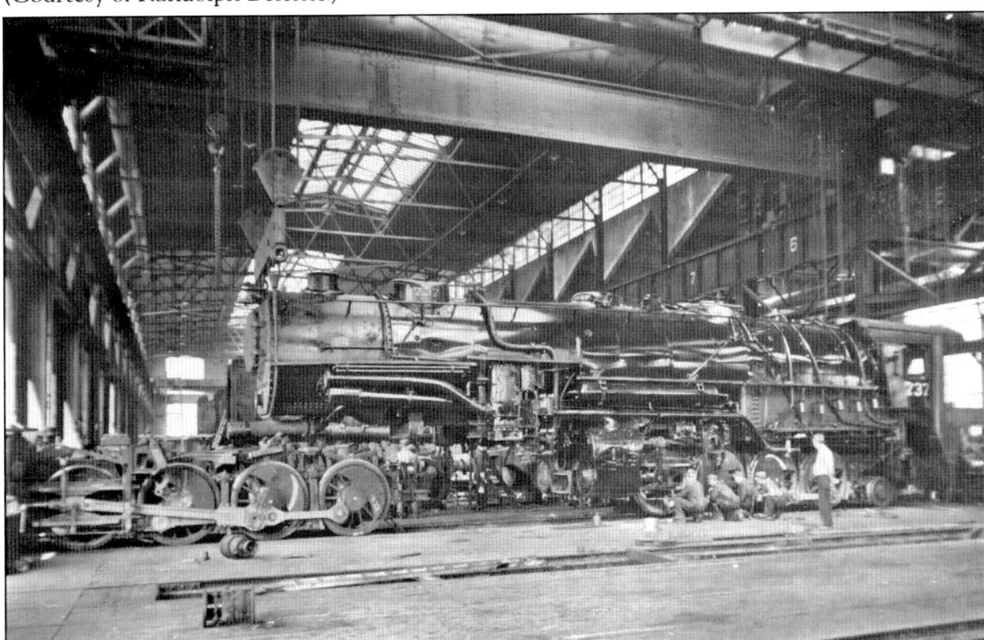

Drivers Away. Virginian workers have removed the front driver from the No. 737. The U.S. E-Class locomotives were originally built for the N&W but soon went into service on the Atchison, Topeka, and Santa Fe line before being bought by the Virginian. Shop workers are shown preparing to remove the rear driver trucks. (Courtesy of Randolph Belcher.)

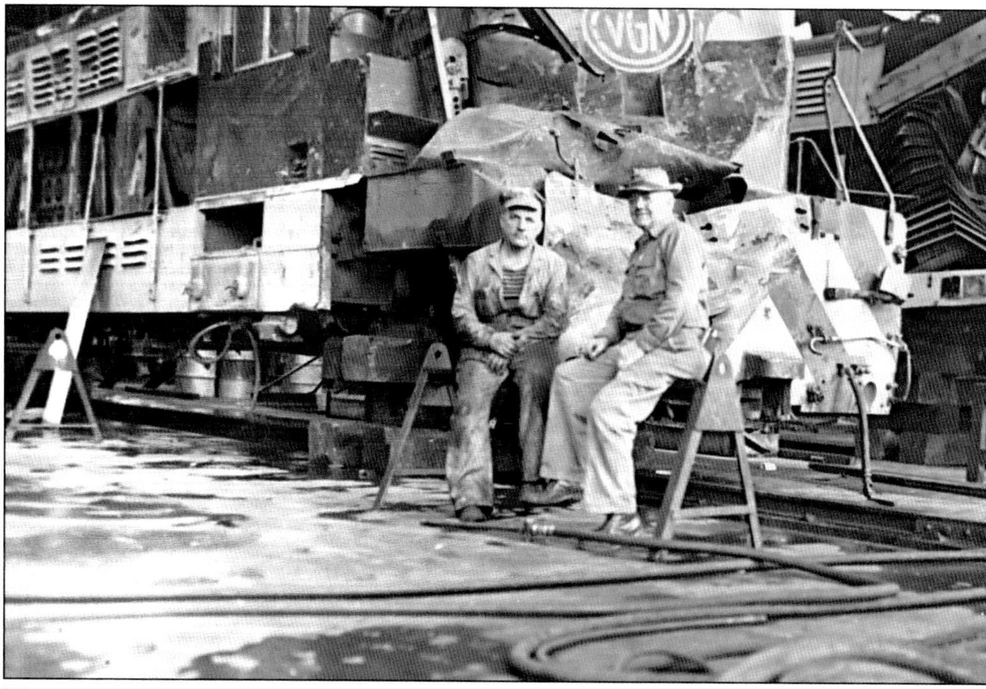

WAITING FOR A WRECK. Ted Malcolm and Amos Bowles are shown here posing in front of a wrecked locomotive before starting to get on with their work. (Courtesy of Randolph Belcher.)

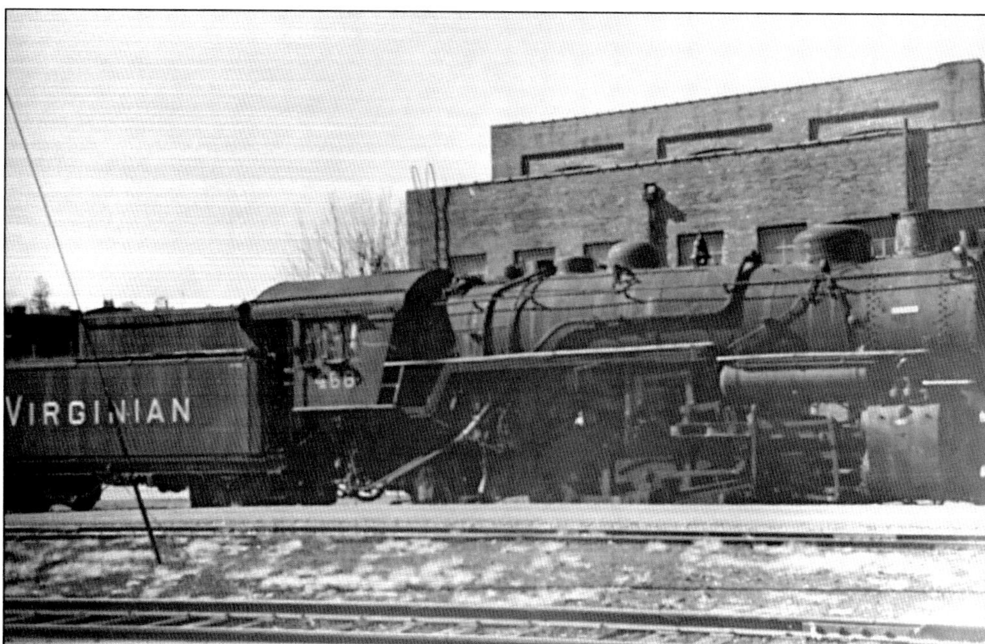

STEAMED. The Virginian 2-8-2 No. 468 saw plenty of work bringing coal out of Wyoming County bound for the Atlantic Coast. (Courtesy of Randolph Belcher.)

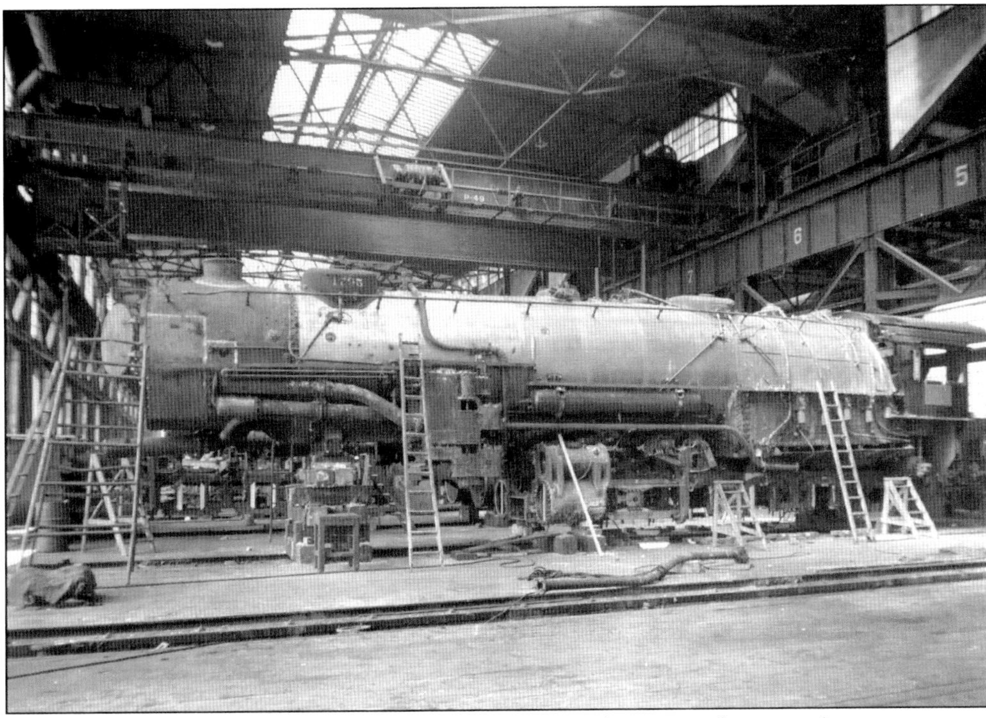

STRIPPED. It's back to work on the old U.S. E-Class No. 737. The exterior fittings and component parts have to be removed as part of the total rebuilding process. (Courtesy of Randolph Belcher.)

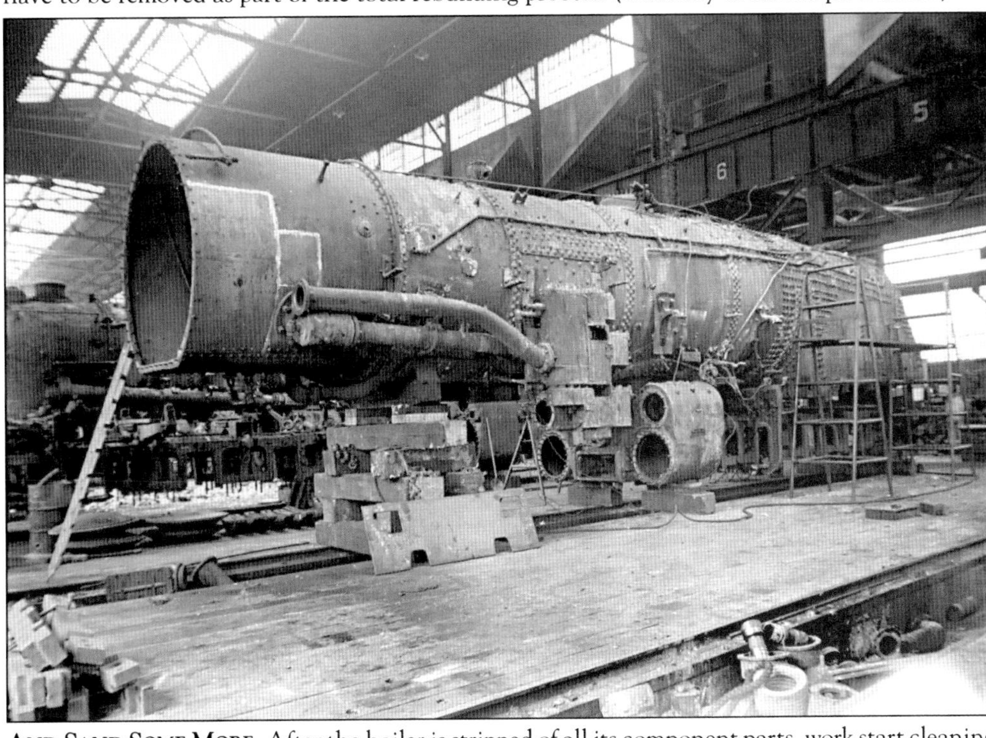

AND SAND SOME MORE. After the boiler is stripped of all its component parts, work start cleaning and preparing the locomotive for rebuilding. (Courtesy of Randolph Belcher.)

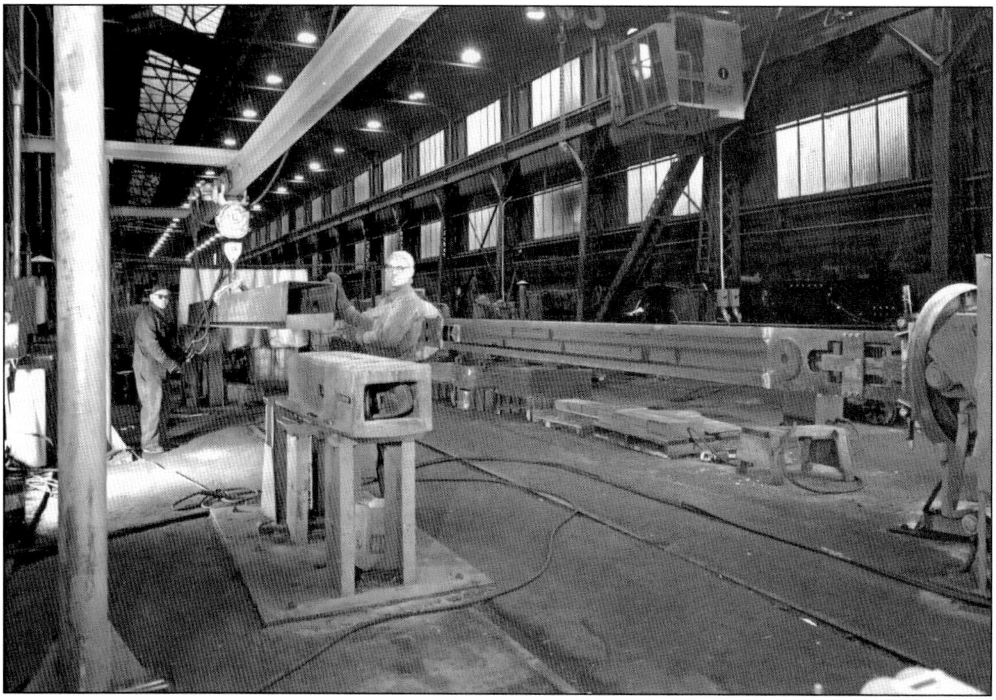

PUTTING IT TOGETHER. Frank Hill, shown here, was a top-flight welder in the Princeton Car Shops. John Waldron recalls that Hill could light a cigarette and not remove it from his mouth when he dropped his welding shield back in place while he worked. (Photograph by Mel Grubb.)

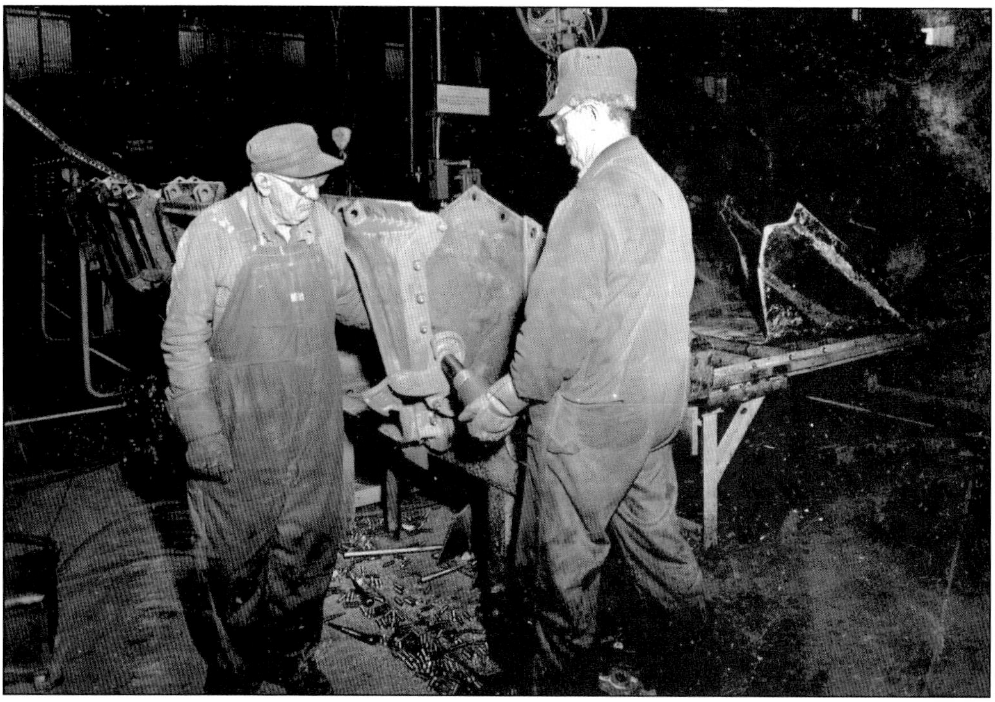

BOLTING. Two unidentified Virginian shop workers are shown assembling parts as part of car assembly work. (Photograph by Mel Grubb.)

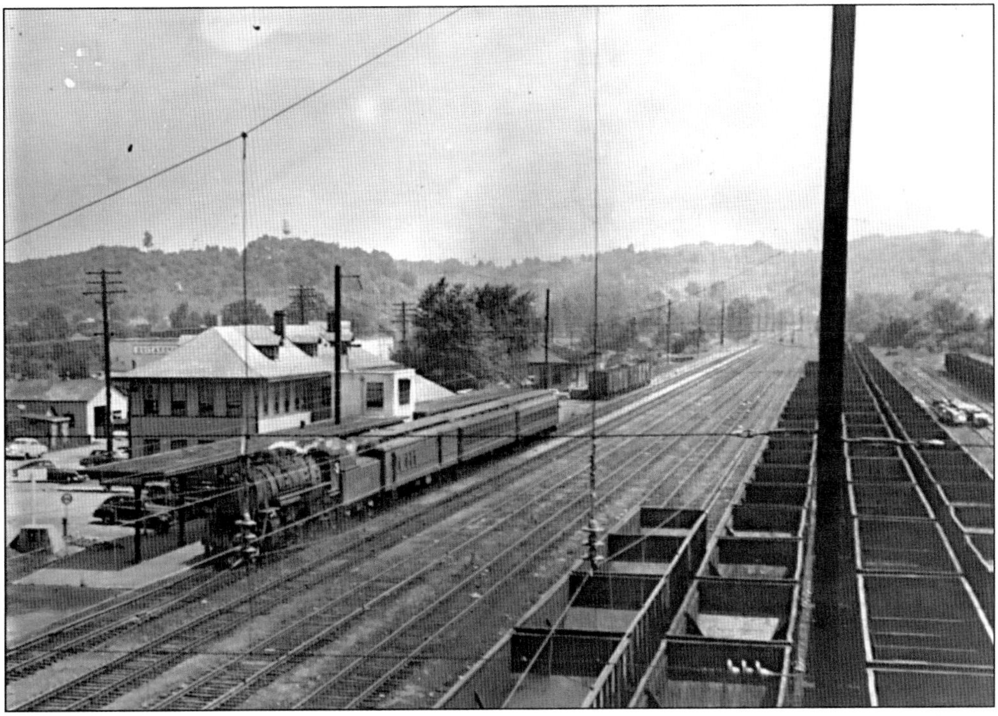

BUSY YARD. A lot of coal, freight, and passengers moved through the Virginian Railway's Princeton yard. The No. 3 and No. 4 passenger trains made their last run through Princeton in 1955. (Courtesy of Elaine Mooney.)

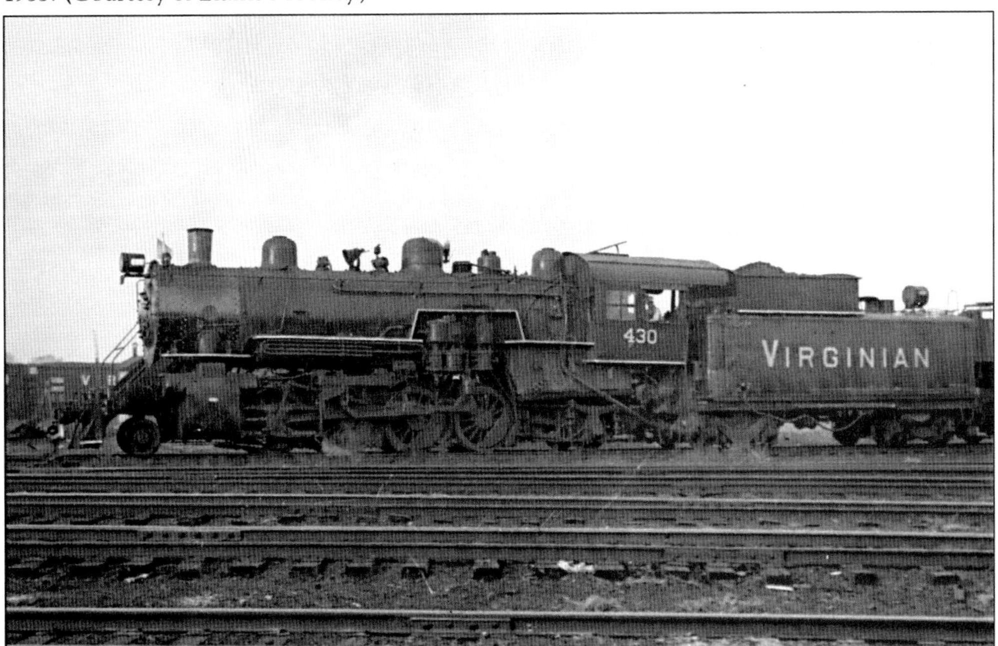

WORKHORSE LOCOMOTIVE. The MB Class 2-8-2 No. 430, a 1909 model locomotive, remained in service at least until 1955 and provided the railroad with the power it needed to move coal from the mountains, down the mainline, and on to Sewalls Point. (Courtesy of Randolph Belcher.)

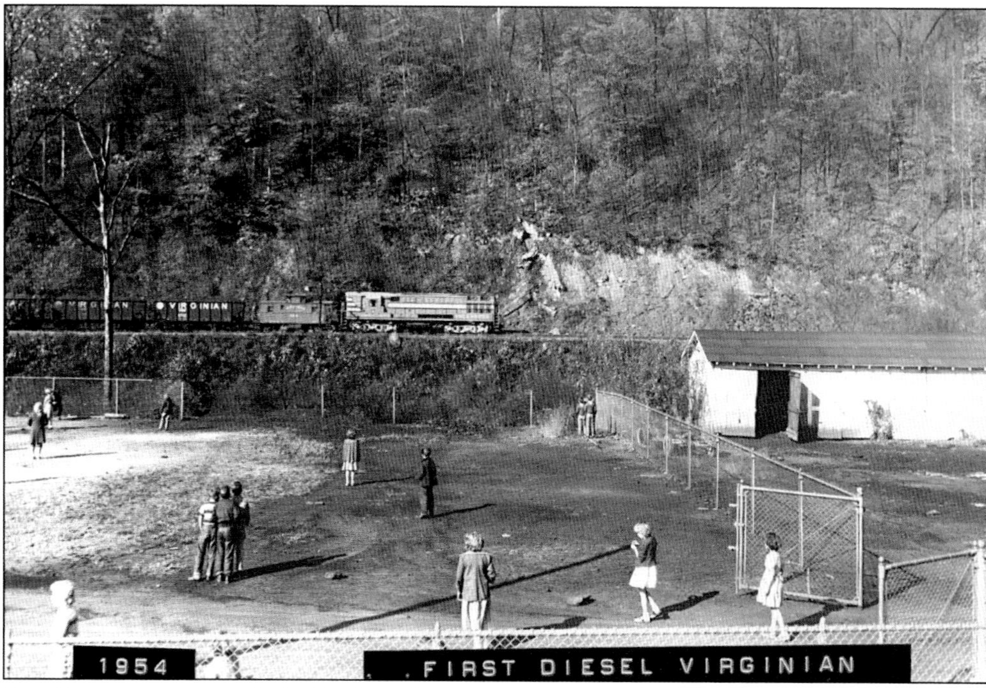

THE DIESELS ARRIVE. E. R. Belcher photographs the arrival of the first diesel locomotive in Princeton in 1954. The locomotive, a Fairbanks-Morse 1600 HP model, changed railroading on the Virginian forever by replacing steam and electric locomotives. (Courtesy of Randolph Belcher.)

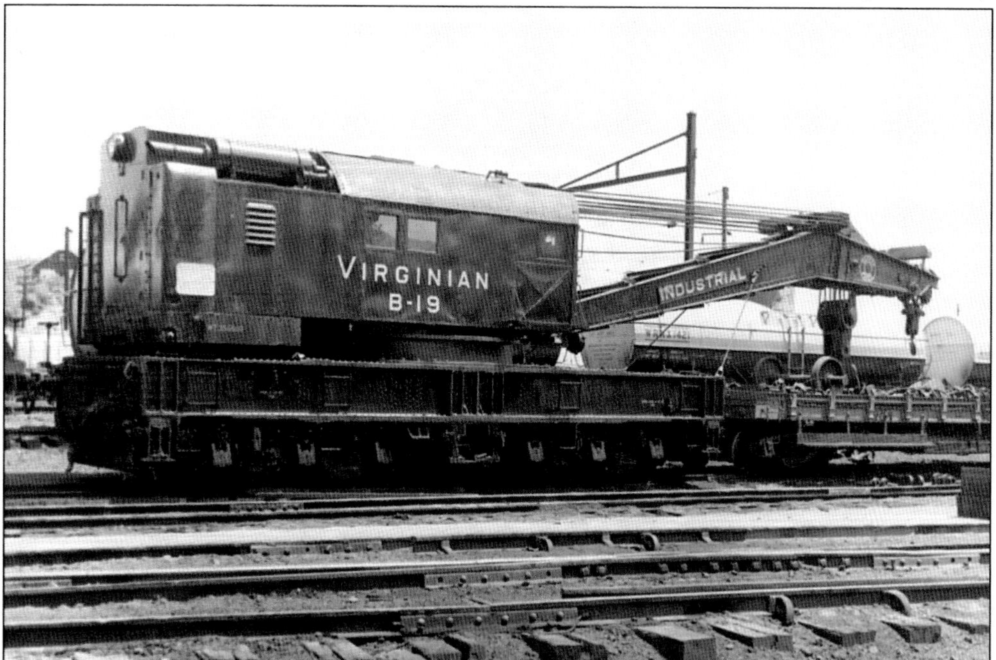

BIG CRANE. The Virginian's mobile crane, the B-19, is shown here in Roanoke, Virginia, after its arrival at the Virginian in 1958. Although it was at Princeton a considerable amount of time, the 250-ton crane could assist anywhere on the line. (Courtesy of Randolph Belcher.)

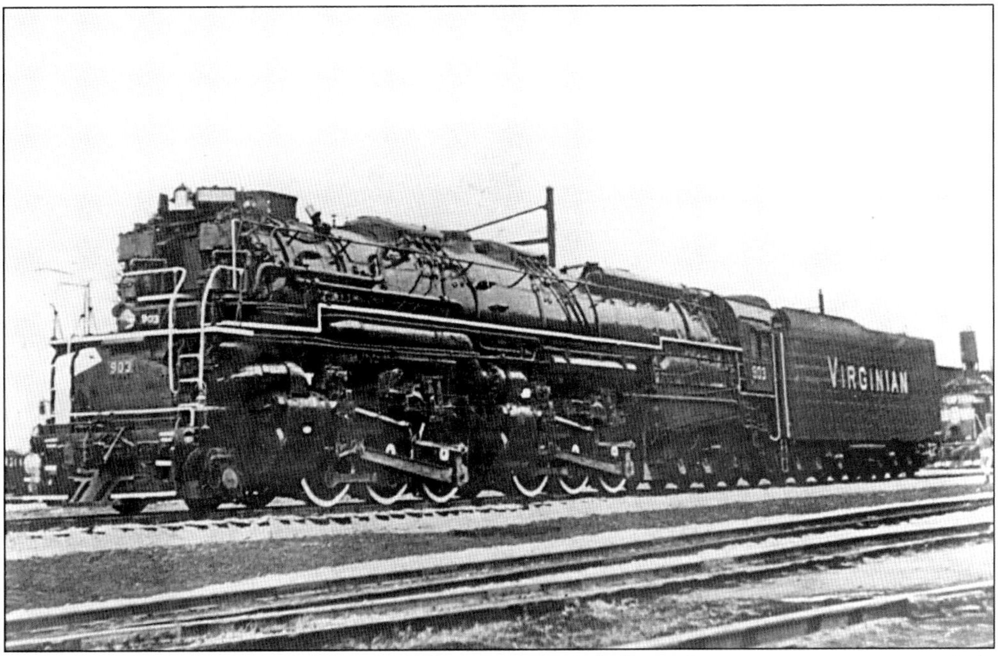

BIG WHEELS KEEP ROLLIN'. The Lima class AG No. 903 shown here went into service in July 1945 but had a short-lived history on the Virginian. The 903 was sold in January 1960, along with the seven other AG 2-6-6-6 locomotives on the former Virginian rails. (Courtesy of Grubb Photo Service.)

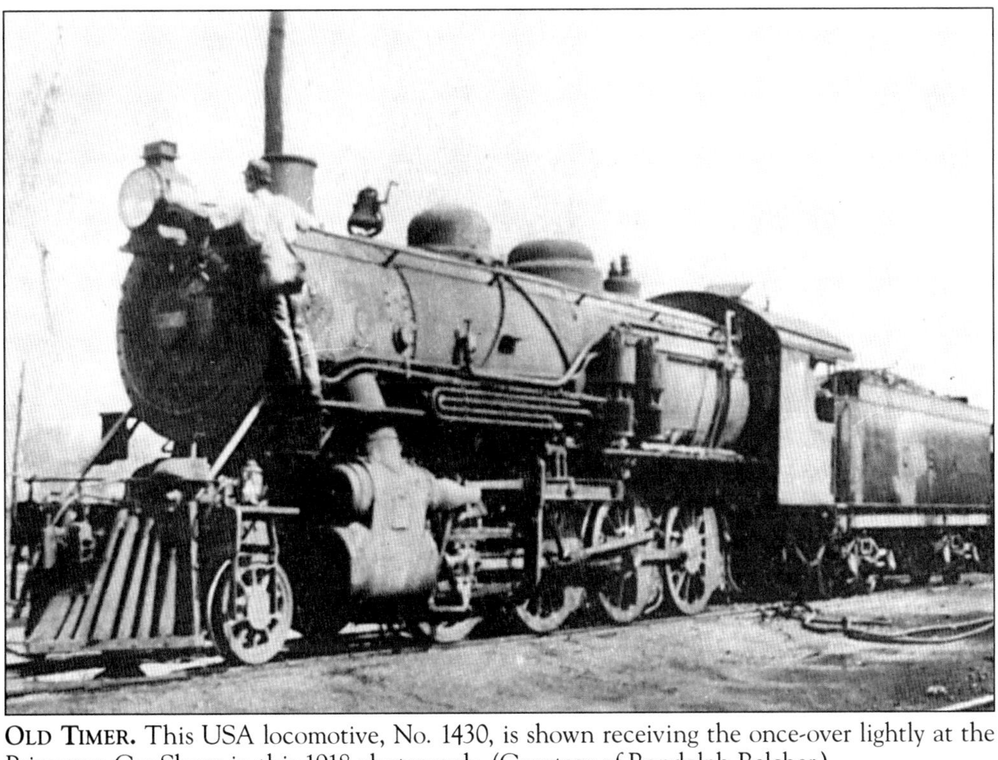

OLD TIMER. This USA locomotive, No. 1430, is shown receiving the once-over lightly at the Princeton Car Shops in this 1918 photograph. (Courtesy of Randolph Belcher.)

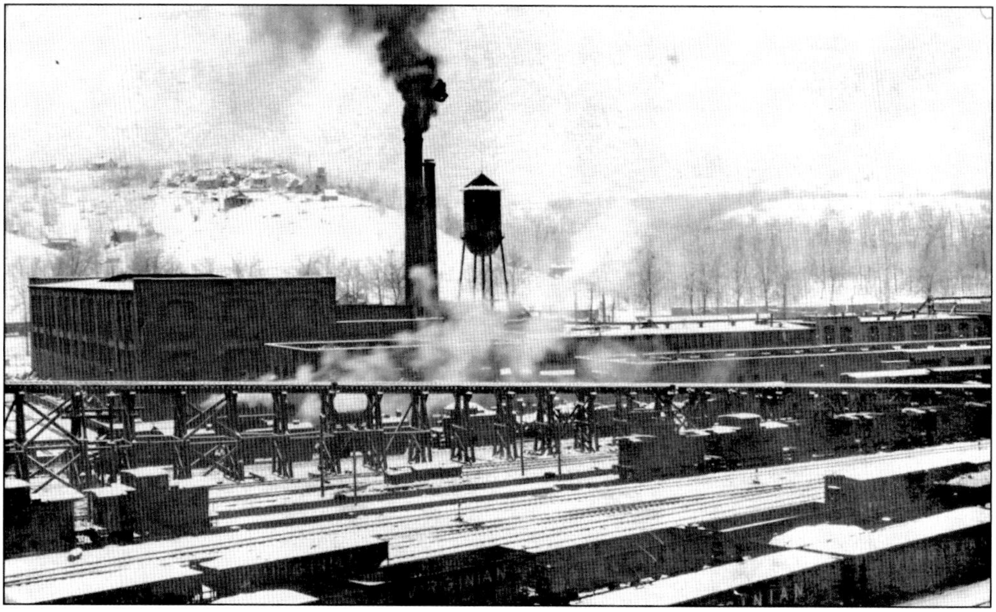

Frigid. It can get cold in Mercer County, as evident in this view of the snow-covered Princeton Car Shops. (Courtesy of Randolph Belcher.)

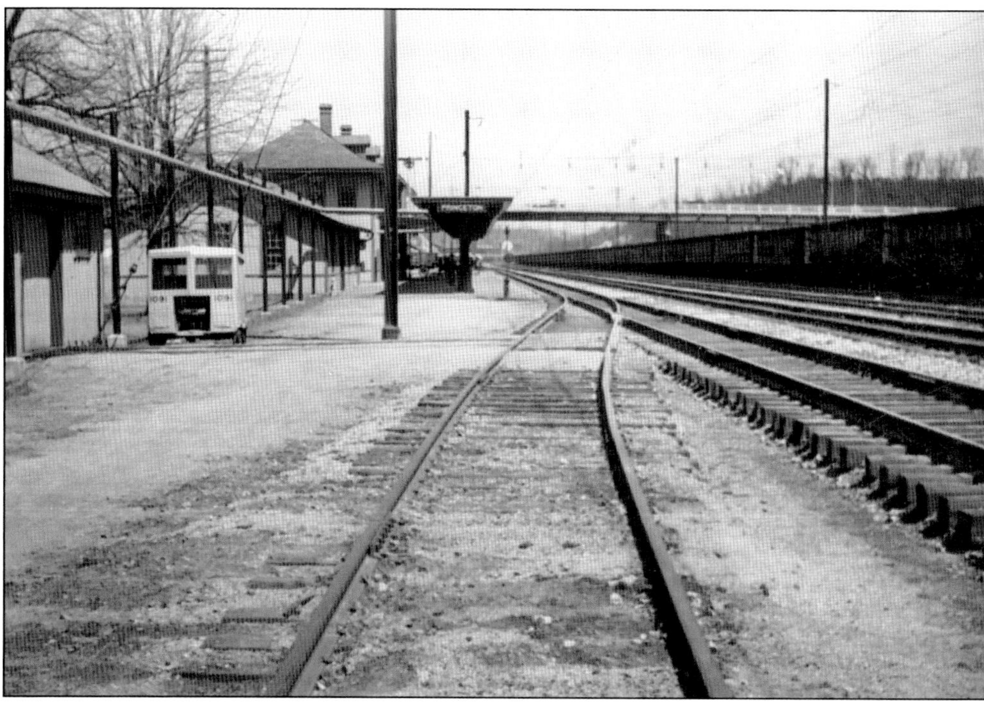

Waiting for a Train. The Princeton passenger station is shown here with no activity at the boarding zone. (Courtesy of Randolph Belcher.)

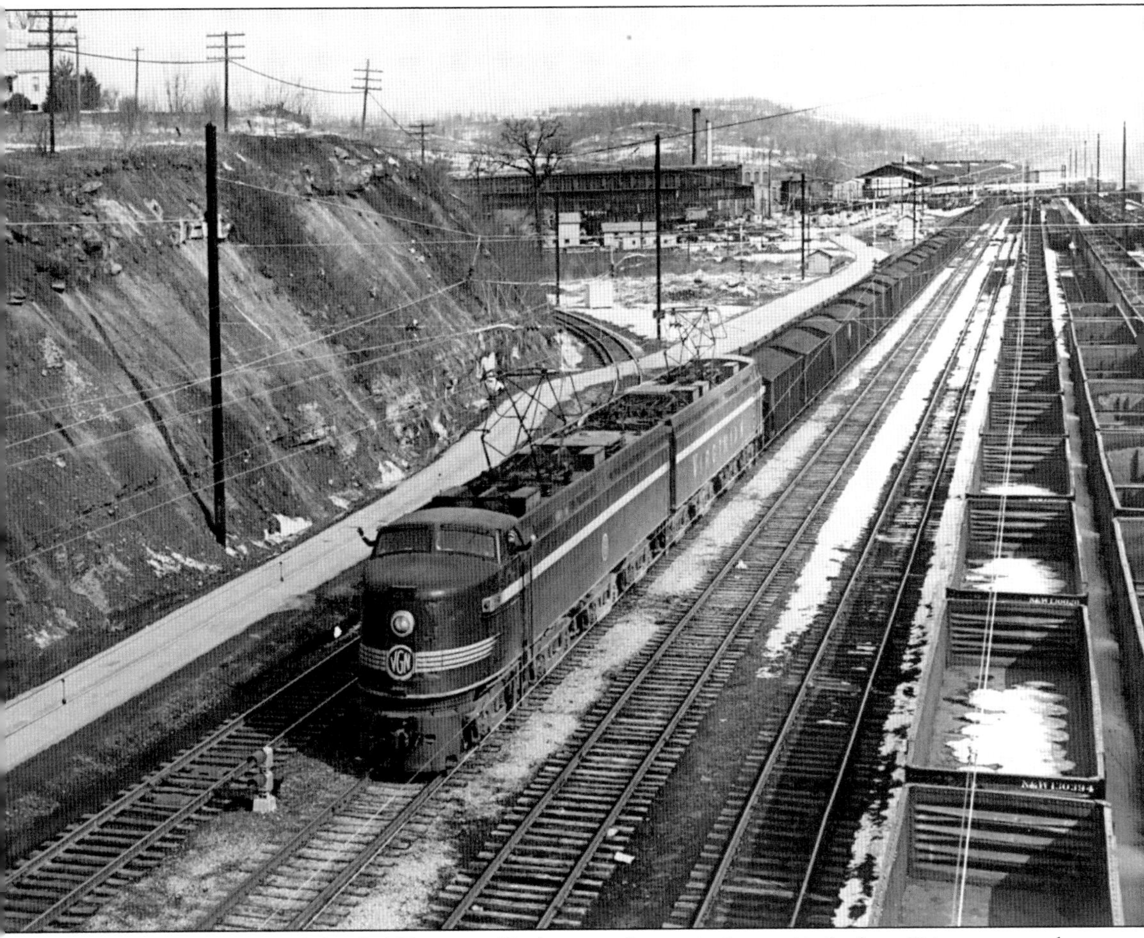

ON THE MAINLINE. A loaded Virginian Railway coal train is shown in the busy Princeton yard. The 125 General Electric power units like the one shown above were placed in service in 1948 and remained with the line through the transition from the Virginian to the Norfolk and Western in 1959. The "biggest electric motors ever built," according to Randolph Belcher, they supplied the electricity to energize the Virginian power mills. (Courtesy of Grubb Photo Service.)

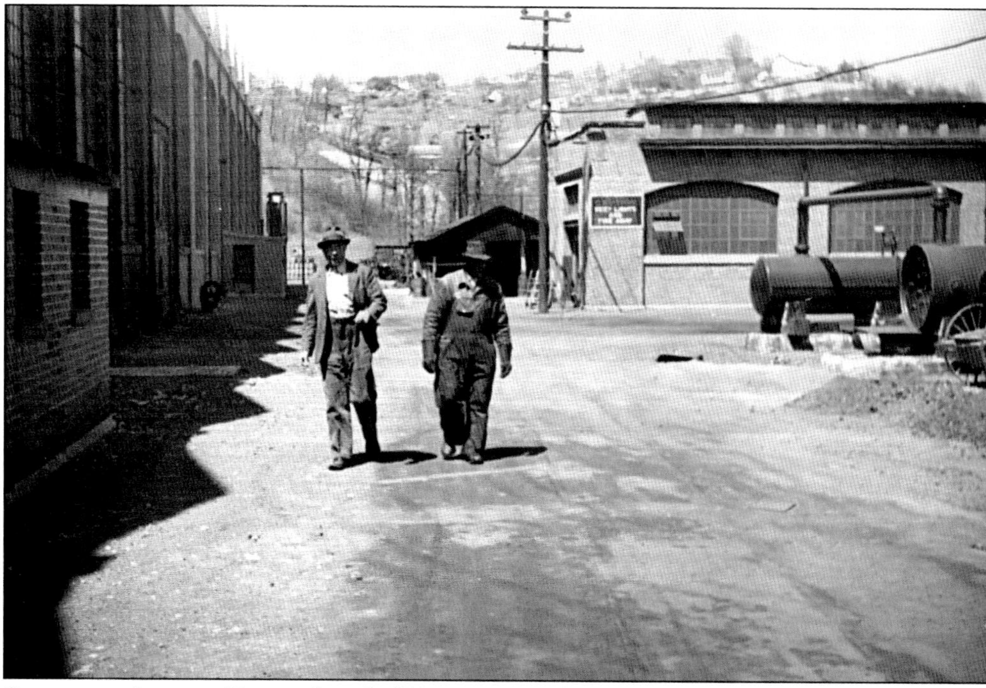

Out for a Stroll. Two unidentified Virginian employees are shown walking on the roadway between buildings of the Princeton Car Shop. (Courtesy of Randolph Belcher.)

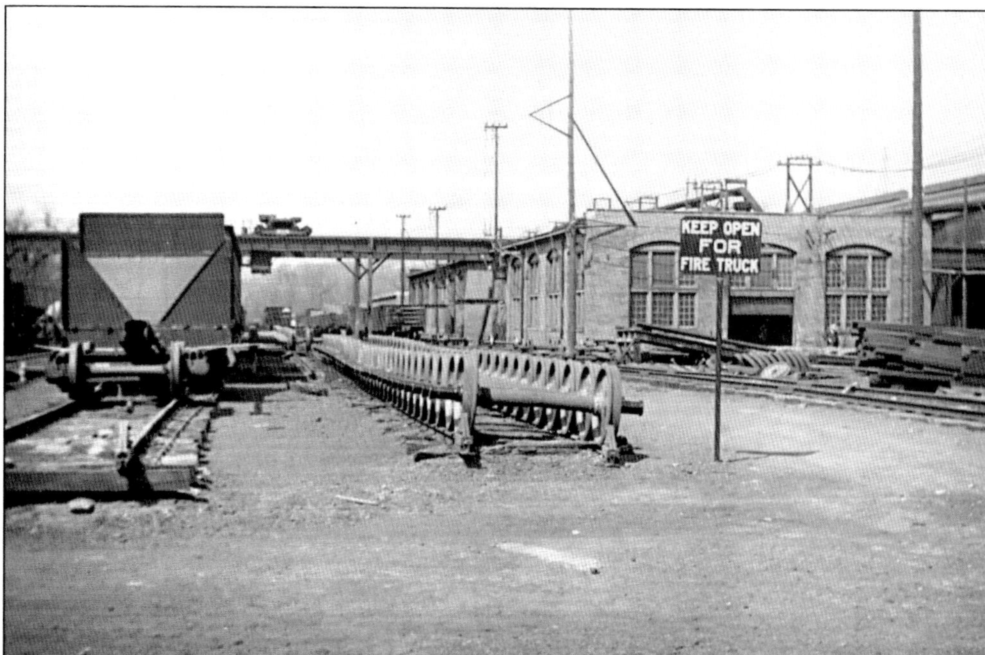

Plenty of Wheels. Car wheels are shown ready to be put into service for new or rebuilt railroad cars. (Courtesy of Randall Belcher.)

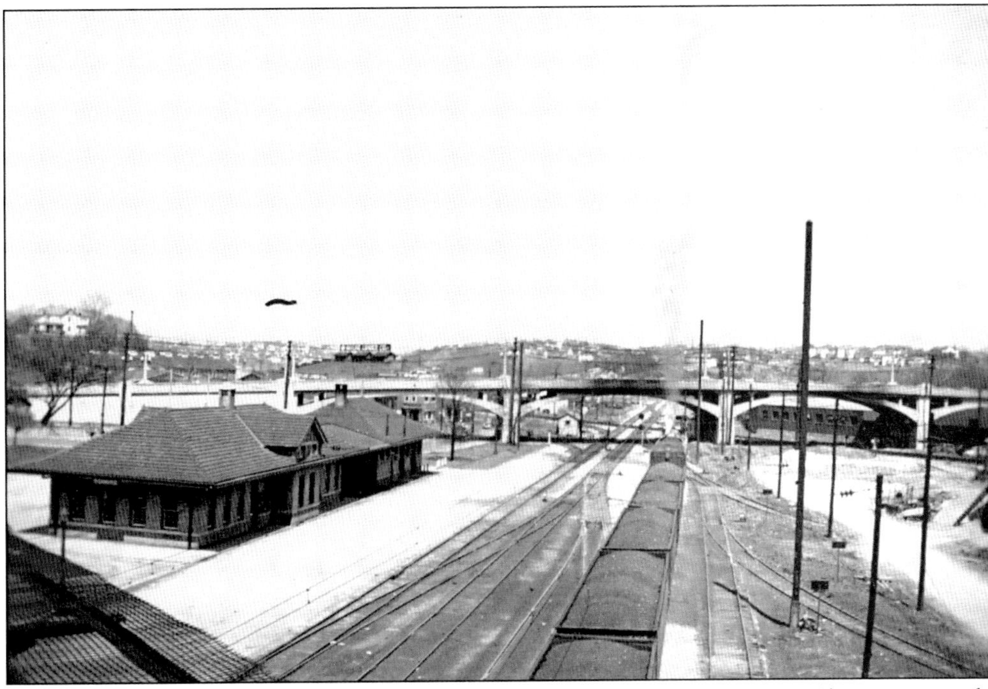

ON THE MOVE. A coal train is shown here moving through the Princeton Car Shop repair yards. (Courtesy of Randolph Belcher.)

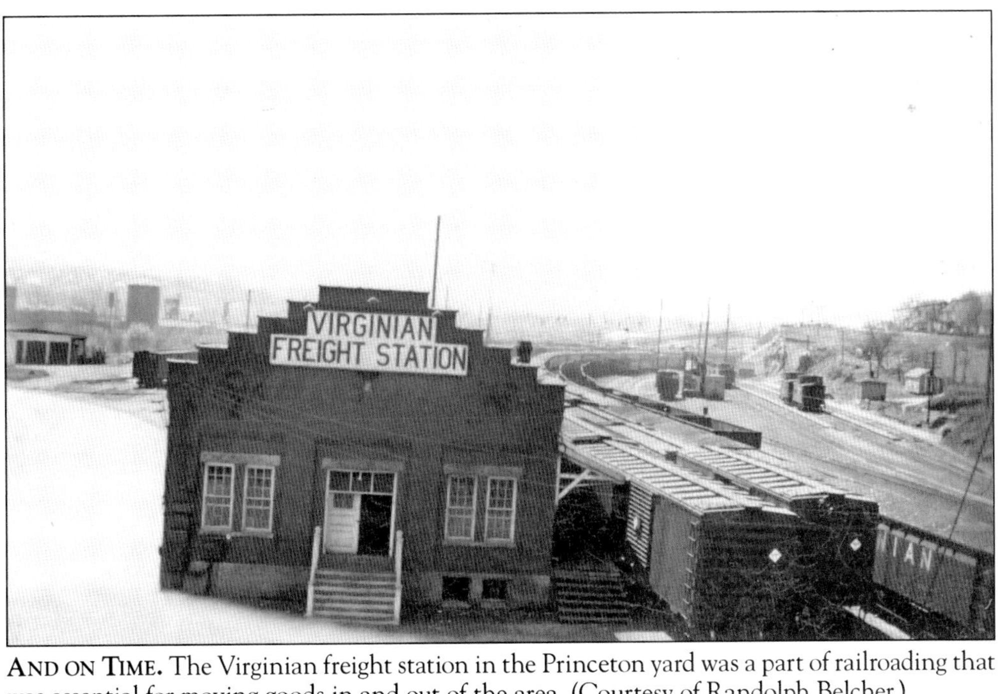

AND ON TIME. The Virginian freight station in the Princeton yard was a part of railroading that was essential for moving goods in and out of the area. (Courtesy of Randolph Belcher.)

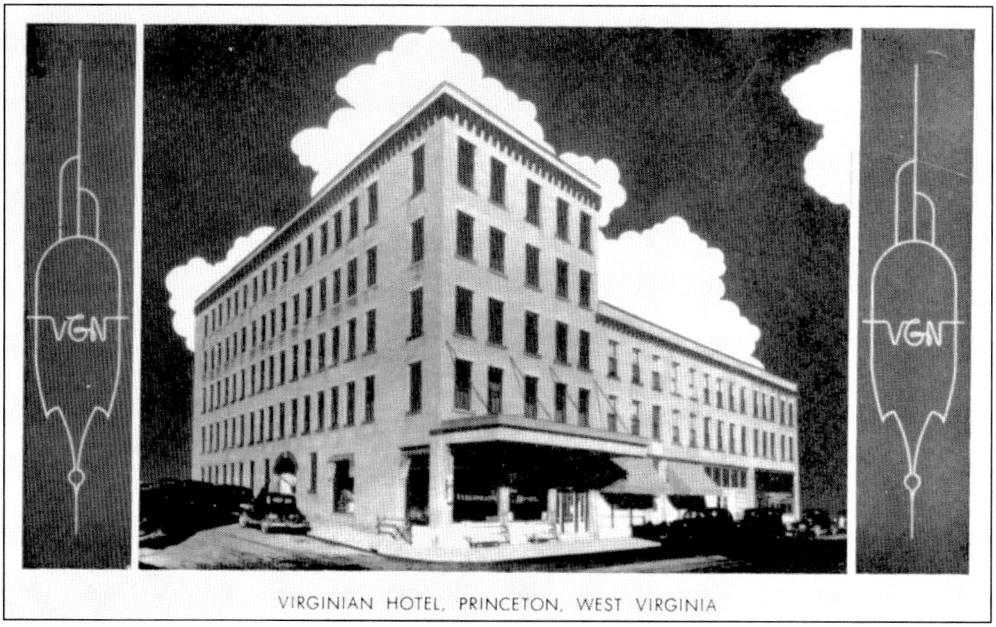

THE HEART OF TOWN. The impressive Virginian Hotel provided visitors to Princeton with first-class accommodations and fine dining. (Courtesy of Eileen Mooney.)

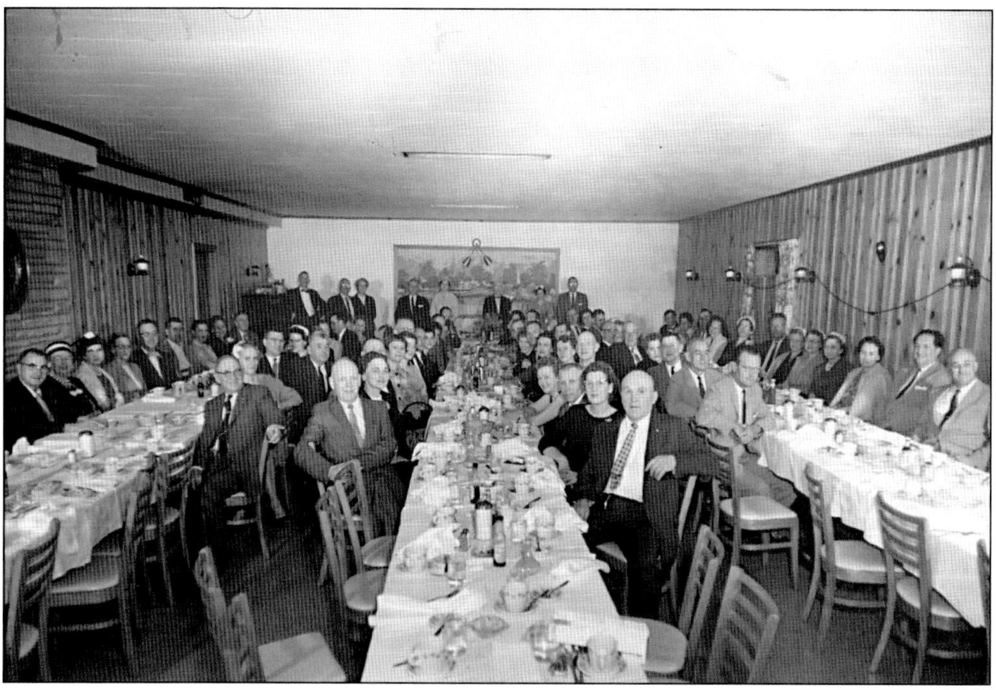

RAILROADERS. Members of Local 736 of the International Brotherhood of Electrical Workers, are shown at the Town-N-Country Restaurant in Princeton, gathered for this April 30, 1960, meeting. (Courtesy of Randolph Belcher.)

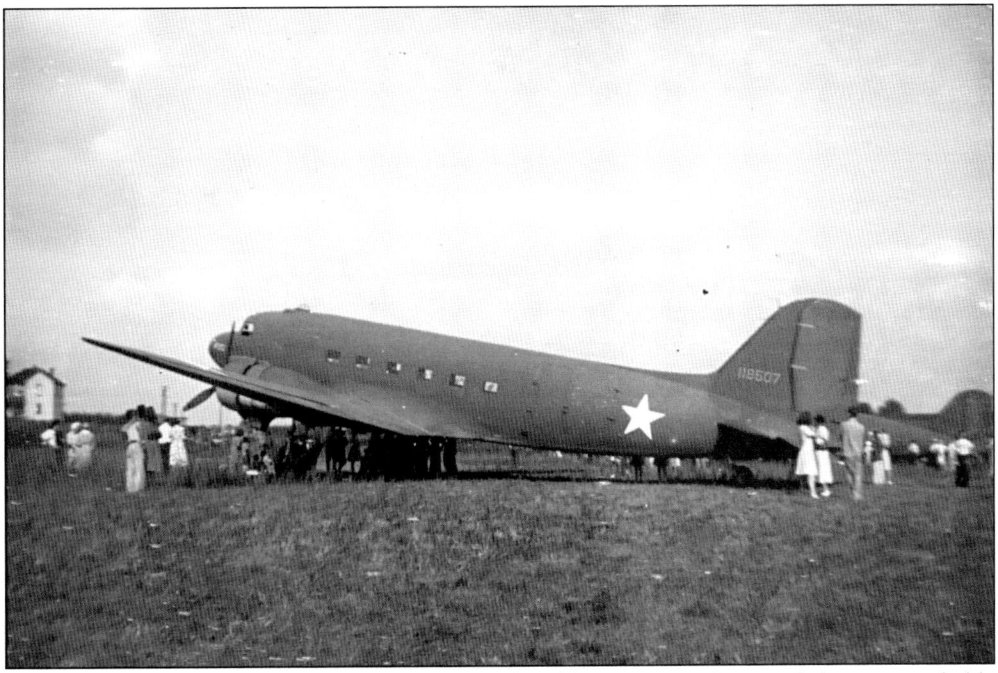

TRANSPORTS. These military DC-3s landed at the old Princeton Municipal Airport, probably sometime in the 1940s. (Courtesy of Reed J. Wheby Jr.)

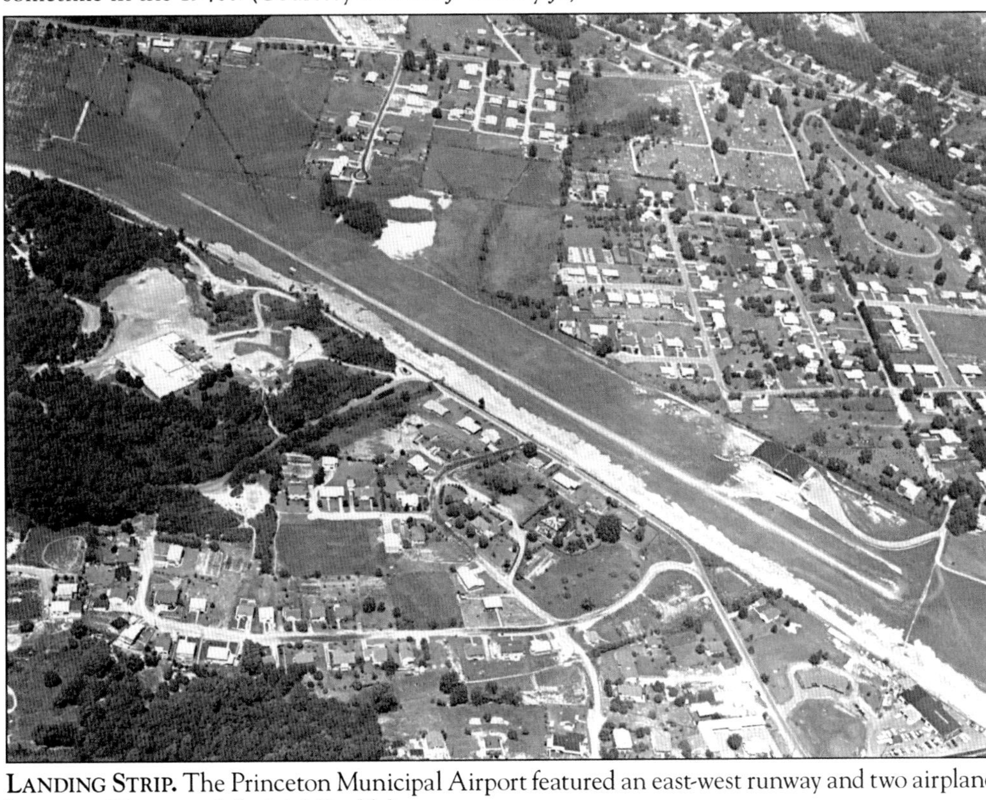

LANDING STRIP. The Princeton Municipal Airport featured an east-west runway and two airplane hangars. (Photograph by Mel Grubb.)

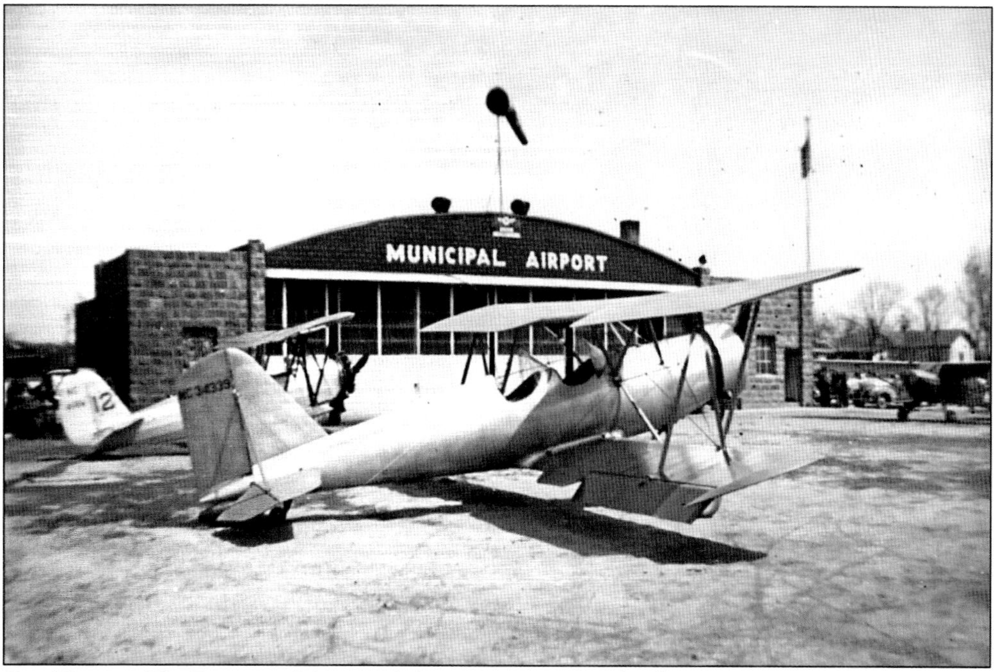

OLD TIMERS. The Princeton Municipal Airport was serving the flying public at least early enough to serve these vintage biplanes. (Courtesy of Reed J. Wheby Jr.)

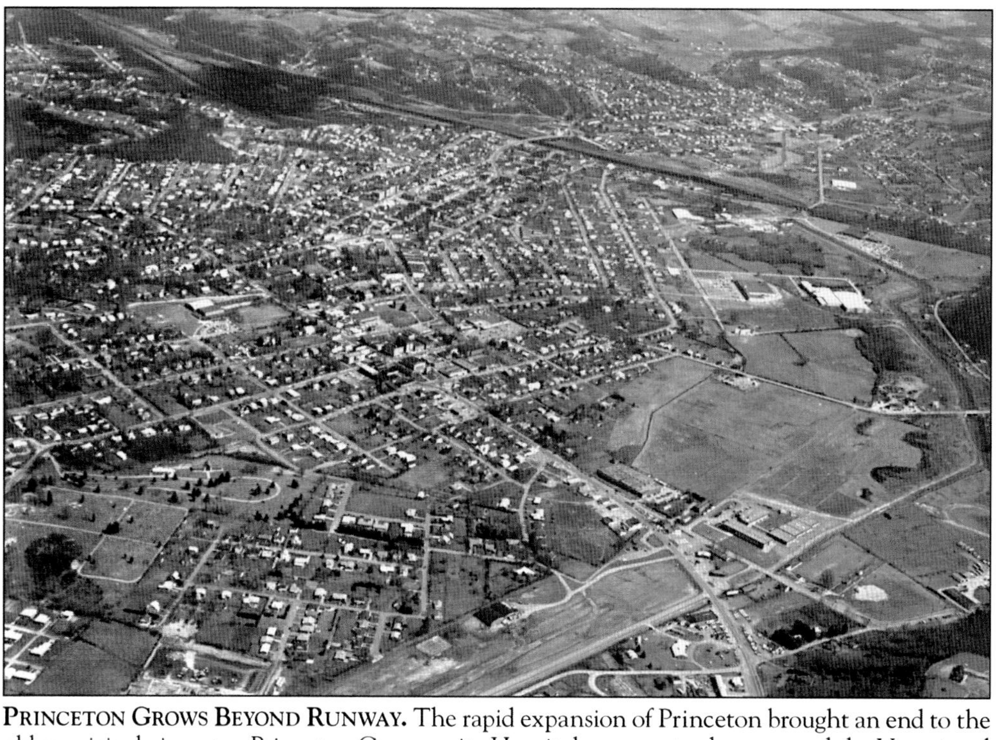

PRINCETON GROWS BEYOND RUNWAY. The rapid expansion of Princeton brought an end to the old municipal airport as Princeton Community Hospital emerges to the west and the Vocational Education Center to the east. The city continues to use the old hangars to store equipment. (Photograph by Mel Grubb.)

Four

Maidenform and More

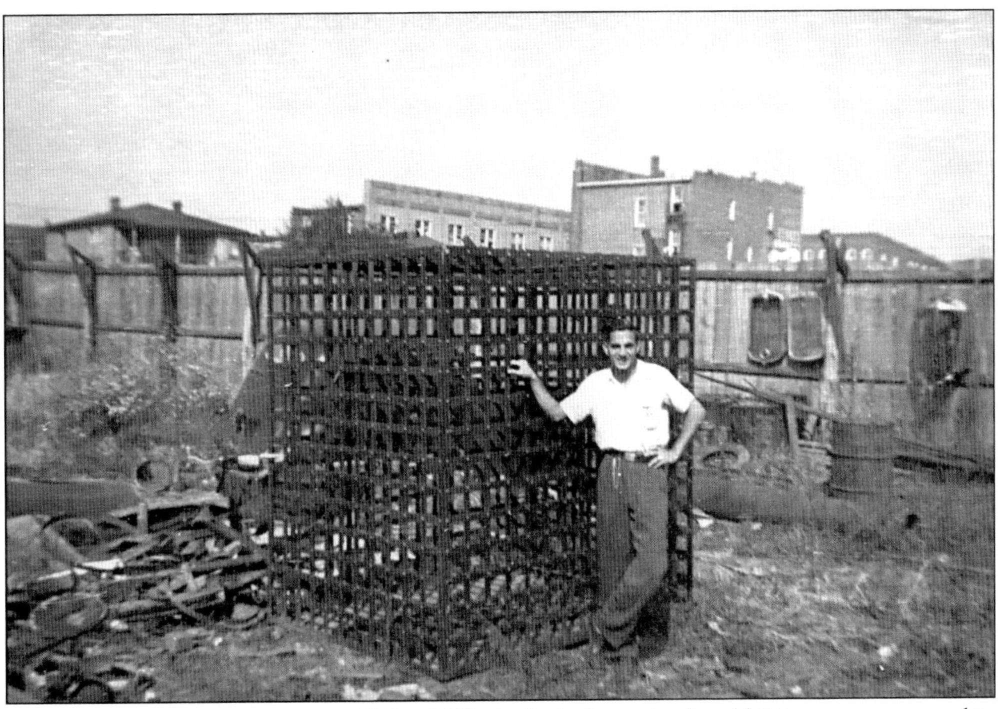

Hanging Out. Seventeen-year-old Reed Wheby Jr. is shown in the old Princeton scrap yard in 1943 resting against the bars of the old Athens jail. Scrap metal drives supplied the American war effort in World War II, but it would take the sacrifice of men like Wheby and many more to successfully fight a war on two fronts and opposite sides of the globe. (Courtesy of Reed J. Wheby Jr.)

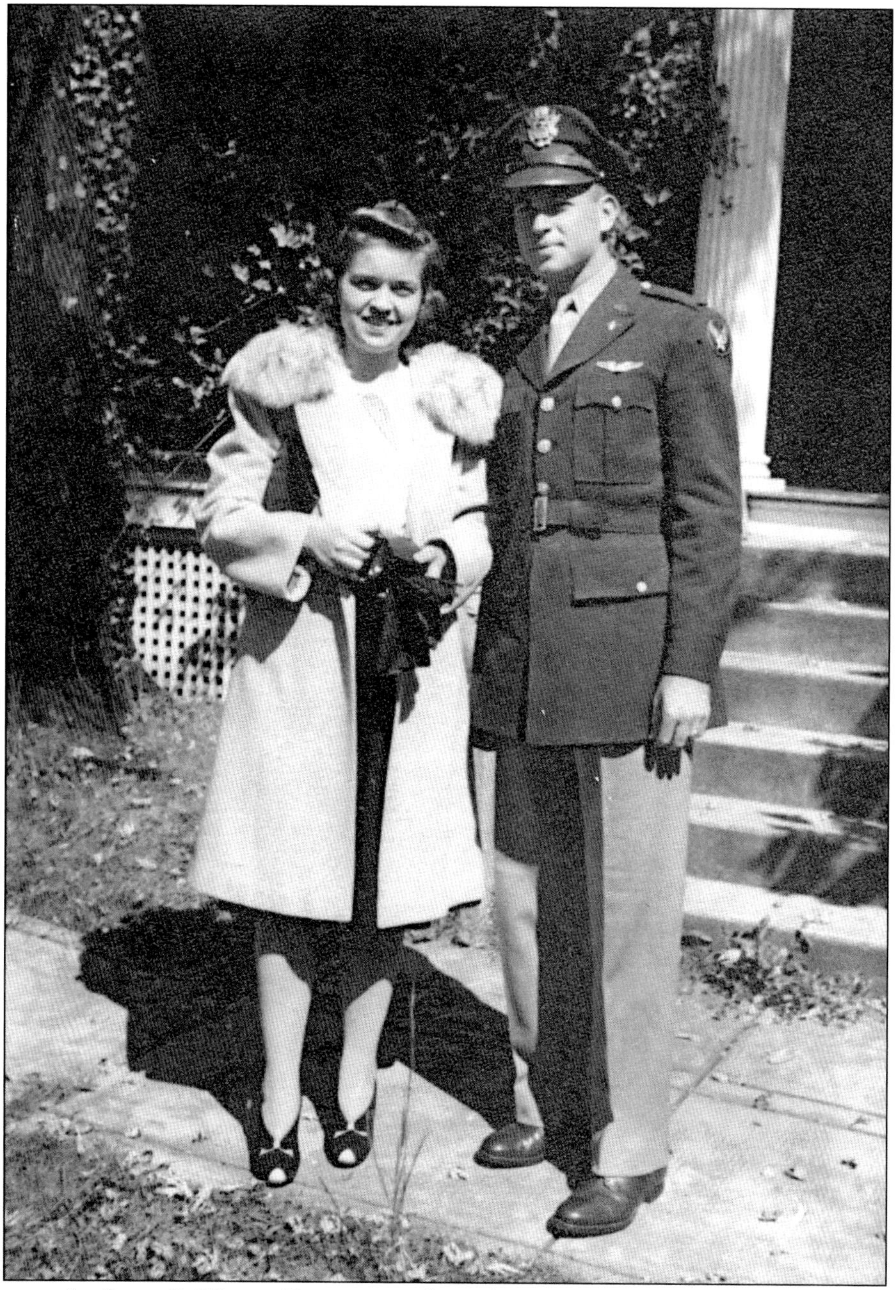

SACRIFICE. Lt. Dana C. White of Princeton is shown here with his hometown sweetheart, Prinny Pendleton, in October 1943, before White shipped off to fly a B-17 in the battle for Europe. White was a Concord College student, but he left school and joined the U.S. Army after being motivated to serve as a result of a speech by Pres. Franklin D. Roosevelt. White was shot down in his B-17 named "Booby Trap" on April 13, 1944, while on a mission to bomb a ball-bearing plant in Schweinfurt, Germany. White was last seen trying to assist one of his crew members; he was killed in action as his plane exploded. According to Tony Whitlow, coordinator of the Mercer County War Museum, White's family had a gospel quartet that was quite popular on the radio. (Courtesy of Mercer County War Museum.)

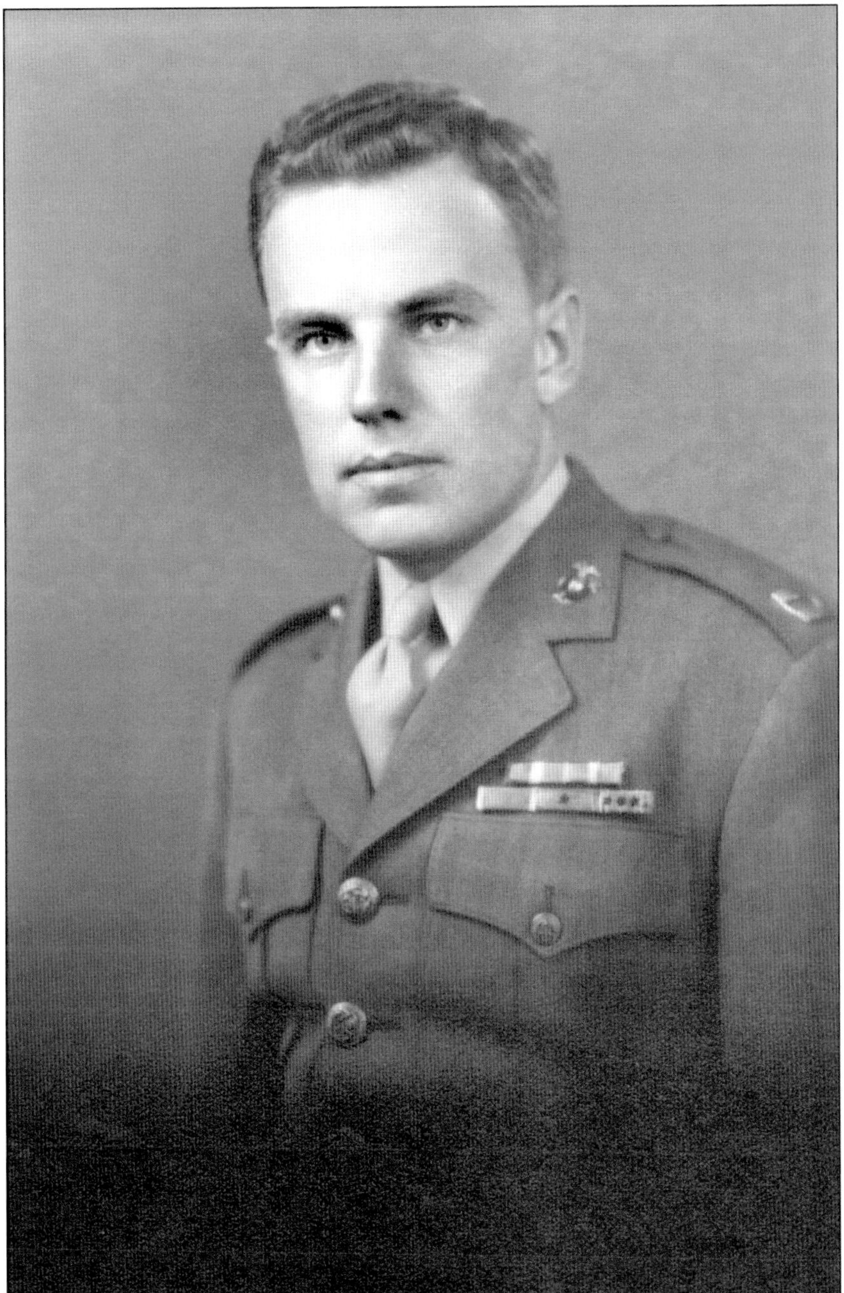

Duty. Honor. Country. First Lt. William Sanders, U.S. Marine Corps, received the Navy Cross personally from Adm. Chester Nimitz after leading his squad to capture three Japanese pillboxes during intense fighting on the Tarawa Atoll of the Gilbert Islands during the Battle of Saipan. Sanders was shot and seriously wounded by an enemy sniper while clearing ammunition from the third pillbox. One of his comrades placed the flag and Samuri sword captured from the Japanese on the litter corpsmen used to transport Sanders to an aid station. Sanders, a prominent Princeton trial lawyer, donated the flag and sword to the Mercer County War Museum. (Courtesy of the Mercer County War Museum.)

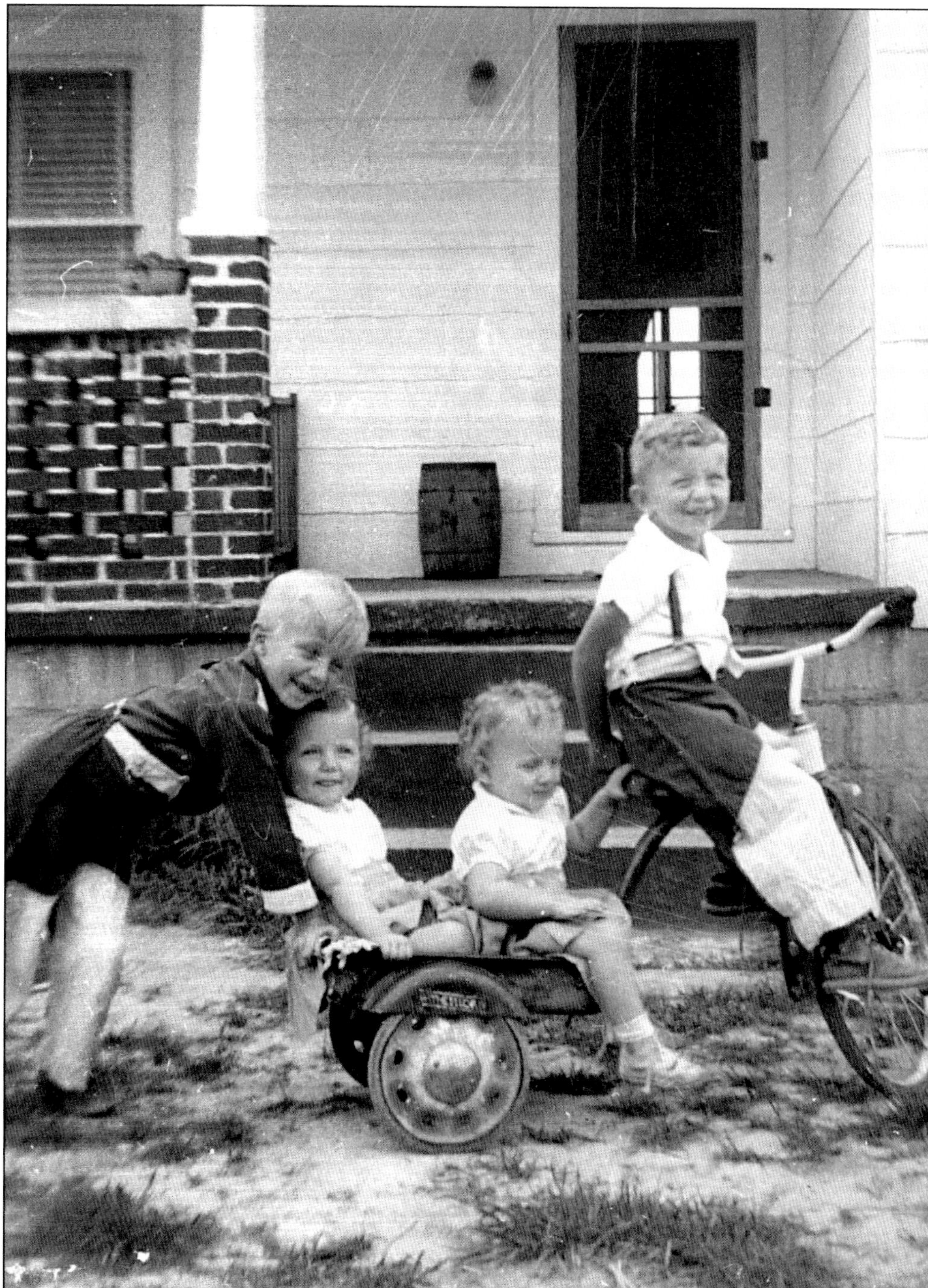

PRINCETON ON THE GROW. After the end of World War II, Bernard and Shelia Shorter married and started a family. Their sons, Bernie (left) and Steve (right), were the first to come along, but they were followed closely by twins, Deb (left center) and Pam (right center). All four children are shown above c. 1953 in front of their Lilly Addition home. The Shorters would have two more sons, Freddie and John, and would build a new home in City View Heights. (Courtesy of Sheila Shorter.)

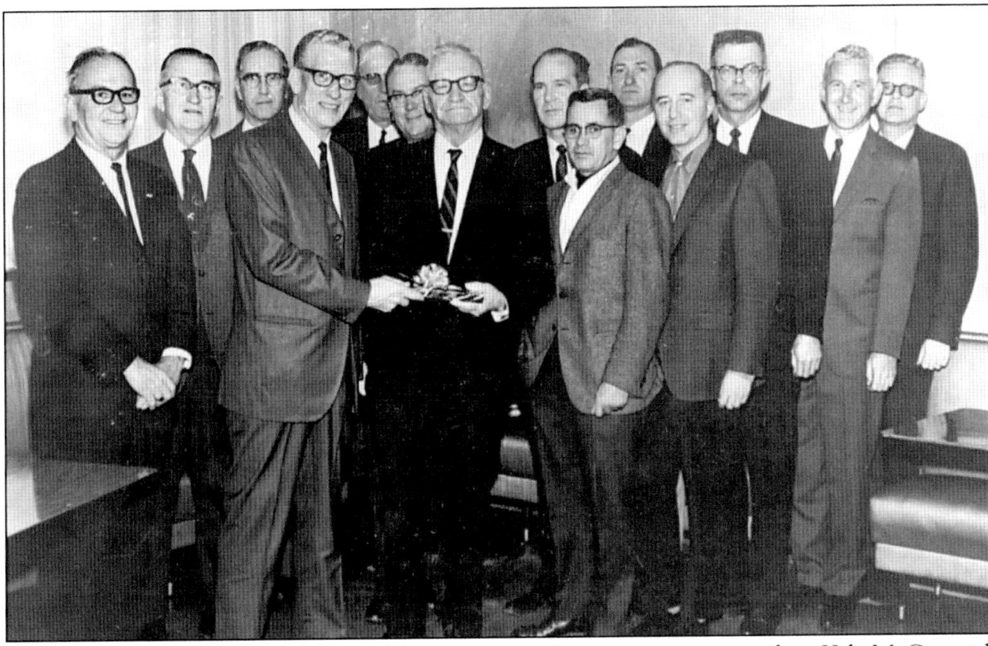

Brother, Can You Spare a Dime? Pete Cook is shown presenting a gift to Kyle McCormick at a gathering of the "10 Cent Millionaire Club." Pictured here from left to right are Price Dyer, Carl Carper, Cam Hunter, Pete Cook, Dan McMullin, Jim Fisher, Kyle McCormick, John McCabe, Orville Wallace, Bob Whittaker, Dick Lilly, Charlie Lane, Dick Copeland, and Tommy Thomas. (Courtesy of Dick Copeland.)

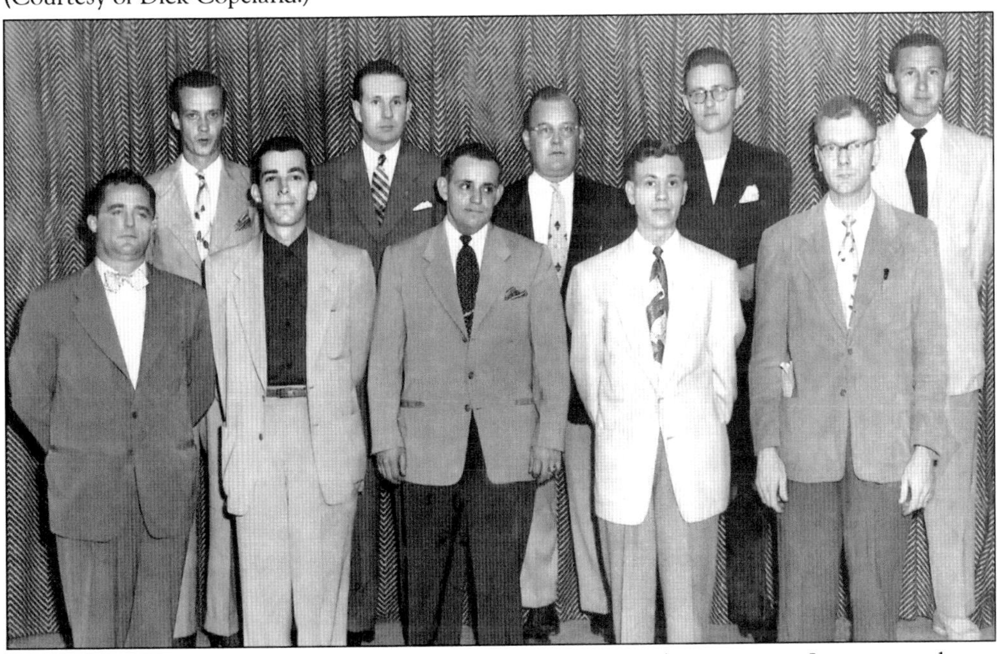

Service to Community. The original charter members of the Princeton Jaycees are shown here. Pictured here from left to right are (first row) Jim Marcum, Bill Meyers, Tommy Seaver, Jack French, and Ted Freeman; (second row) Walt Dempsey, Ed Rasnich, Jim Kelley, Ben White, and Dick Copeland. (Courtesy of Dick Copeland.)

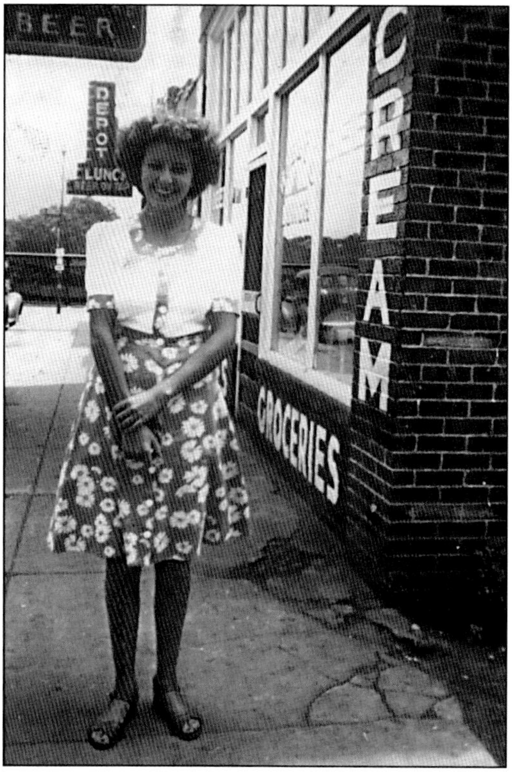

EAST MERCER STREET. Louise Ryan is shown standing in front Wheby's Grocery Store in this 1943 photograph. Ryan was among the first group of seamstresses to work for Maidenform when the company opened its Princeton factory. (Courtesy of Reed J. Wheby Jr.)

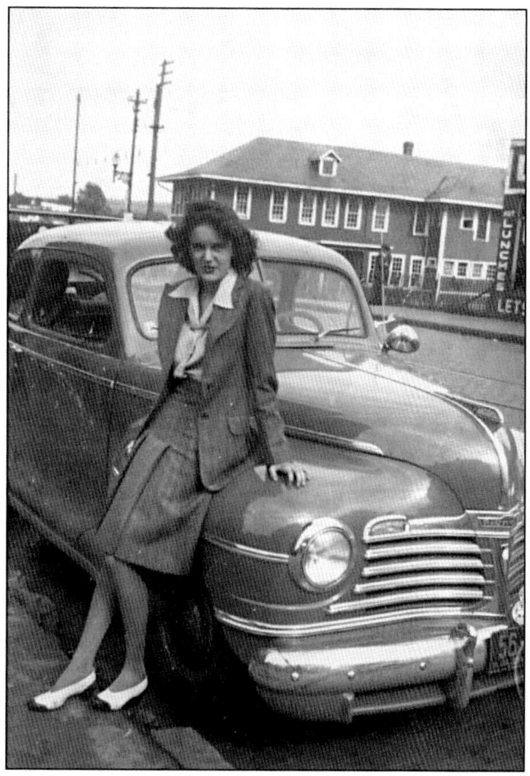

LOOKING GOOD. Lois Lucas is sitting pretty on the fender of a sedan parked on East Mercer Street. Note the Princeton passenger station in the background. (Courtesy of Reed J. Wheby Jr.)

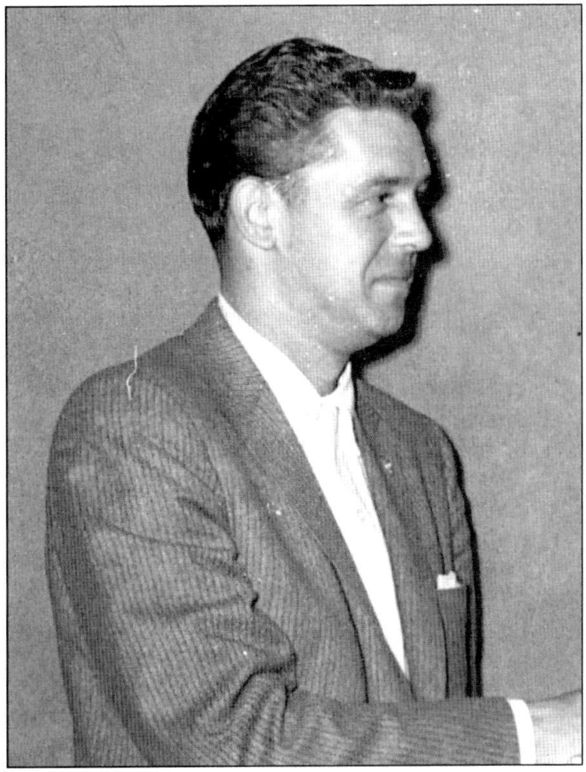

NEW DIRECTIONS. Princeton adopted the city manager–council form of government in the early 1950s and selected Duke England to serve as the first city manager. A series of strong city managers through the years combined to help the city grow. (Courtesy of Dick Copeland.)

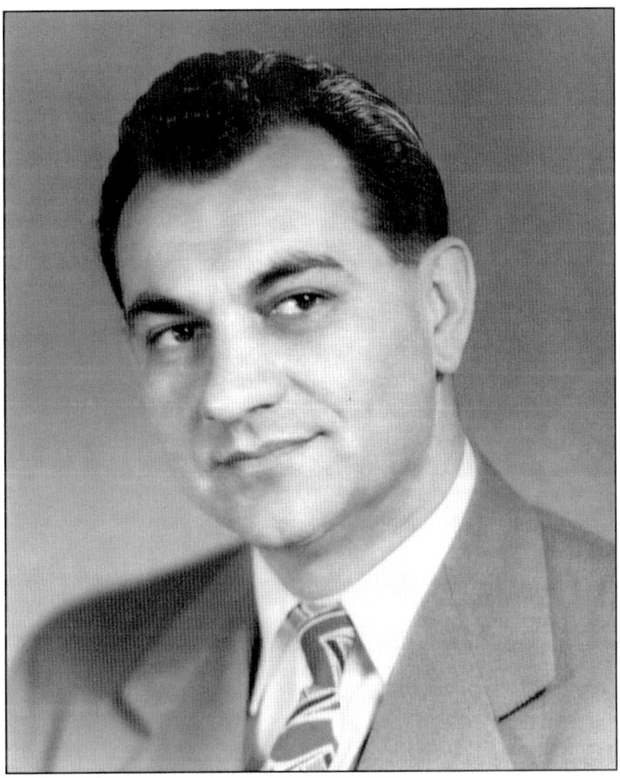

CIVIC LEADER. W. Grady Carper Sr. was a dynamic force in Princeton, southern West Virginia, and in the entire region. He built the first modern motel in the region at the southern terminus of the West Virginia turnpike, branched out into the insurance business, and became active in civic affairs. (Courtesy of Bill Carper.)

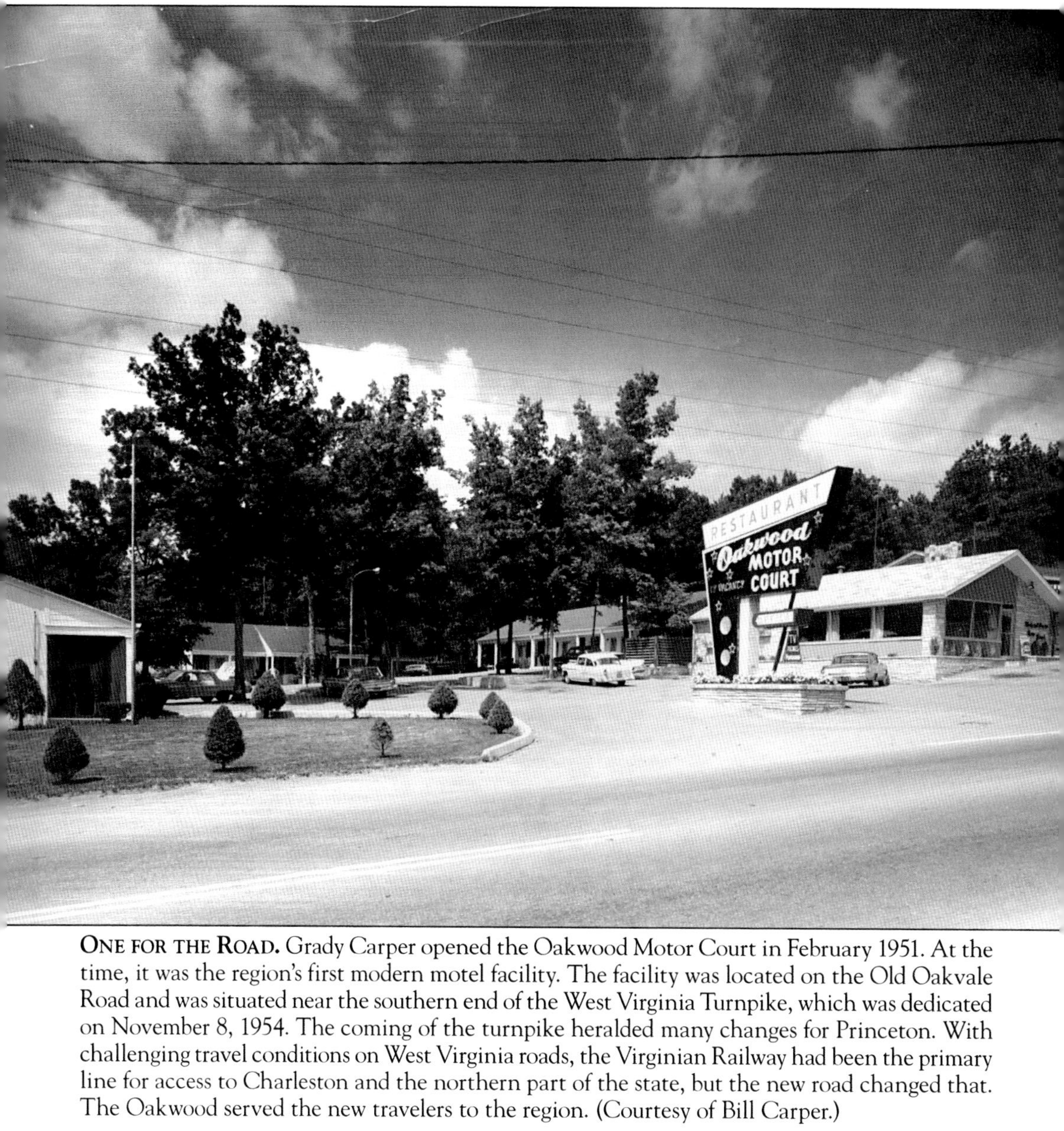

ONE FOR THE ROAD. Grady Carper opened the Oakwood Motor Court in February 1951. At the time, it was the region's first modern motel facility. The facility was located on the Old Oakvale Road and was situated near the southern end of the West Virginia Turnpike, which was dedicated on November 8, 1954. The coming of the turnpike heralded many changes for Princeton. With challenging travel conditions on West Virginia roads, the Virginian Railway had been the primary line for access to Charleston and the northern part of the state, but the new road changed that. The Oakwood served the new travelers to the region. (Courtesy of Bill Carper.)

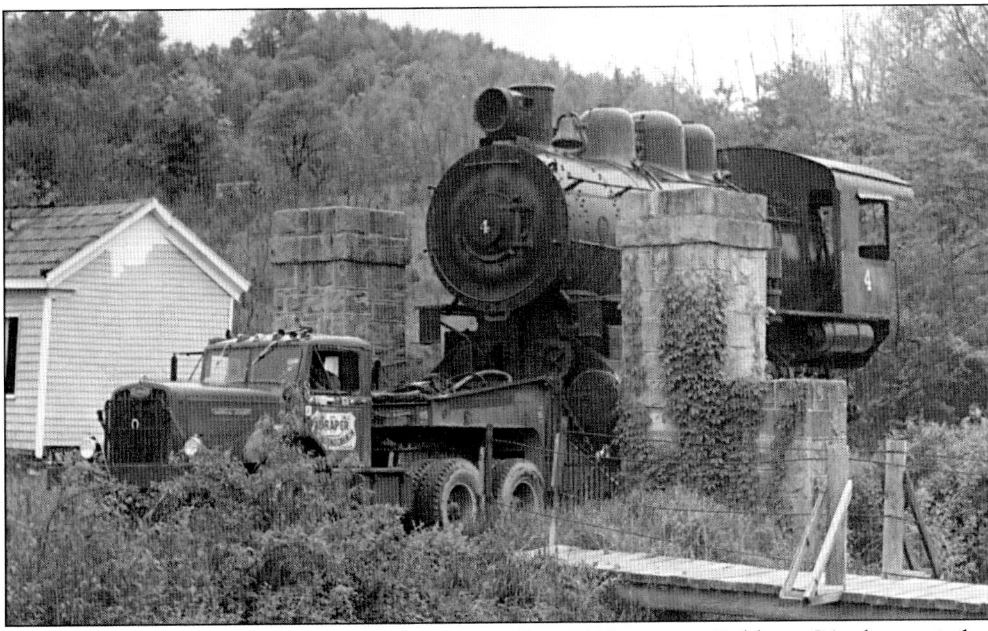

CHANGING ERA. The Virginian Railway retired its 1910-vintage Baldwin SA class switcher locomotive known as the "Four Spot" and donated it to the city of Princeton in May 1957. The city's Park Association leaders put the old locomotive in the new city park—a 40-acre park with swimming pool and lighted baseball field. But the Four Spot was not secure and was victimized by vandals. (Courtesy of Bill Carper.)

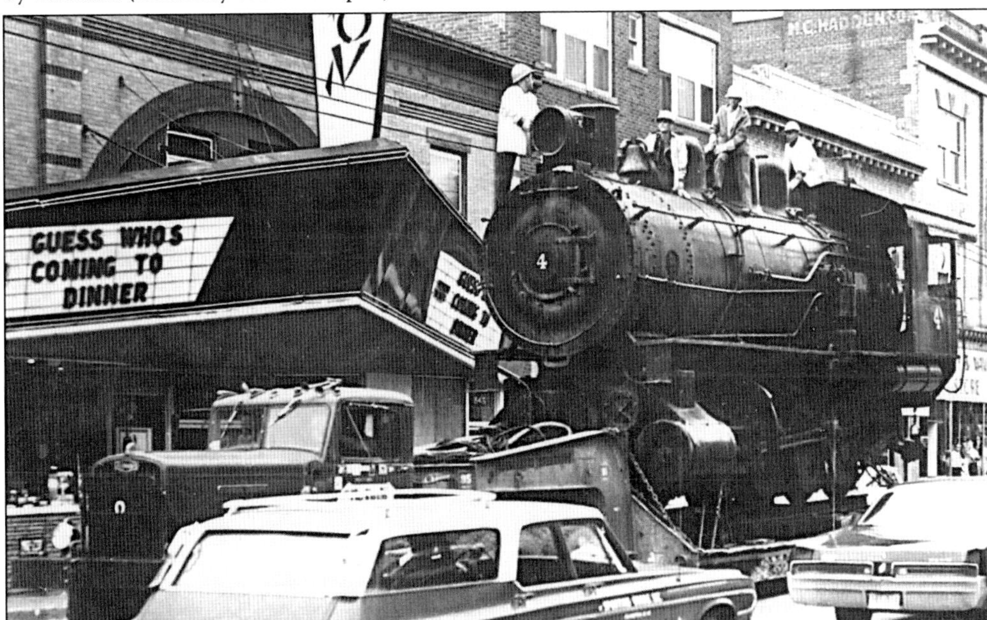

CHANGING TIMES. Grady Carper and the Park Association decided to give the Four Spot to the Railroad Museum in Roanoke, Virginia, for restoration. The Four Spot went to Roanoke for restoration and was made a permanent part of the Transportation Museum, despite an effort by Princeton to block the move to Roanoke. (Courtesy of Bill Carper.)

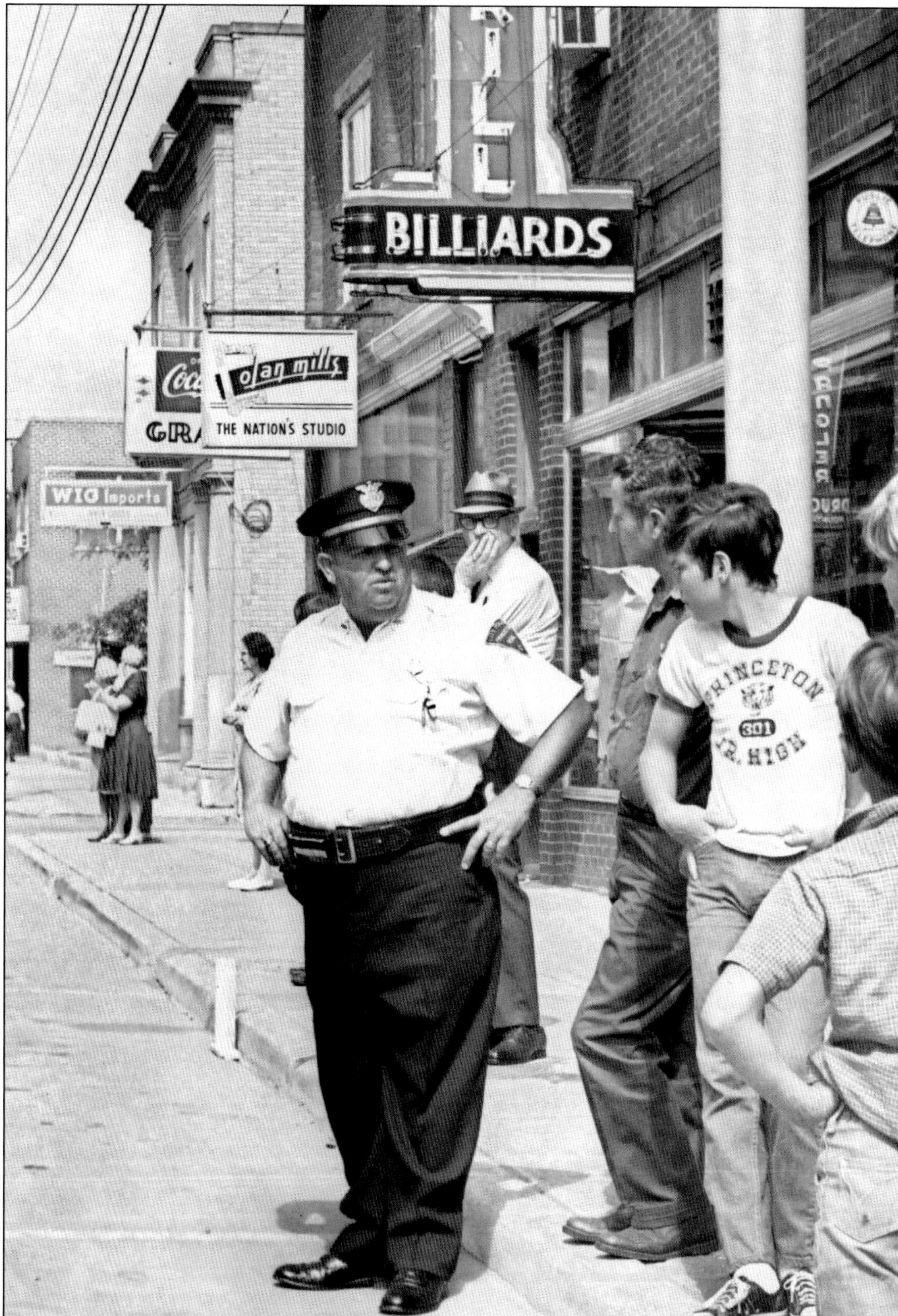

CHIEF-O-POLICE. Alfred Lucas was director of the public works department but moved up to serve as Princeton's chief of police. In 1960, the city maintained a force of 13 officers and one police cruiser, but the force grew to meet the changing demands. (Courtesy of *Princeton Times* archives.)

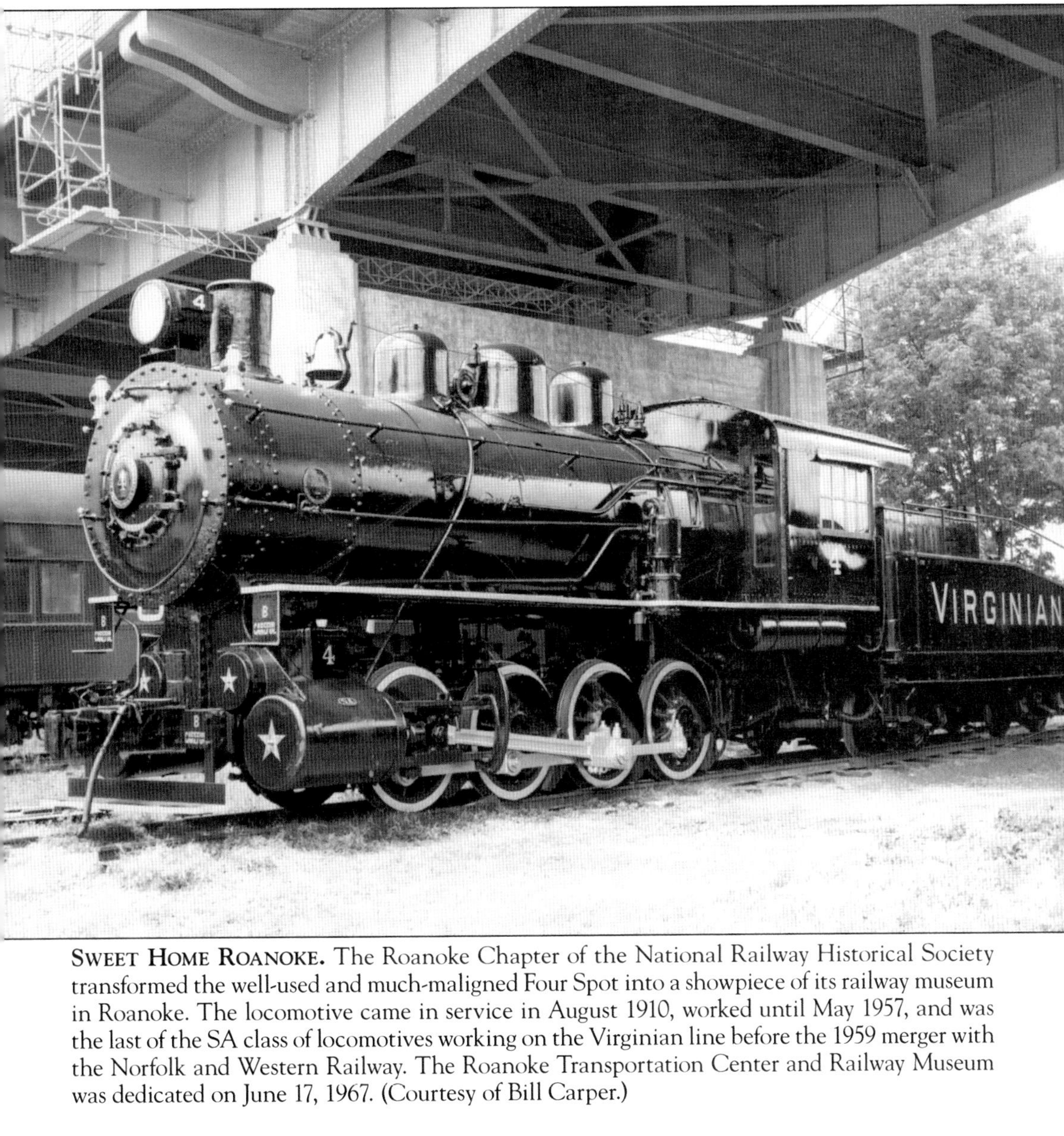

SWEET HOME ROANOKE. The Roanoke Chapter of the National Railway Historical Society transformed the well-used and much-maligned Four Spot into a showpiece of its railway museum in Roanoke. The locomotive came in service in August 1910, worked until May 1957, and was the last of the SA class of locomotives working on the Virginian line before the 1959 merger with the Norfolk and Western Railway. The Roanoke Transportation Center and Railway Museum was dedicated on June 17, 1967. (Courtesy of Bill Carper.)

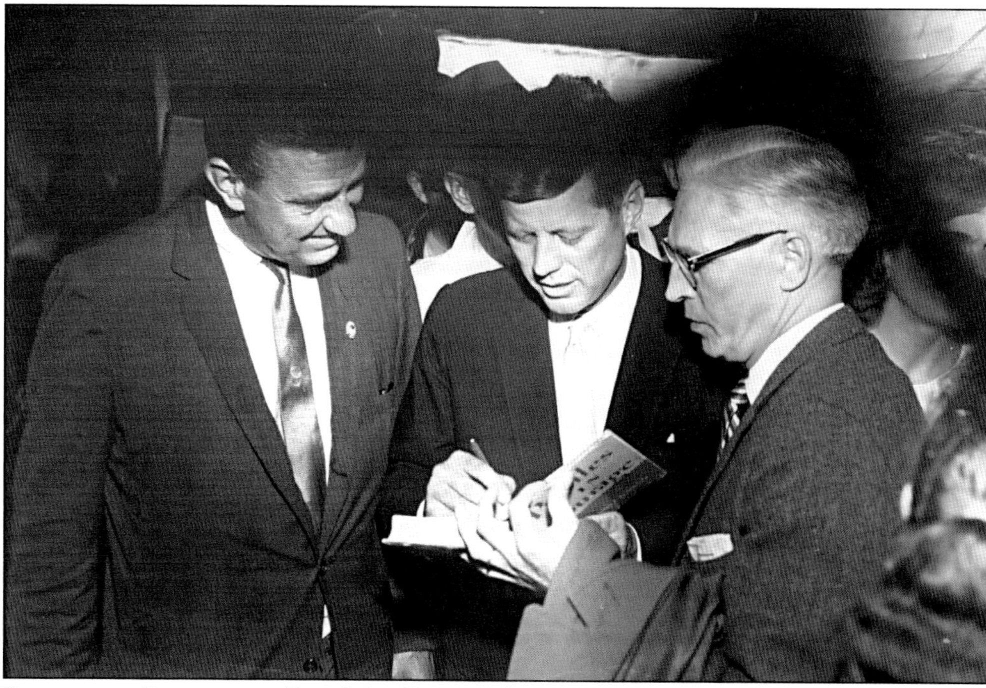

PROFILES IN PRESIDENTS. Pres. John F. Kennedy visited Princeton in late April 1960 during his campaign for the Democratic party's nomination. The West Virginia primary election was considered to be pivotal in Kennedy's run for the White House. (Photograph by Mel Grubb.)

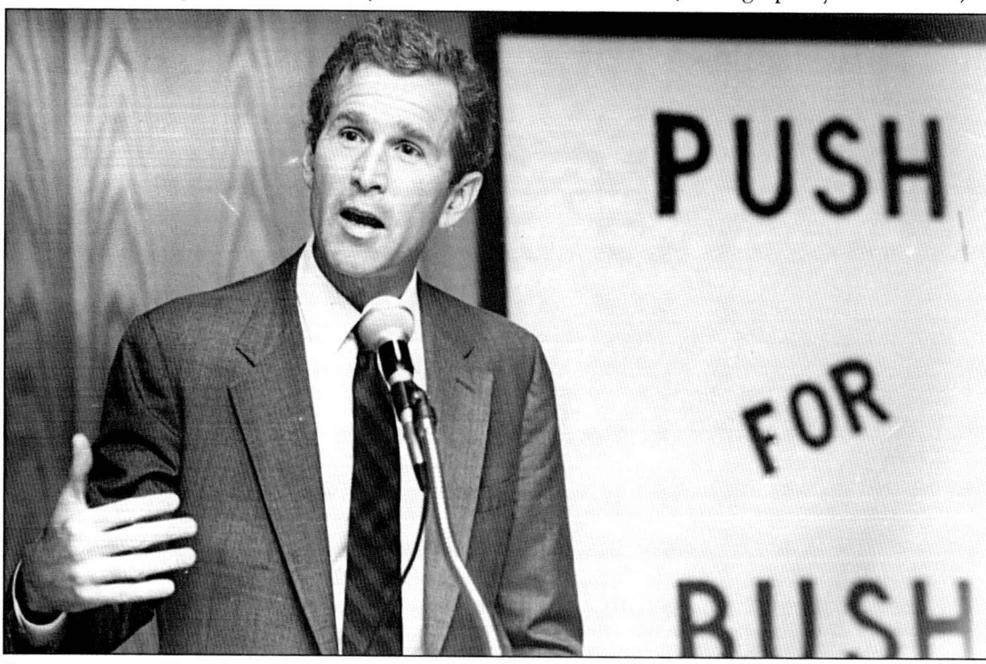

STUMPING FOR DAD. Pres. George W. Bush is shown here addressing Mercer County Republicans in the summer of 1987 on behalf of his father, former president George H. W. Bush, who went on to win the presidential race that year. The elder Bush returned the favor in 2000 by coming to Mercer County to campaign for his son. (Courtesy of *Princeton Times* Archives.)

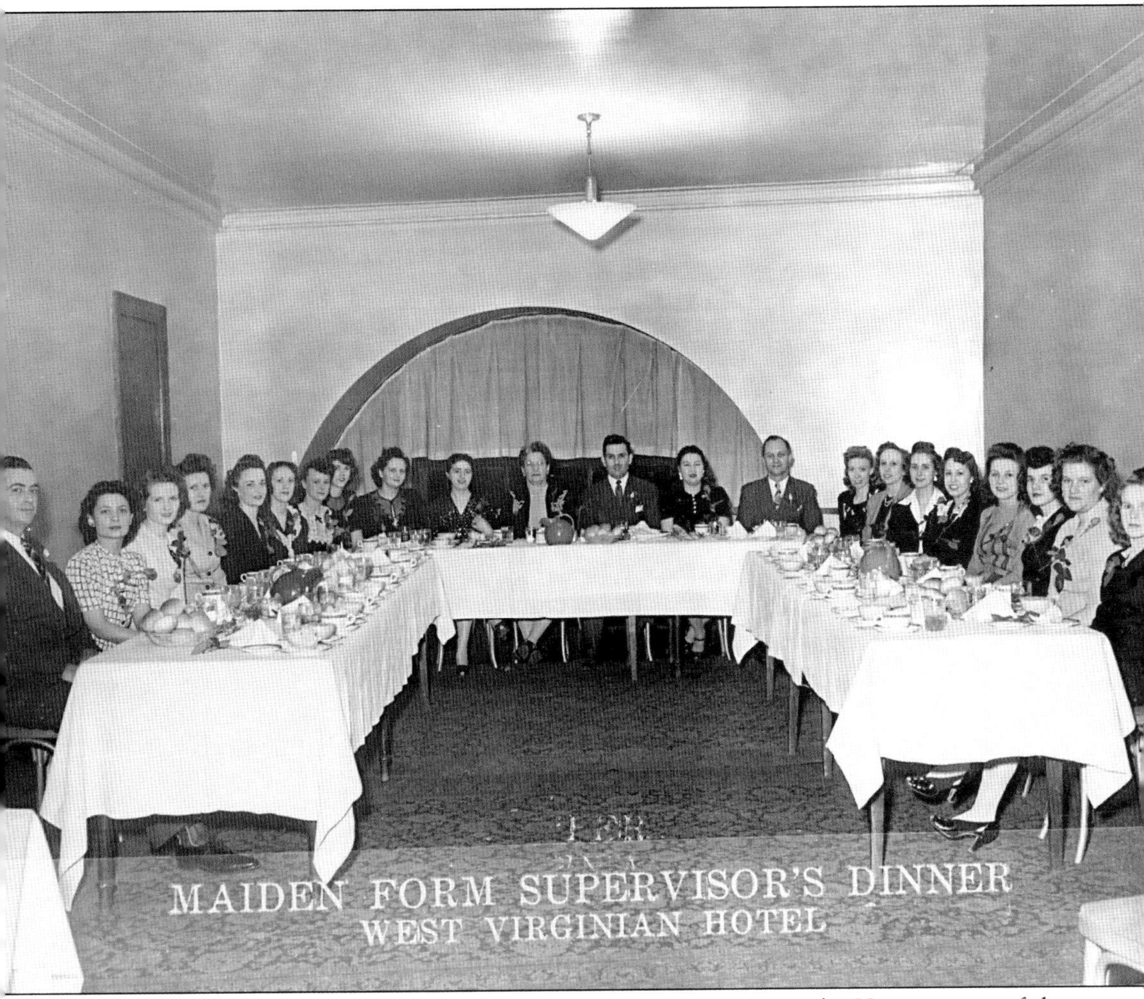

I DREAMED I CAME TO PRINCETON IN MY MAIDENFORM BRA. Marsha Hammer, one of the original seamstresses who created the first Maidenform bras, was the guest at the Maidenform supervisors' dinner held in 1944 at the West Virginian Hotel. Pictured here from left to right are Raymond Thomas; Alma Archer; Virginia Lovern; Helen Alvis; Polly Lovern; Inez W. Goodwin; Bea Huffman; Lucille M. Barbour; Frances Borowski; Geraldine Franisano; Marsha Hammer; plant manager Samuel Laufer and his wife, Frances Laufer; Fred Precht; Isabelle Vaught; Charlotte Marquis; Helen Barr; Ruth W. Setliff; Sheila Simmons; Alma Belcher; Kathryn Bailey; and unidentified. William K. Woltz and Ellis and Mae Rosenthal of Bayonne, New Jersey, also attended. (Courtesy of Sheila Shorter.)

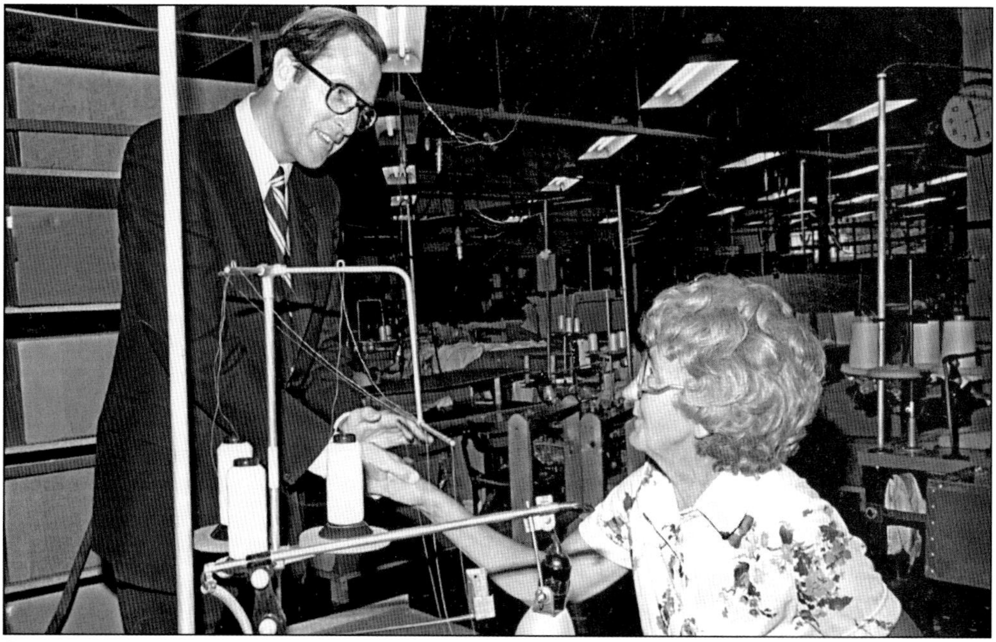

STITCH IN TIME. Former governor (now U.S. senator) John D. "Jay" Rockefeller IV is shown pressing the flesh for a photograph opportunity with Maidenform employee Billie Blankenship. Russian Jewish émigrés Enid Bissett and Ida Rosenthal started Maidenform in 1922 when they were both seamstresses at Enid Frocks, a small dress shop in New York City. The first Maidenform plant opened in Bayonne, New Jersey, in 1926, and the company opened the Princeton plant in 1943 in a building on Straley Avenue. (Courtesy of Billie Blankenship.)

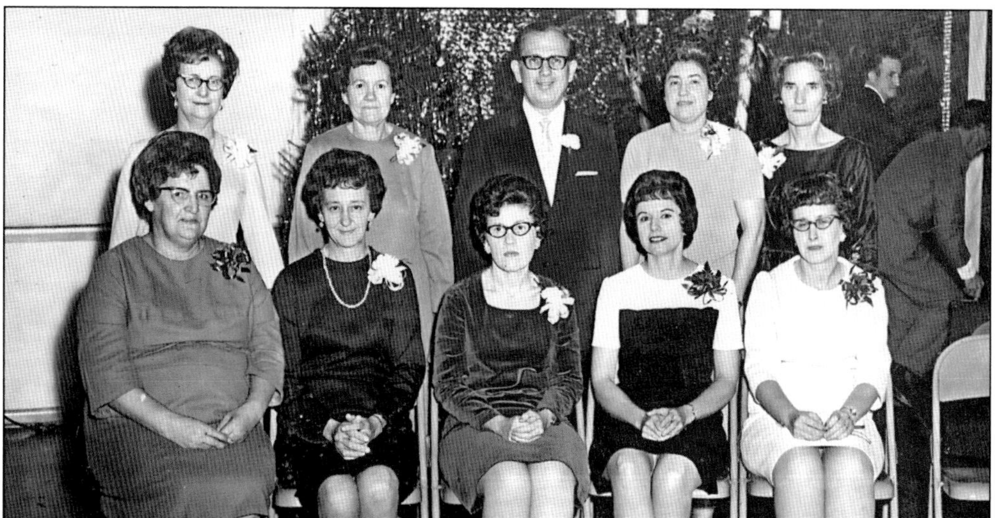

SEW NICE. Maidenform employees are shown at a holiday gathering. Pictured here from left to right are (front row) Pearl Warden, Billie Blankenship, Dean Karnes, Wanda Parcell, and Kathryn Davis; (second row) Ina Shaffer, Dean Pendleton, Sam Lauffer (plant manager), Carrol Thorne, and Frances Crockett. Maidenform made the "pigeon vest" for soldiers to transport carrier pigeons during World War II and also made silk parachutes for the war effort. (Courtesy of Billie Blankenship.)

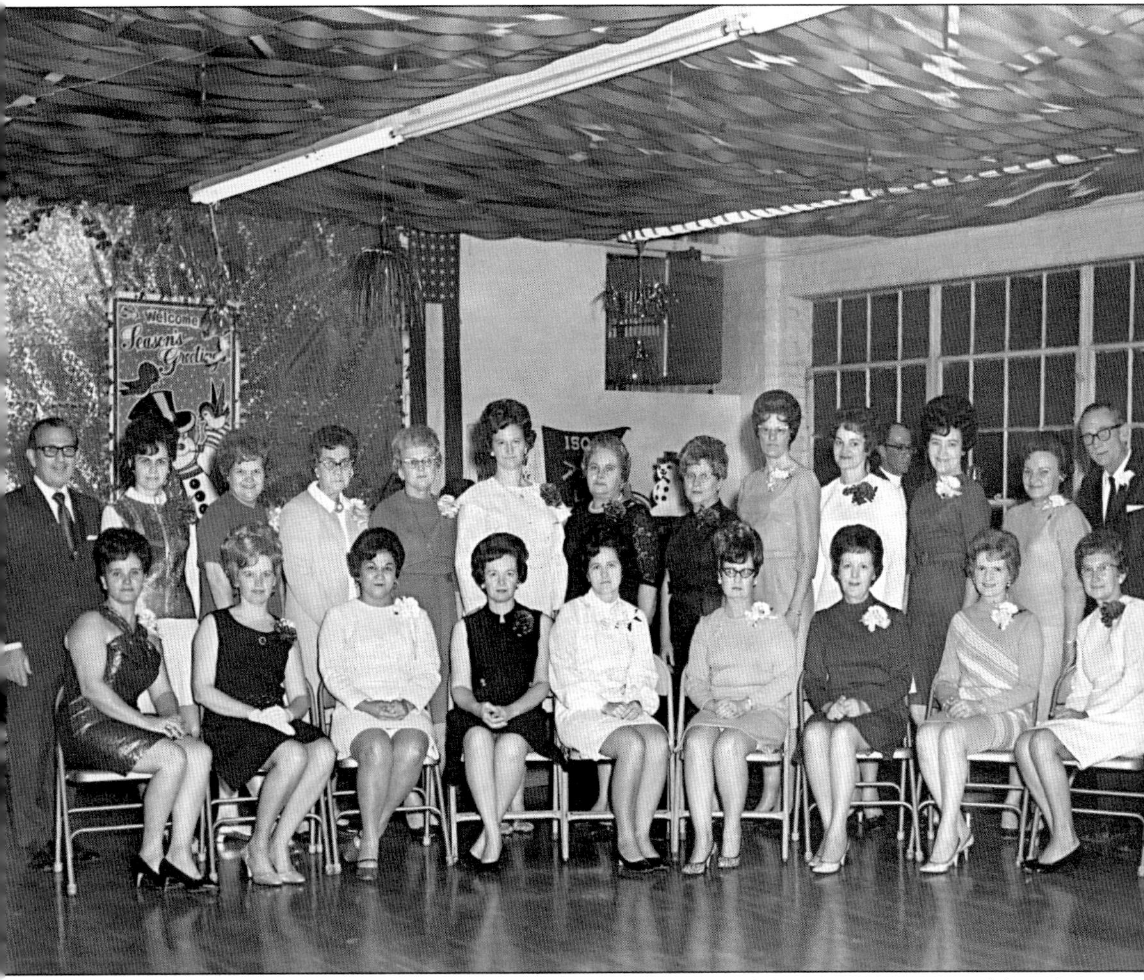

HOLIDAY EVENT. Maidenform employees are gathered for a holiday event in 1969. Although not identified, the employees here were receiving awards for 25 years of service according to the March 1970 edition of the "Maiden-forum," the employee newsletter. At the time, Maidenform had plants in Clarksburg, Huntington, and Princeton, West Virginia, as well as New York City, Bayonne, and Perth Amboy, New Jersey. Bernice Coleman was Maidenform president in 1970. (Courtesy of Lynn Whitteker.)

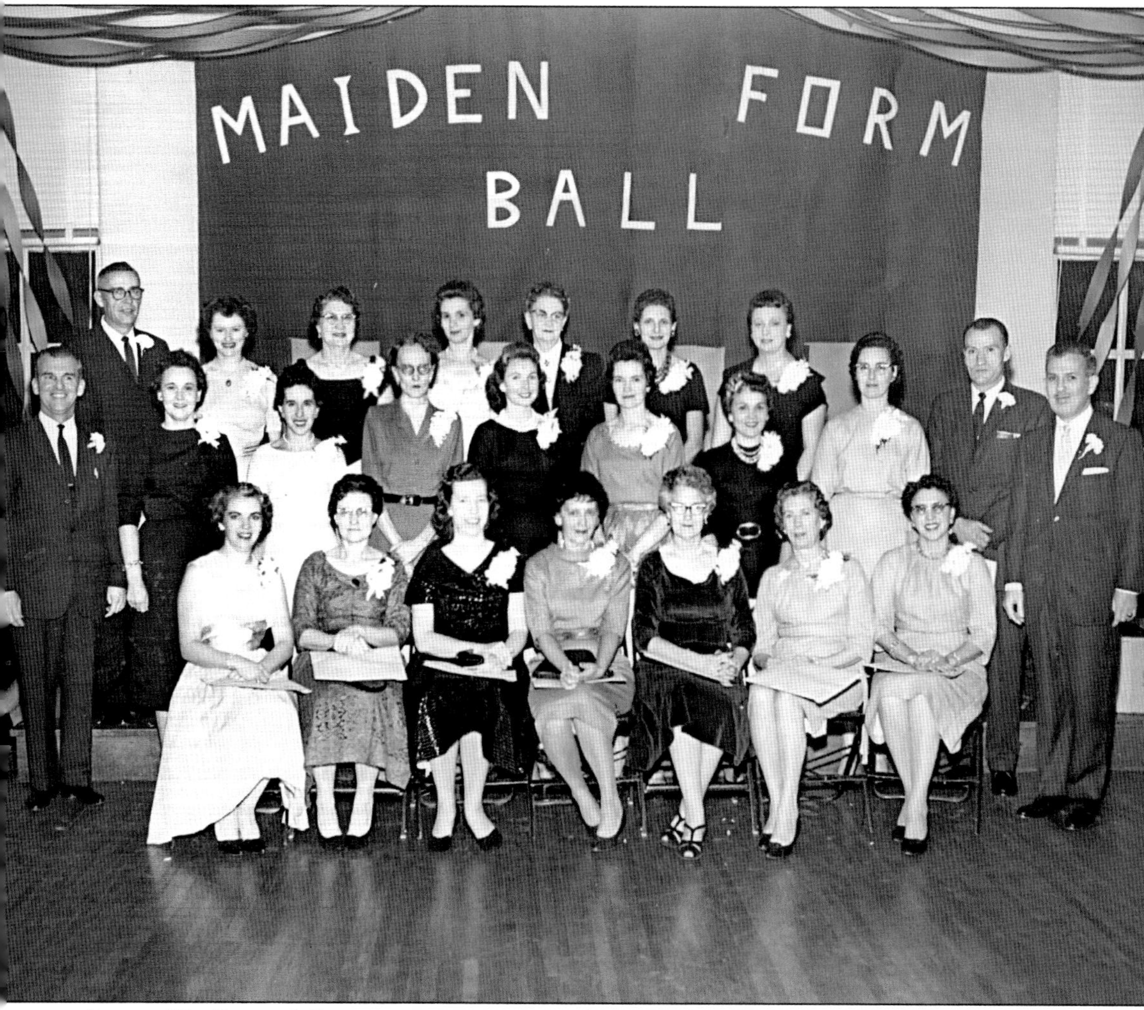

Shall We Dance? Company executives are shown with an honored group of Maidenform employees at the "Maiden Form Ball." Maidenform workers were represented by Local 260 of the ILGWU (International Ladies Garment Workers Union). After starting out at the old armory on Straley Avenue, the plant opened a Mercer Street annex at the end of World War II and, in 1951, opened a Thorn Street annex location before consolidating operations and moving to Courthouse Road in June 1952 in a building initially built by H. P. Hunnicutt as a Pepsi plant but never used for that purpose. Maidenform hit its peak employment in September 1953, when 763 workers were at the Princeton plant—15 were men, and the rest were ladies. The Maidenform story is a fascinating one. The first brassieres were given away free with the dresses made at the Enid Frocks dress shop in New York but soon became very popular as an independent garment. The Princeton plant served as a place of employment for many women of the region until it closed in 1992. (Courtesy of Beulah Shrewsbury.)

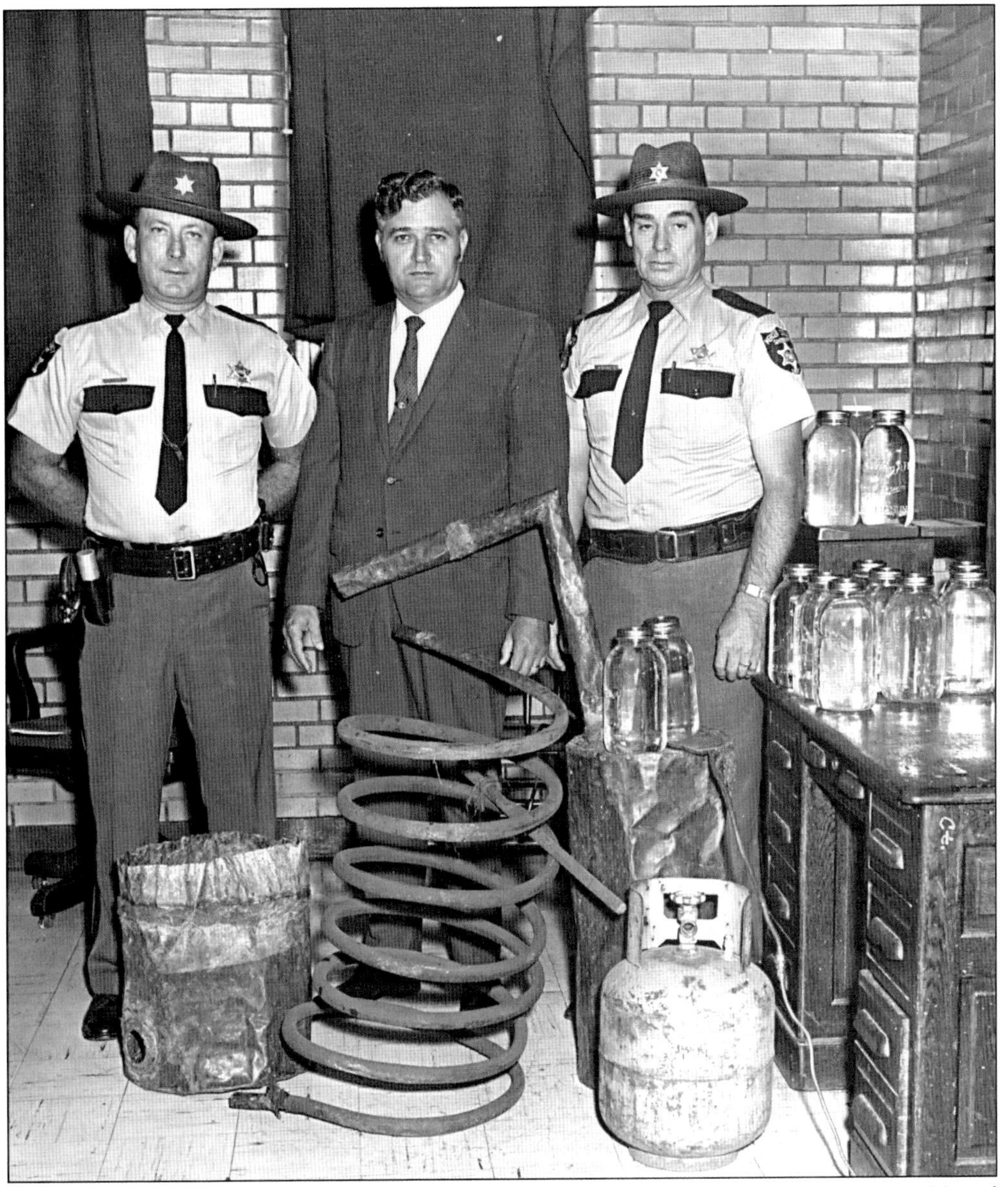

STILL LIFE. Mercer County sheriff Winfrey Shrewsbury (center) served from 1969 to 1973 and presided over several raids to break up the region's illegal moonshine business. He is shown with two deputies, Emory Fleming (left) and E. R. "Shorty" Simons, in this c. 1970 photograph of a moonshine still confiscated in a raid near Athens. Shrewsbury was also in office when his officers made the first large marijuana arrest in the county on June 25, 1970. Shrewsbury held five elective offices and served 32 years in Mercer County government, including an 18-year period as county assessor. (Courtesy of Winfrey Shrewsbury.)

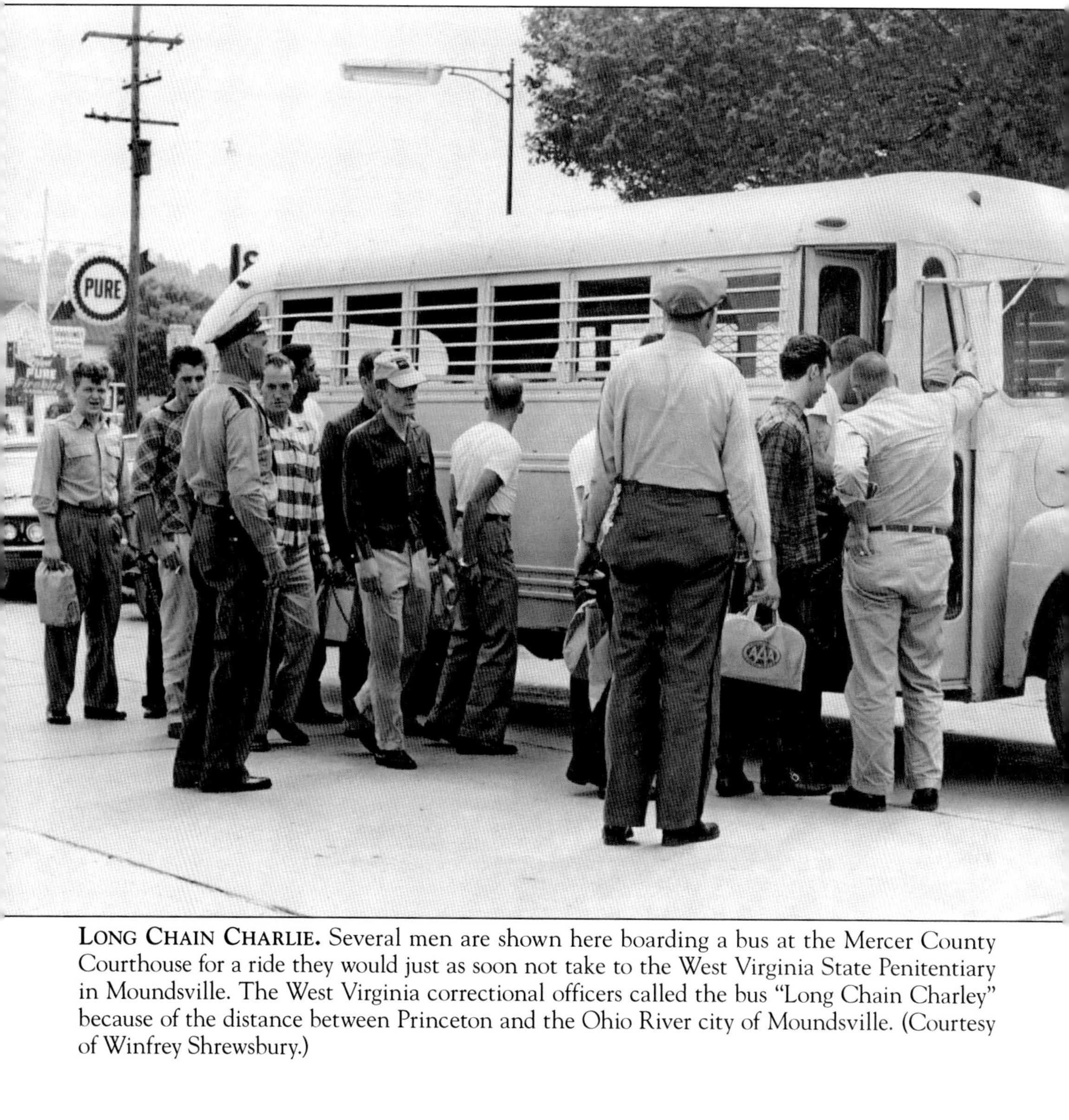

LONG CHAIN CHARLIE. Several men are shown here boarding a bus at the Mercer County Courthouse for a ride they would just as soon not take to the West Virginia State Penitentiary in Moundsville. The West Virginia correctional officers called the bus "Long Chain Charley" because of the distance between Princeton and the Ohio River city of Moundsville. (Courtesy of Winfrey Shrewsbury.)

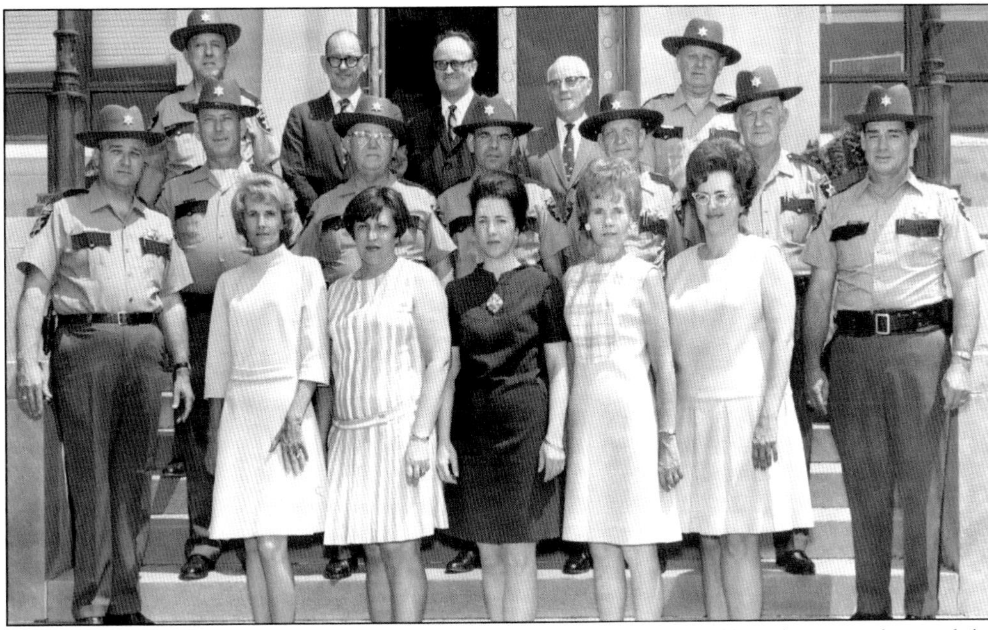

PROTECT AND SERVE. Sheriff Winfrey Shrewsbury (front row at left) is shown in front of the Mercer County Courthouse with deputies, members of his administrative staff, and fellow county officials. Shrewsbury served as a constable before being elected sheriff. (Courtesy of Winfrey Shrewsbury.)

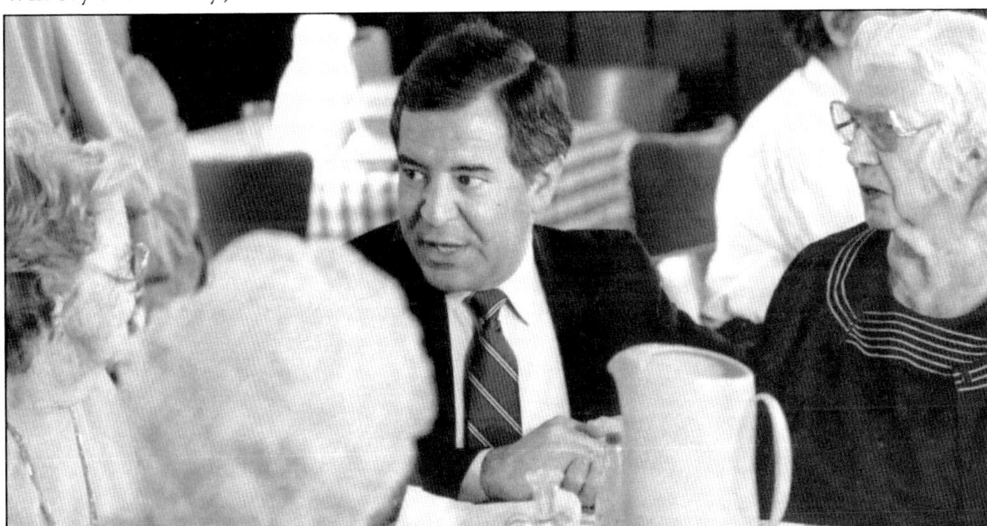

IN THE NICK OF TIME. U.S. Rep. Nick J. Rahall, a Democrat from West Virginia, has served West Virginia's Third Congressional District since 1977 and has proven to be a champion of issues that benefit coal miners and the Appalachian Regional Commission. Perhaps his greatest strength is his work on shaping the nation's highways. He has played a significant role in every highway bill passed by Congress since he was first elected and was a key architect in the creation of the Transportation Equity Act for the 21st Century, known as TEA 21. Despite having a huge district, Rahall makes regular visits to Princeton and surrounding communities. (Courtesy of *Princeton Times* archives.)

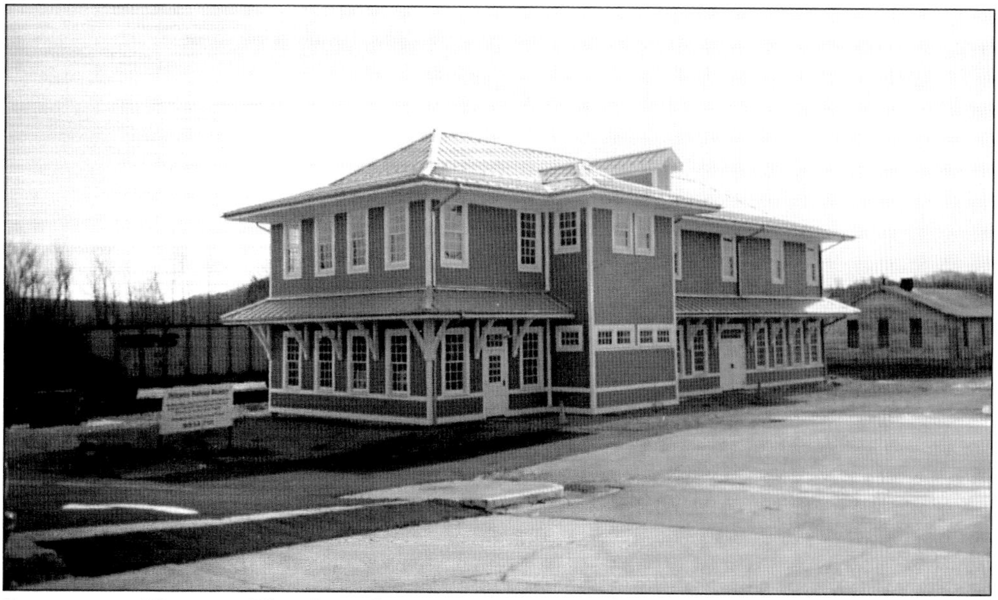

REBUILDING HISTORY. The City of Princeton received a $934,712 Transportation Equity Act (TEA 21) grant to totally rebuild the old Princeton passenger station in the early part of the 21st century. The station is one of the highlights of a comprehensive restoration effort in the area that includes the dynamic East Mercer Street Streetscape project. (Photograph by the author.)

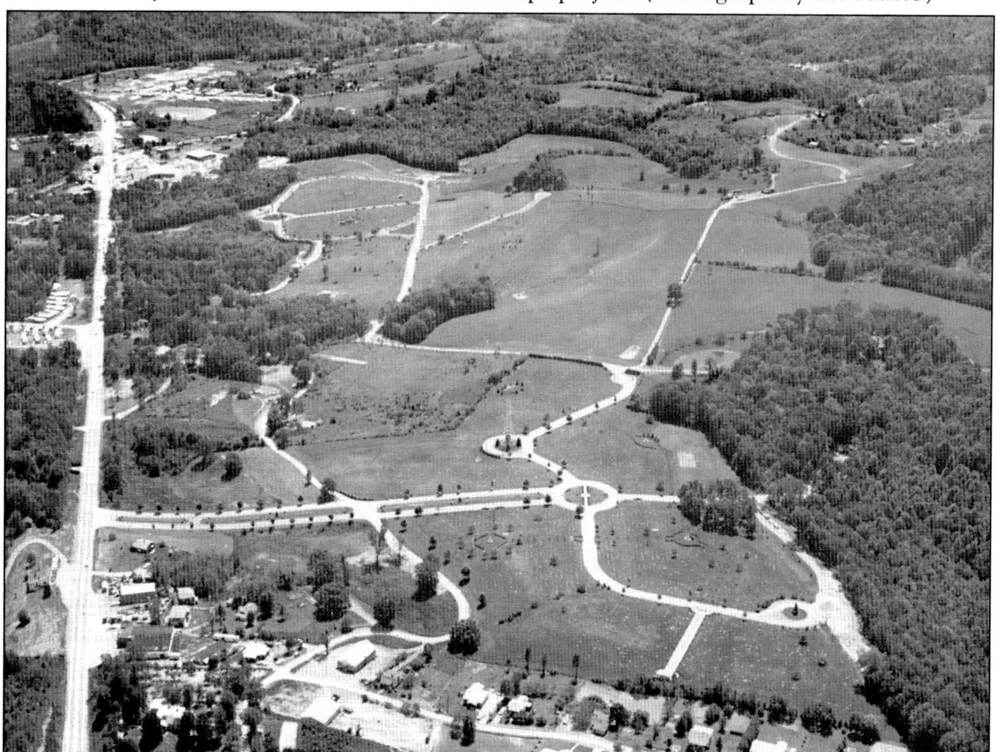

FINAL RESTING PLACE. Roselawn Cemetery on the Courthouse Road, with City View Heights in the foreground, encompasses several acres just south of the city limits. (Courtesy of Sheila Shorter.)

Five

FROM RAIL TO ROAD

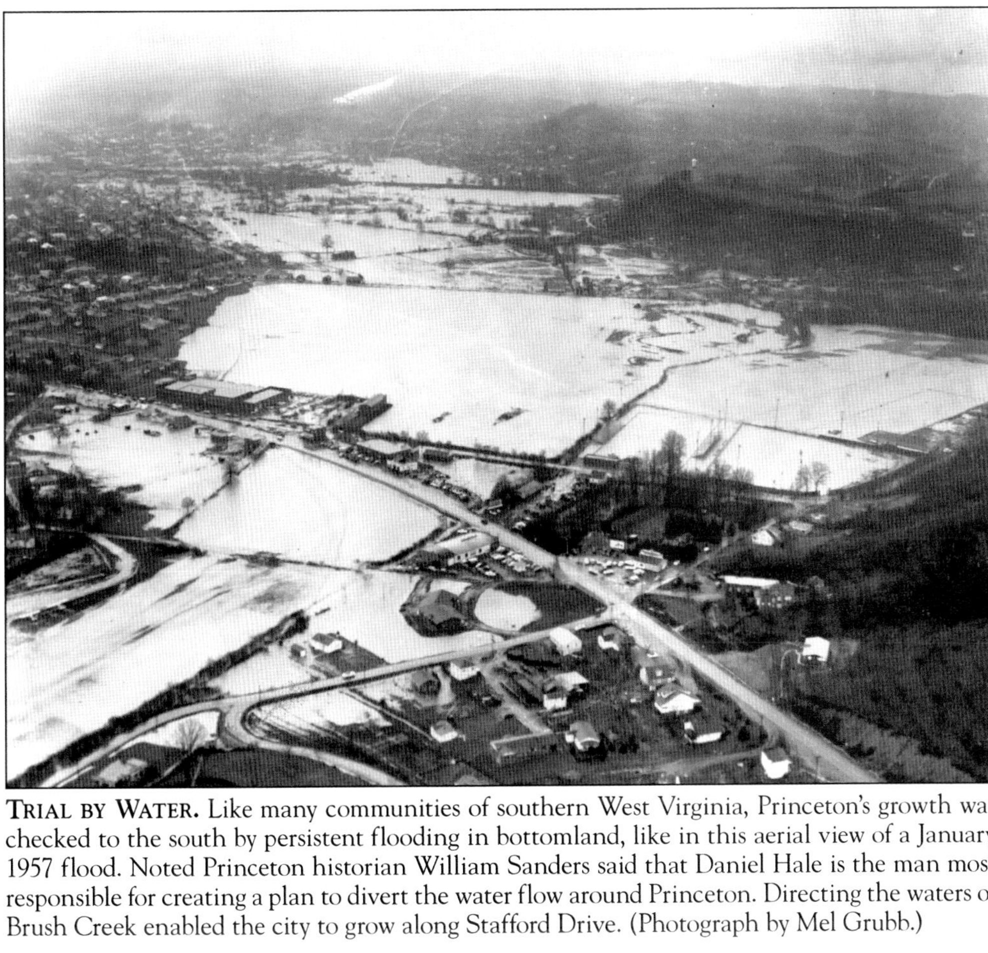

TRIAL BY WATER. Like many communities of southern West Virginia, Princeton's growth was checked to the south by persistent flooding in bottomland, like in this aerial view of a January 1957 flood. Noted Princeton historian William Sanders said that Daniel Hale is the man most responsible for creating a plan to divert the water flow around Princeton. Directing the waters of Brush Creek enabled the city to grow along Stafford Drive. (Photograph by Mel Grubb.)

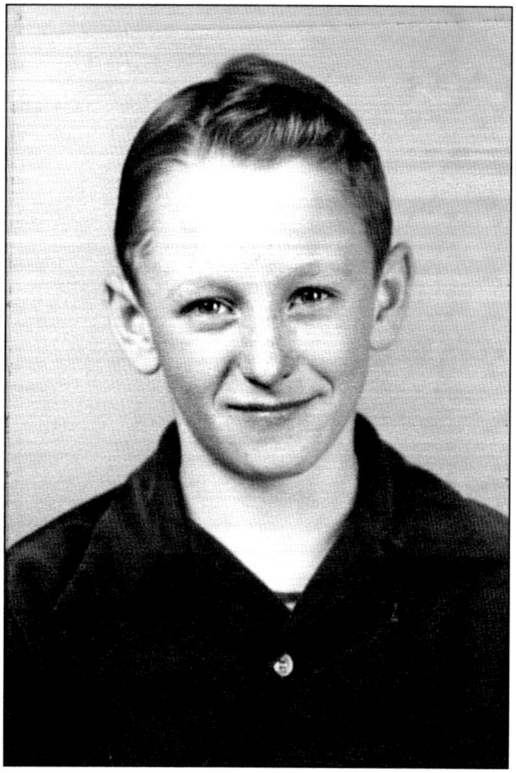

ONE COOL SIXTH GRADER. Rod Thorn, West Virginia University All-American basketball star, NBA great, and now president of the New Jersey Nets, is shown in his sixth-grade photograph. (Courtesy of Rod Thorn.)

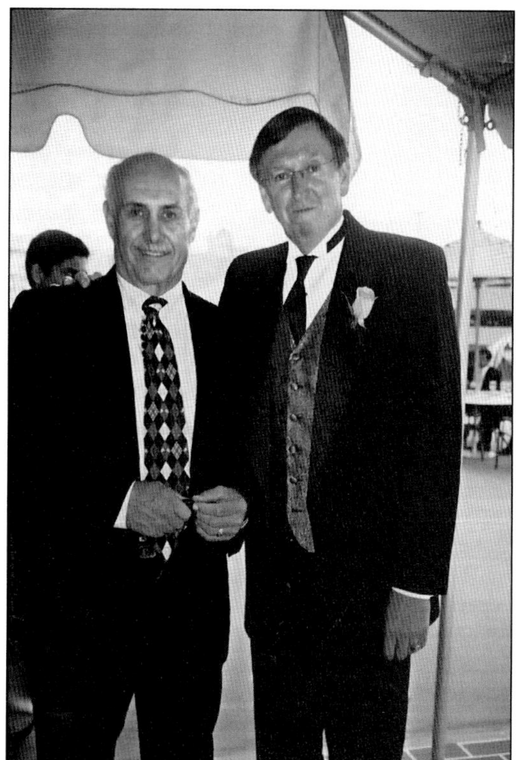

PALS. Ted Gillespie is shown here with Rod Thorn attending a wedding in Charleston in 2001. While Thorn, who drafted Michael Jordan into the NBA as coach of the Chicago Bulls, made an impact on the NBA, Gillespie made an impact by developing new generations of Princeton youth as a principal of both the junior and senior high schools of Mercer County. (Courtesy of Rod Thorn.)

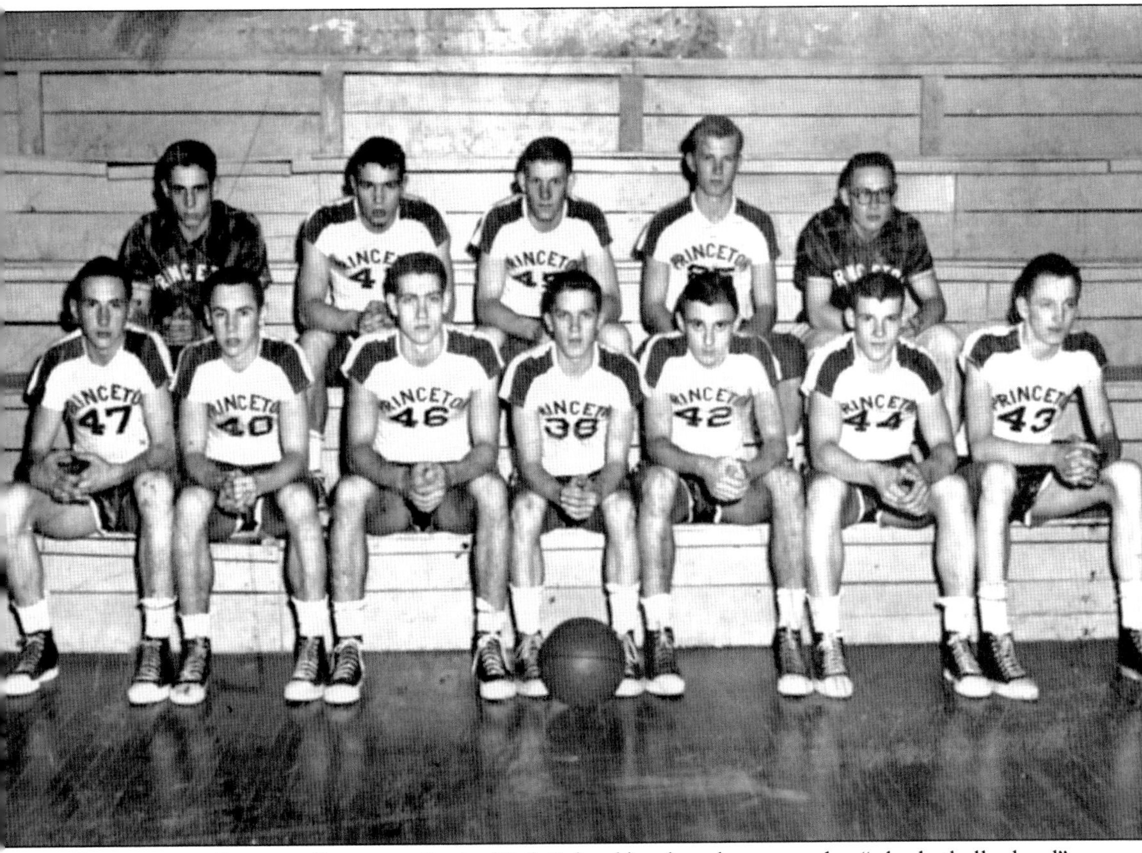

BASKETBALL SCHOOL. Princeton Senior High School has long been noted as "a basketball school" in state circles. The team shown here at the old Princeton Senior High School before it was destroyed by fire was Rod Thorn's first varsity team. Thorn started as a ninth grader and kept on playing. Pictured from left to right are (first row) Jim Miller, Tony Mandible, Roger Little, John Porterfield, Dale Thompson, David Steorts, and Rod Thorn; (second row) Ted Gillespie (manager), Don Tennant, Jim Sayers, Steve Bird, and David Brown. (Courtesy of Rod Thorn.)

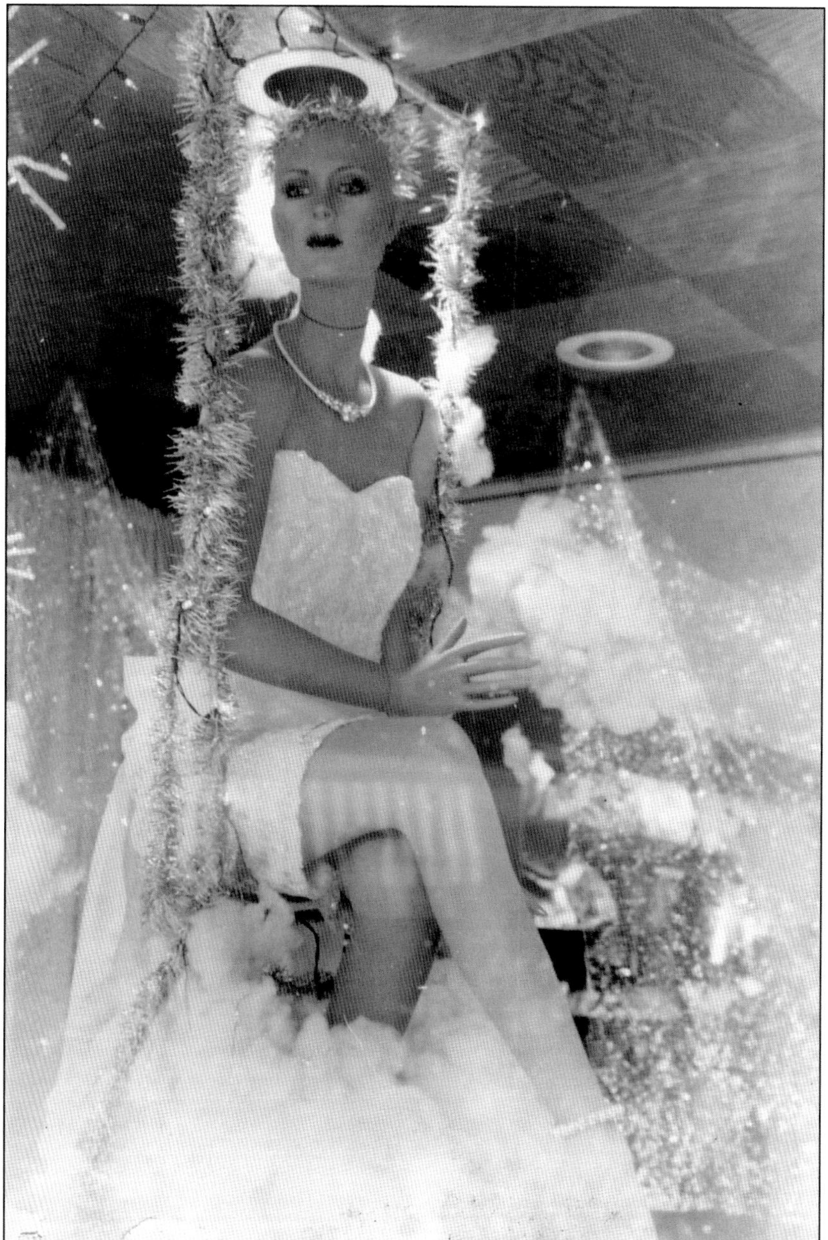

SOMEPLACE SPECIAL. Santon's on Mercer Street in the heart of downtown Princeton was well known throughout the region for its elegant fashions and appeal to lady customers seeking to keep abreast with national trends. "The Captain," George Santon, a brilliant person who devoted his time and talents to the betterment of his community, was at the helm of the store when competitive market forces adversely impacted the family business he took over from his parents, N. E. and Marie Saleh Santon. George was a former Princeton mayor and executive director of the Princeton–Mercer County Chamber of Commerce from 1992 to 2002. His wife, Donna "Biddy" Santon, had an unequalled passion for the region's social scene and wrote about that scene under the pen name "Muffy Vanderbilt," a popular column for *the Observer*, a weekly newspaper that served the region. (Courtesy of *Princeton Times* Archives.)

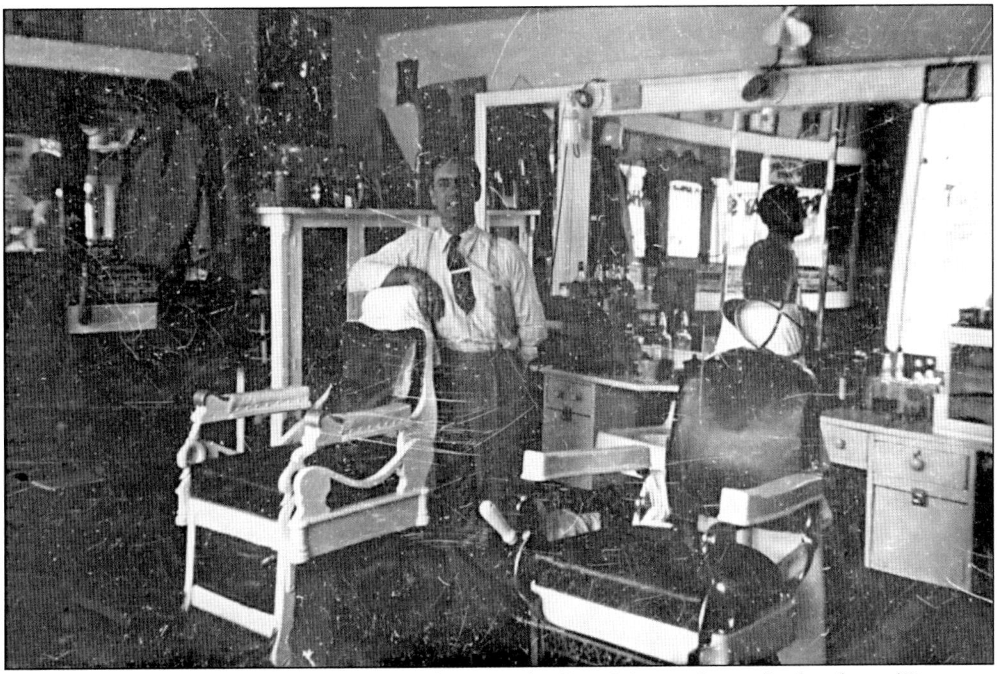

JUST A TRIM. Ted Treadway is shown at his popular East Mercer Street barbershop. (Courtesy of Reed Wheby Jr.)

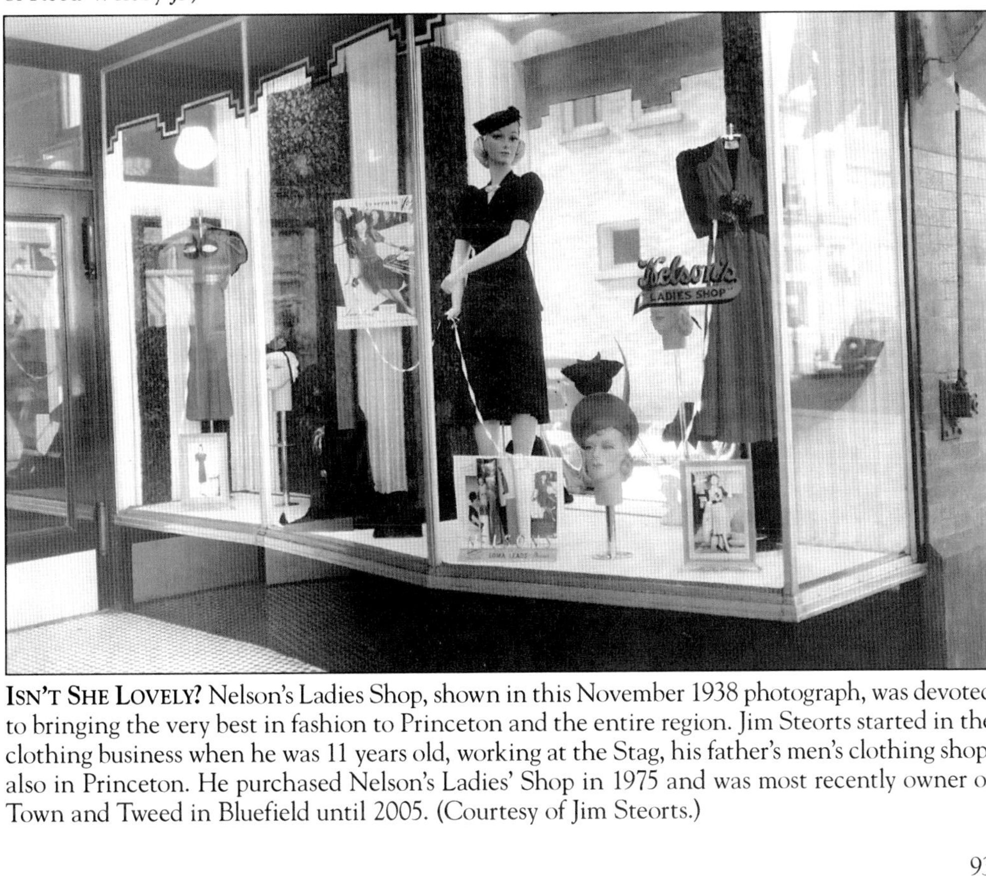

ISN'T SHE LOVELY? Nelson's Ladies Shop, shown in this November 1938 photograph, was devoted to bringing the very best in fashion to Princeton and the entire region. Jim Steorts started in the clothing business when he was 11 years old, working at the Stag, his father's men's clothing shop, also in Princeton. He purchased Nelson's Ladies' Shop in 1975 and was most recently owner of Town and Tweed in Bluefield until 2005. (Courtesy of Jim Steorts.)

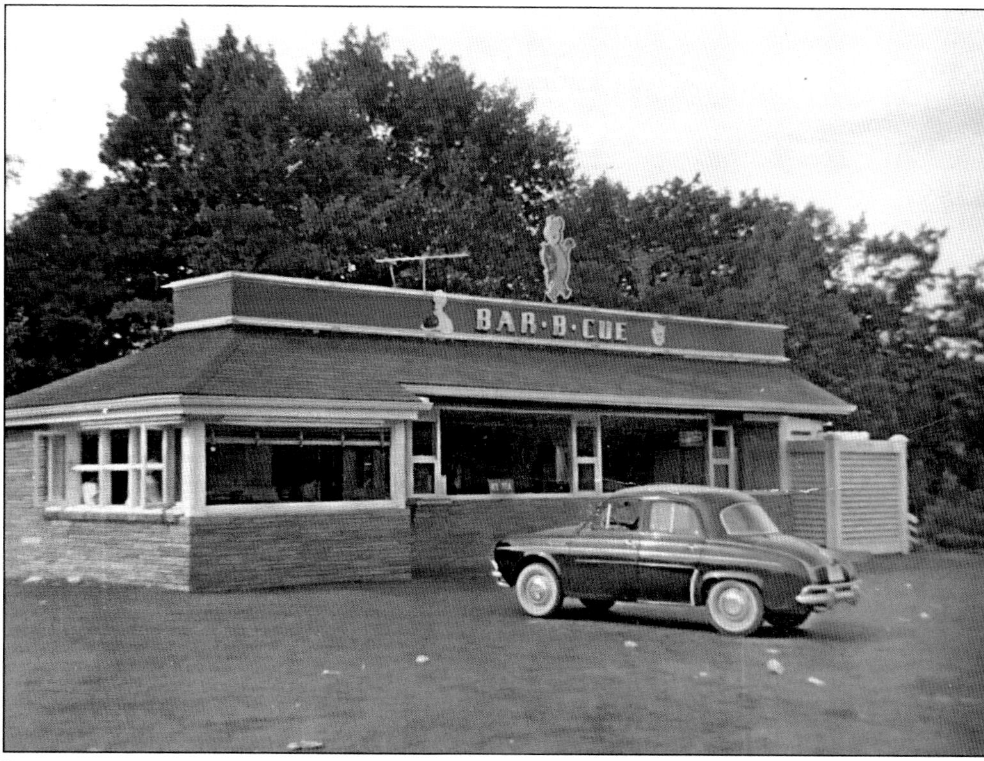

INSTITUTION. Mooney's Drive-In, overlooking the city from its perch on Courthouse Road, was a popular hangout for young people for many years. The drive-in served the public from 1956 through 1985 through the efforts of its founder, M. T. Mooney, and later David Coburn, who leased the business. (Courtesy of Eileen Mooney.)

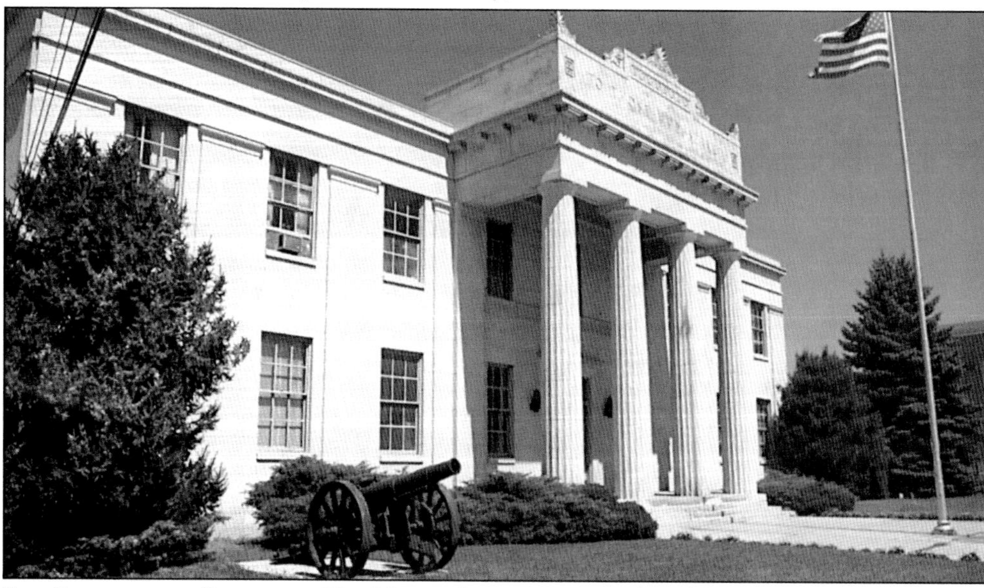

FOR SERVICE AND SACRIFICE. The Mercer County Memorial Building was dedicated on April 3, 1931, by the American Legion of Princeton and later named the Memorial Building on June 20, 1935. (Courtesy of Winfrey Shrewsbury.)

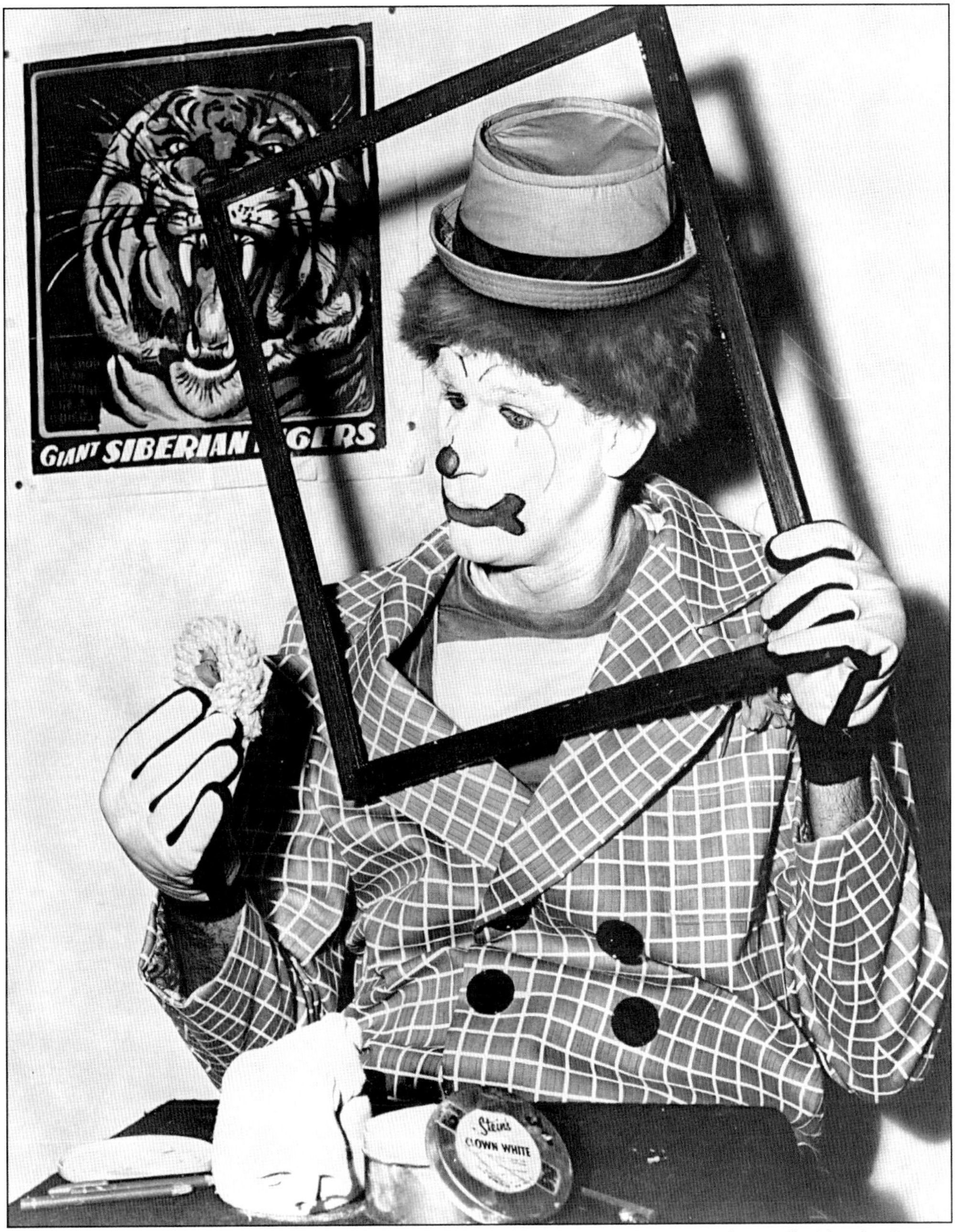

SMELL OF THE GREASEPAINT AND ROAR OF THE CROWD. At 7 feet, 3 inches tall, Charles Logan "Buck" Buxton was a big man on the Princeton Senior High School campus, and while people encouraged him to play basketball, the lanky Buxton joined a chimpanzee act in the late 1950s and toured the world for the next 33 years, billing himself as the "World's Tallest Clown." Buxton appeared in several films under the name Buck Nolan and turned down the role of Darth Vader because he was under contract to do another film at the same time. He was born in 1936 and retired to his Front Street home, where he was a frequent visitor at regional flea markets. He died November 9, 2004. (Courtesy of Judith Buxton Collins.)

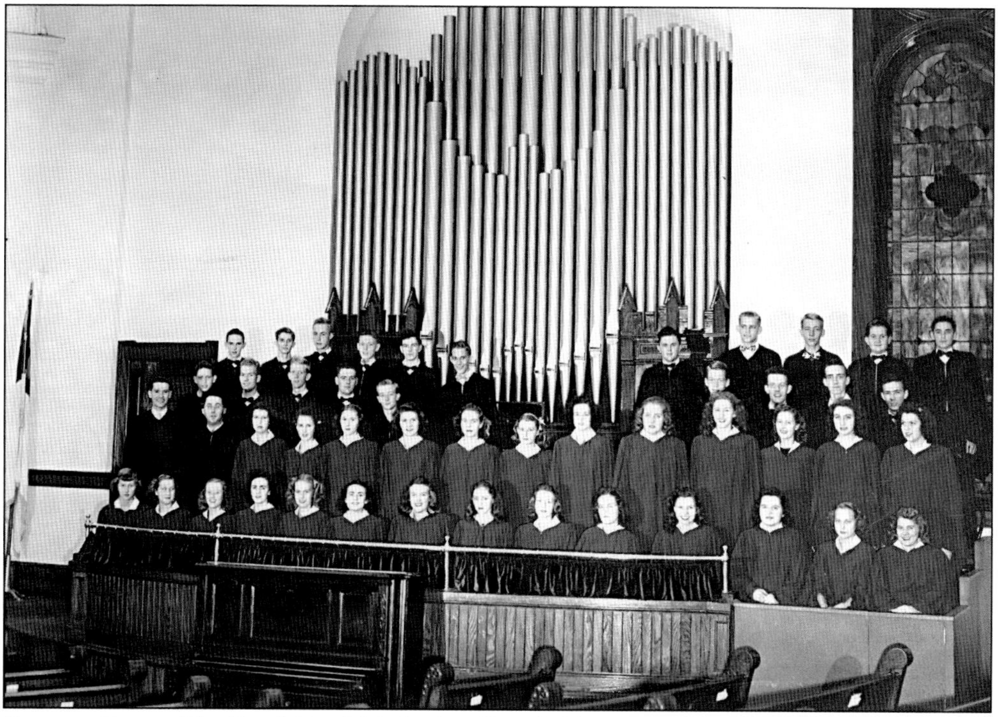

SONG OF FAITH. The First United Methodist Church Choir is seen in this undated photograph. The choir was well known throughout the city and the region. (Courtesy of Shirley Smith.)

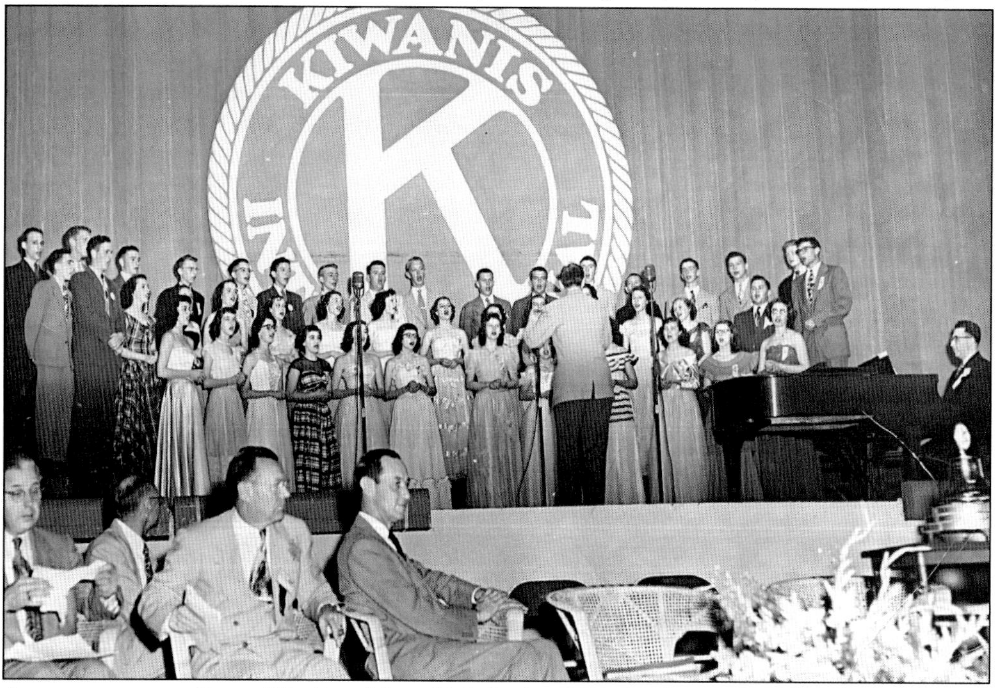

AMBASSADORS OF SONG. The First United Methodist Church Choir traveled to Miami, Florida, where they were invited to perform at a Kiwanis International annual convention. (Courtesy of Shirley Smith.)

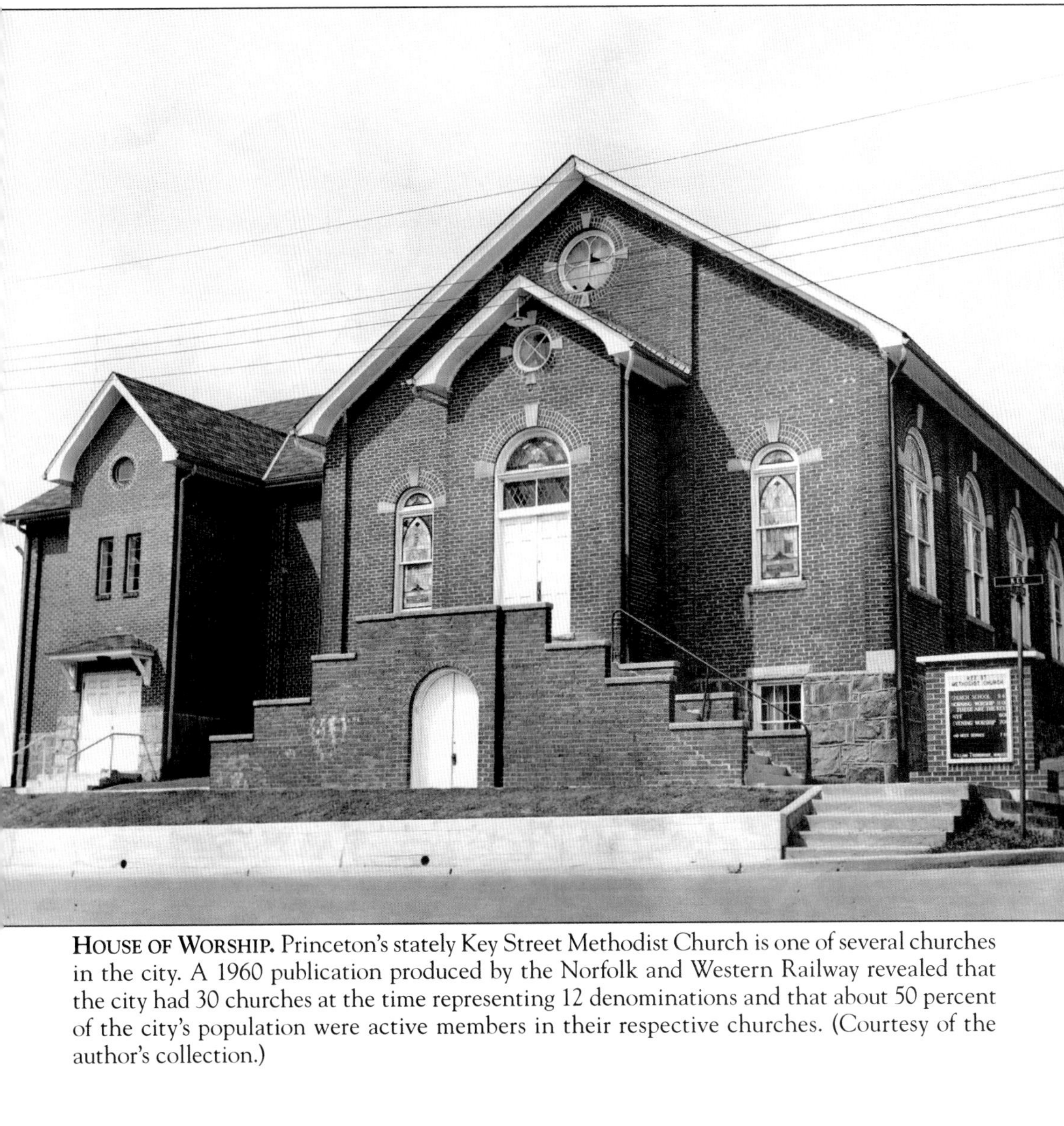

HOUSE OF WORSHIP. Princeton's stately Key Street Methodist Church is one of several churches in the city. A 1960 publication produced by the Norfolk and Western Railway revealed that the city had 30 churches at the time representing 12 denominations and that about 50 percent of the city's population were active members in their respective churches. (Courtesy of the author's collection.)

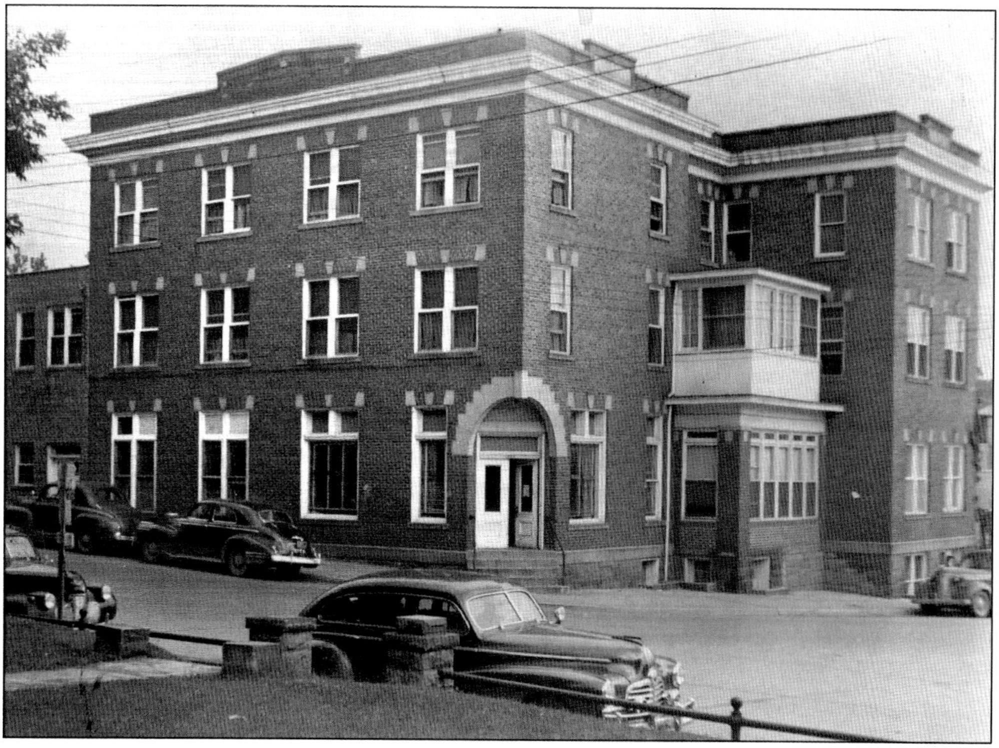

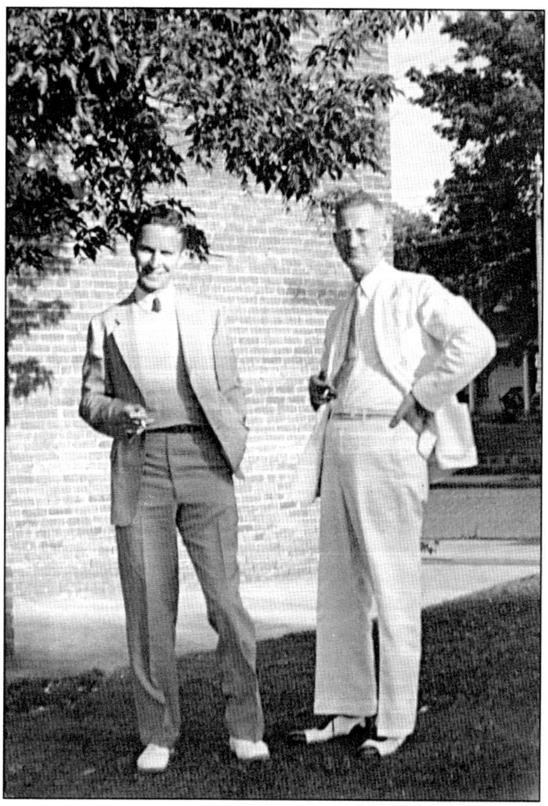

To Your Health. The health care needs of Princeton residents were met at the old Mercer Memorial Hospital located on Main Street. Dr. Gordon Todd transformed the hospital into a not-for-profit facility. The hospital underwent a major expansion in 1957. (Courtesy of Rixie Todd.)

Pair of Docs. Dr. Gordon L. Todd Sr. (right) and Dr. Gordon L. Todd Jr. are shown in this photograph from the 1940s. The senior Dr. Todd died at age 50, and Dr. Todd Jr. became Memorial president. (Courtesy of Rixie Todd.)

More Power to You. Dr. James E. Powers served as general surgeon at Memorial and made the transition in that same capacity to Princeton Community Hospital, where he served from 1970 to 1993. (Courtesy of Princeton Community Hospital.)

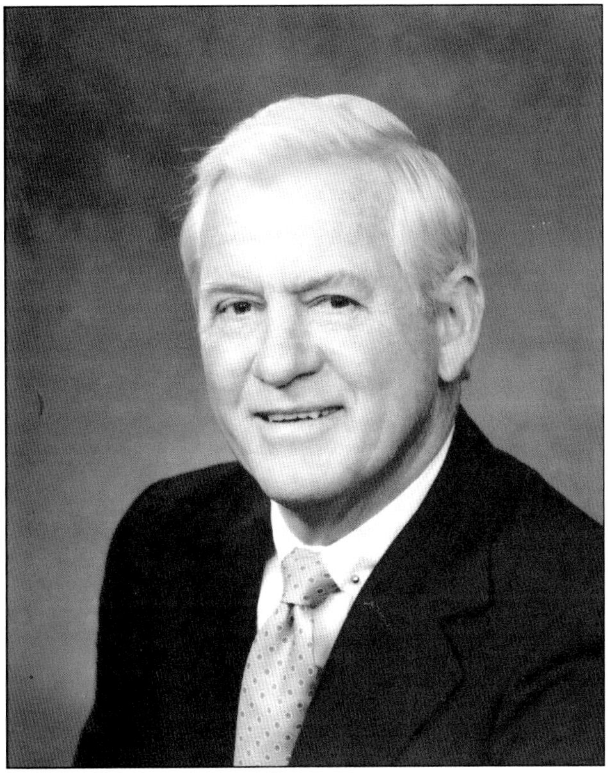

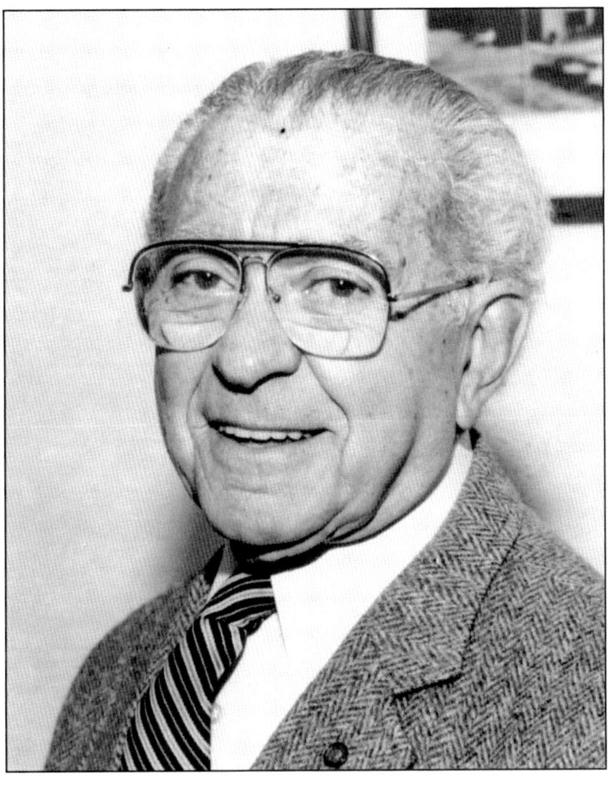

Pace Yourself. In addition to being an excellent physician, Dr. Lawrence Pace was also a community-minded individual who put his considerable talents and energy behind the development of a new community hospital. (Courtesy of Princeton Community Hospital.)

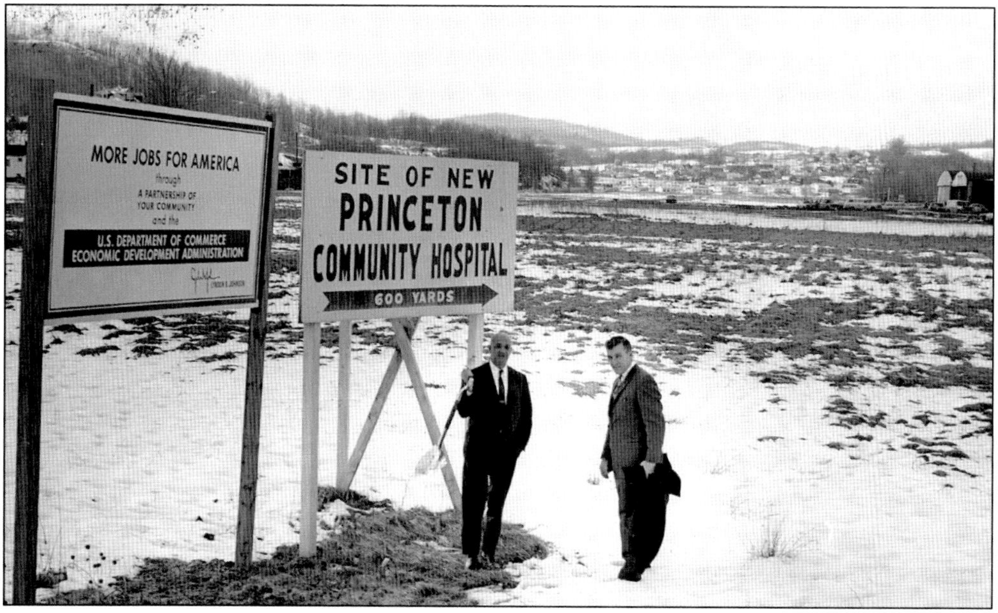

The Big Dig. Dr. James Powers (right) and Harold Tomchin are shown at the 1967 groundbreaking ceremony for Princeton Community Hospital (PCH). Powers served as the first PCH chief of staff and Tomchin, owner of Tomchin Furniture, was on the PCH board of directors. (Courtesy of Princeton Community Hospital.)

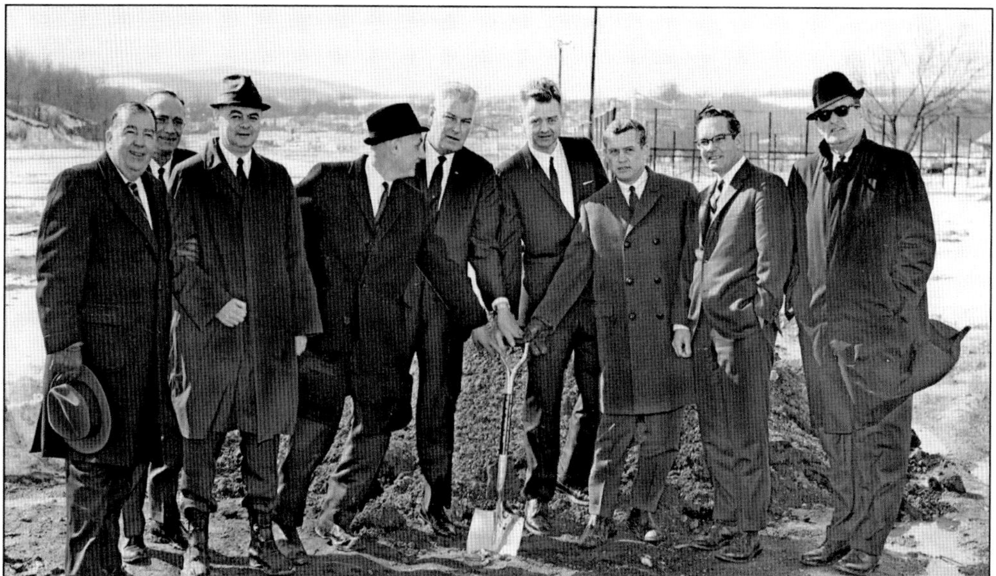

Dignitaries Dig. Several area dignitaries participated in the PCH groundbreaking. Pictured here from left to right are U.S. senator Jennings Randolph; U.S. representative James Kee; Harry Finkelman, professor at Concord College; Harold Tomchin, owner of Tomchin Furniture; James Morrison, plant manager at North American Rockwell; Odell Huffman, PCH legal counsel; James Powers, chief of staff; James Thompson, president and board chairman at Mercer County Bank; and O. D. "Bus" Compton, owner of Compton Construction Company. (Courtesy of Princeton Community Hospital.)

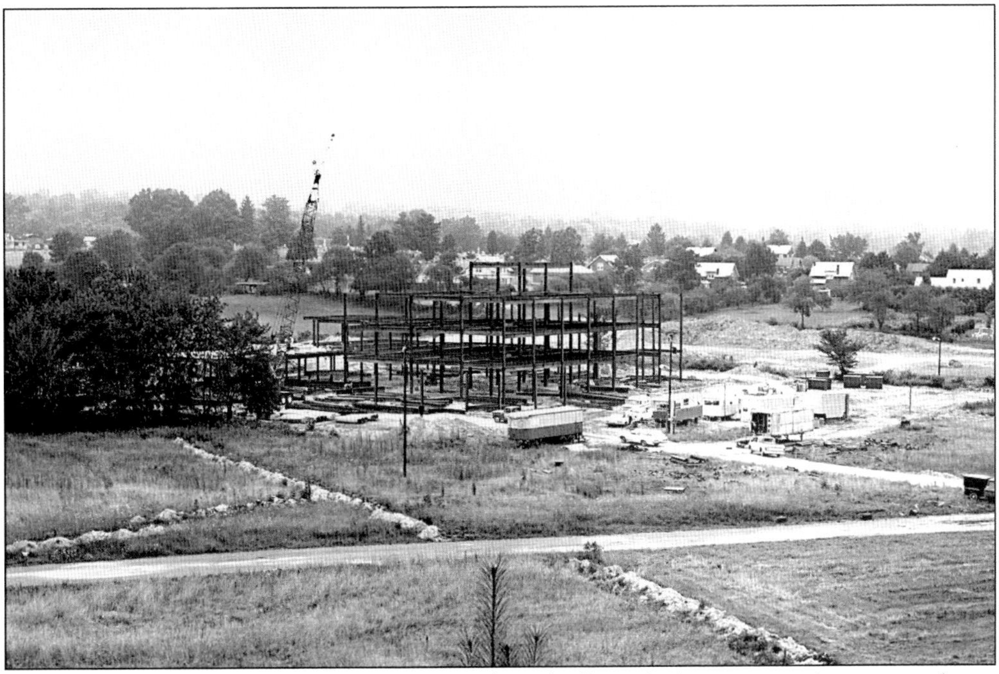

STEEL WORK. Princeton Community Hospital gradually took shape, as can be seen in this *c.* 1968 photograph by Mel Grubb. The emergence of the hospital near the end of the old Princeton Municipal Airport ignited dramatic growth in this section of the city. (Courtesy of Princeton Community Hospital.)

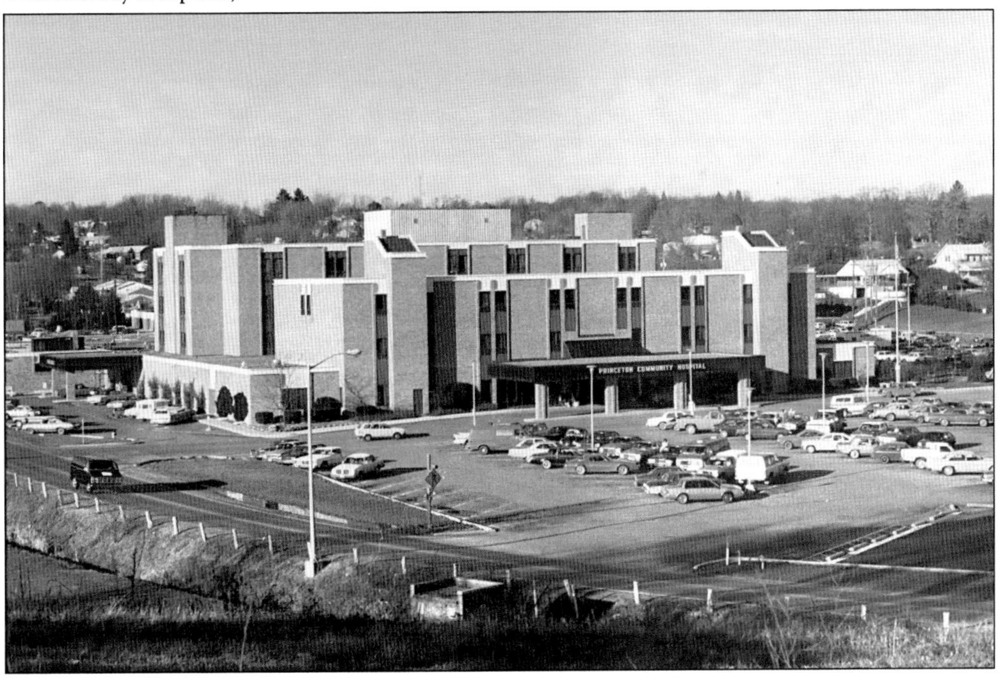

OPEN FOR PATIENTS. Princeton Community Hospital was open and ready to start admitting patients in December 1970. While the hospital's core remains essentially the same, the hospital complex has grown considerably since its beginnings. (Courtesy of Princeton Community Hospital.)

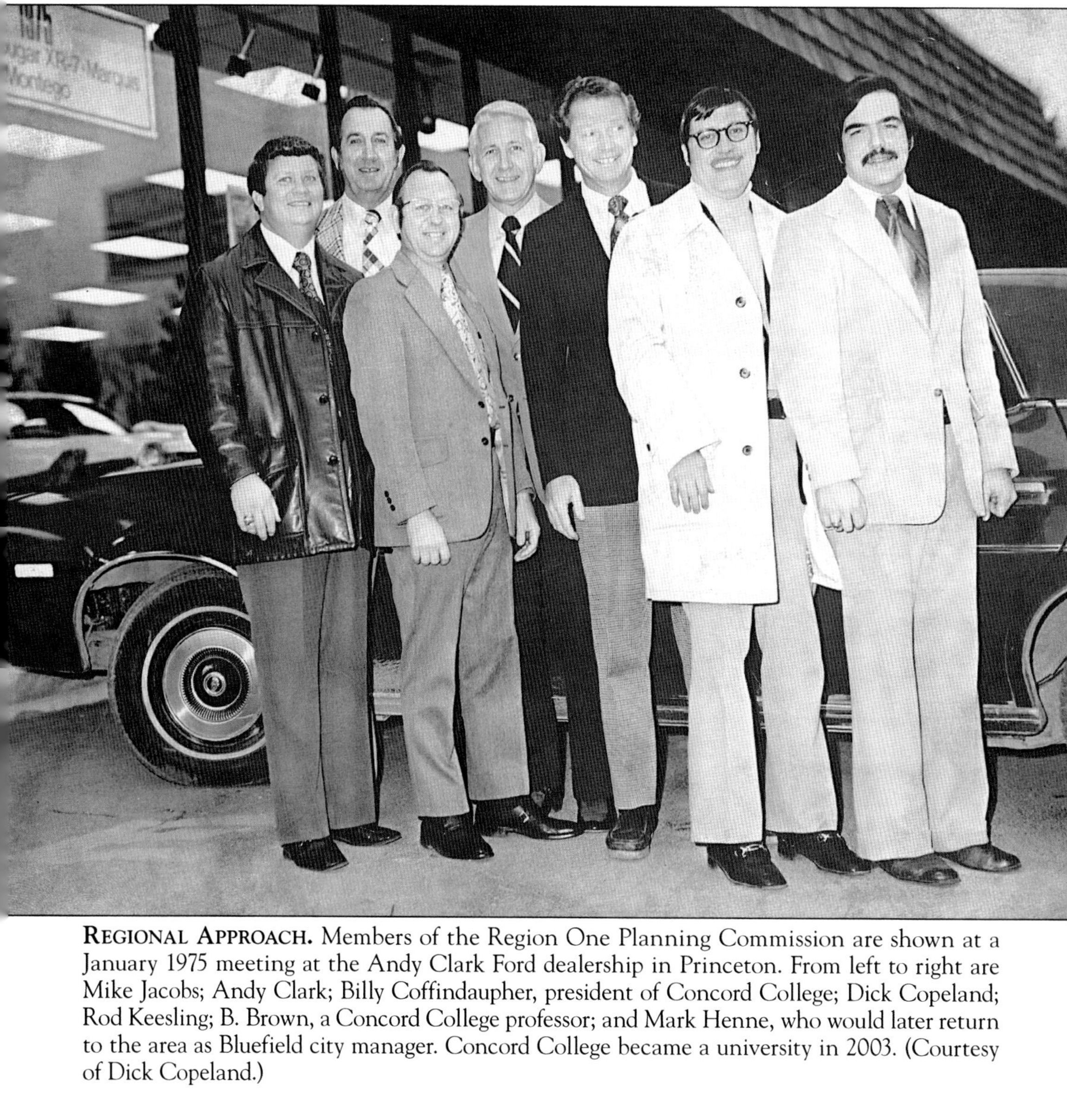

REGIONAL APPROACH. Members of the Region One Planning Commission are shown at a January 1975 meeting at the Andy Clark Ford dealership in Princeton. From left to right are Mike Jacobs; Andy Clark; Billy Coffindaupher, president of Concord College; Dick Copeland; Rod Keesling; B. Brown, a Concord College professor; and Mark Henne, who would later return to the area as Bluefield city manager. Concord College became a university in 2003. (Courtesy of Dick Copeland.)

Six

The Artistry of a City

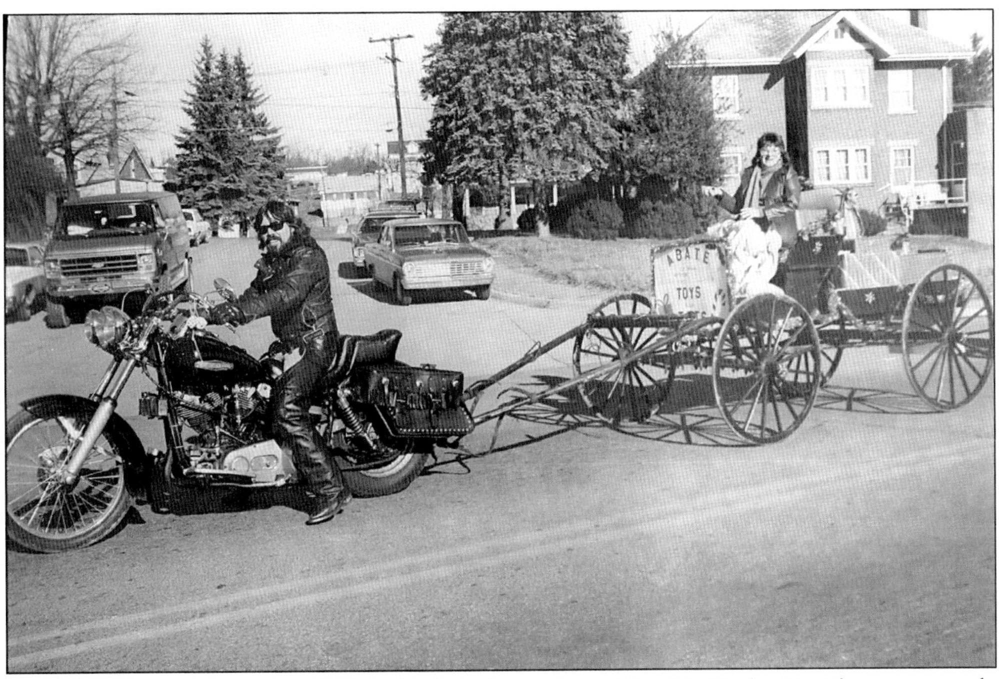

Hog and Buggy Days. Ace "Winky" Lilly is shown here riding his Harley Davidson motorcycle hitched to a buggy at the intersection of Fourth Street and Straley Avenue for the 1990 Princeton Christmas Parade. Princeton's Abate and, later, the Brothers of the Wheel motorcycle clubs have operated a children's holiday toys program for several years. Diana Luciano is the passenger in the buggy. (Courtesy of *Princeton Times* archives.)

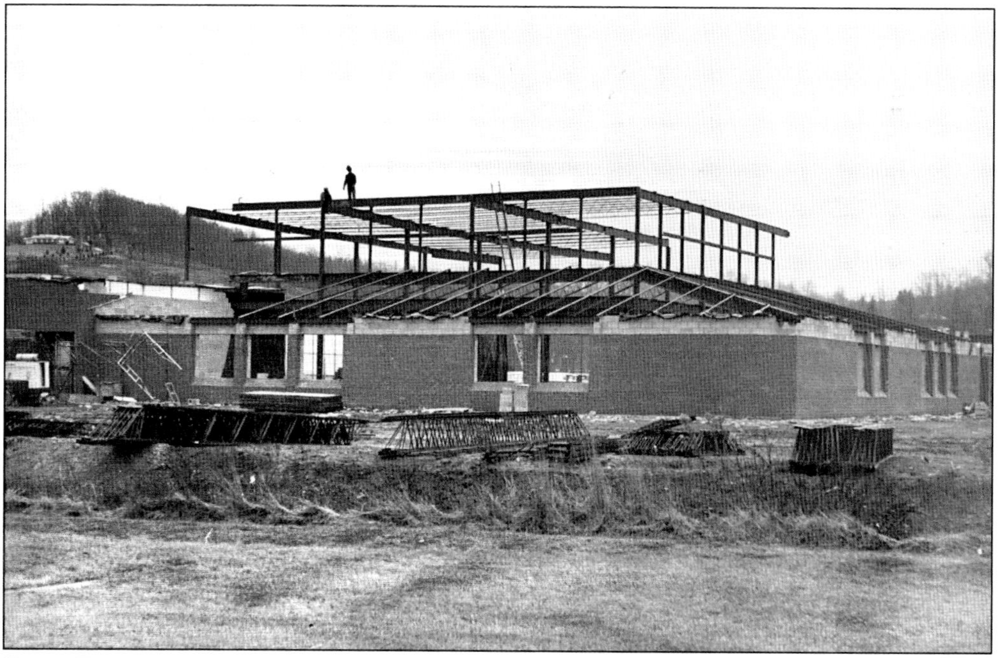

TIGER TOWER. Construction of the new Princeton Senior High School (PSHS) is shown here. The old PSHS was destroyed by fire *c.* 1975. PSHS was recognized as a National Blue Ribbon School in 1996–1997, among many honors achieved by the school through the years. (Courtesy of *Princeton Times* archives.)

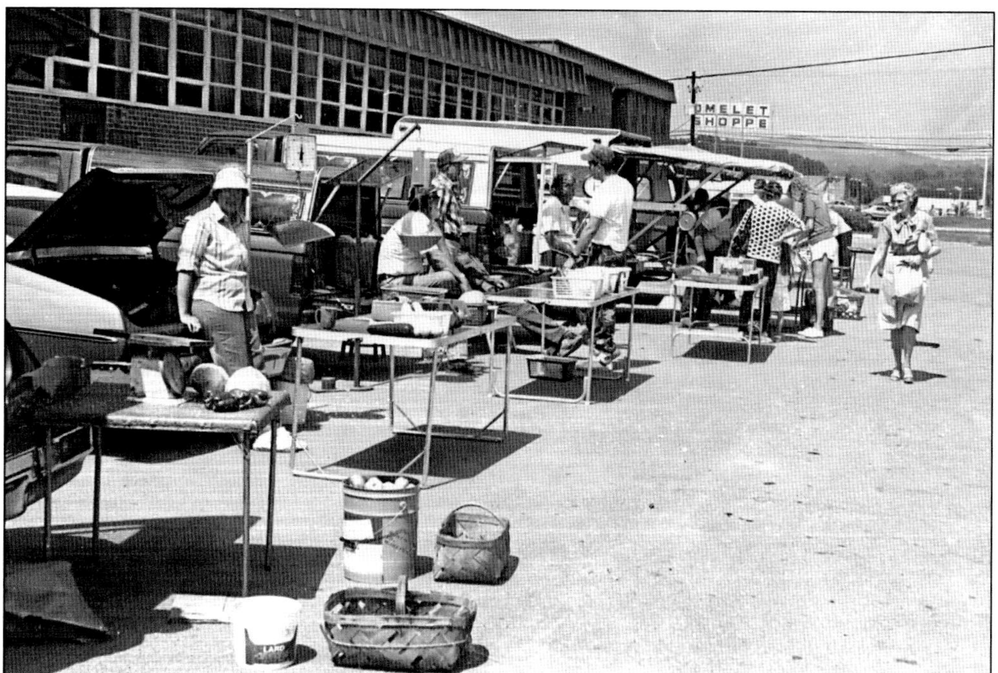

AN APPLE A DAY. Princeton's popular farmer's market in the parking lot of the Mercer County Technical Educational Center has been a popular place for area farmers to sell their produce. (Courtesy of *Princeton Times* archives.)

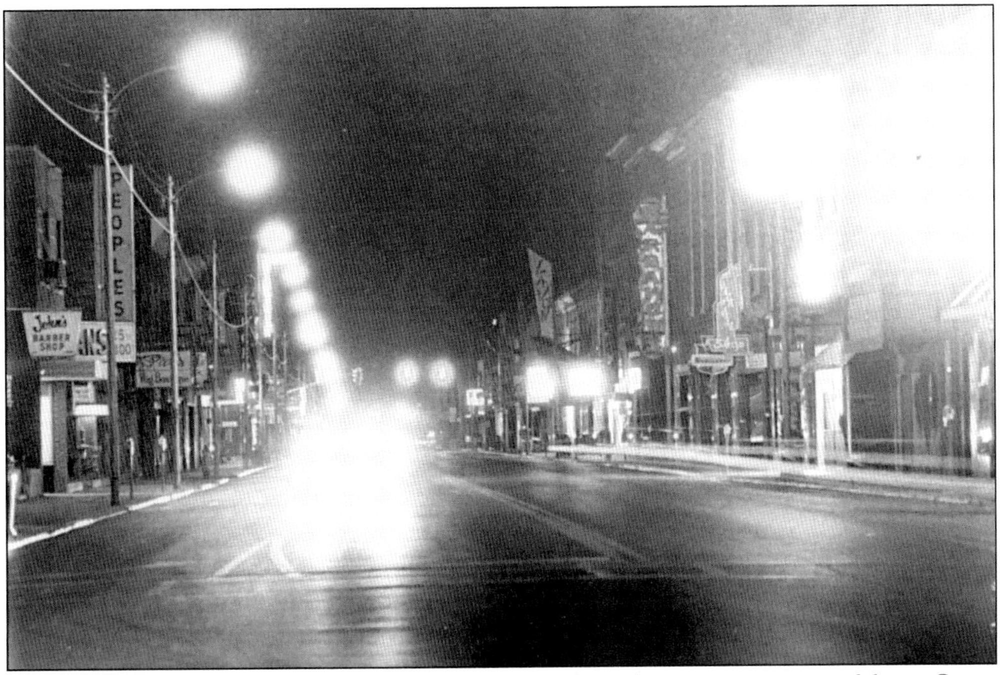

CRUISIN'. One of the hugely popular activities for youth in the area is to come to Mercer Street on Friday evenings and cruise. The city has made attempts to control or even curtail the popular activity, but has had limited success. (Courtesy of *Princeton Times* archives.)

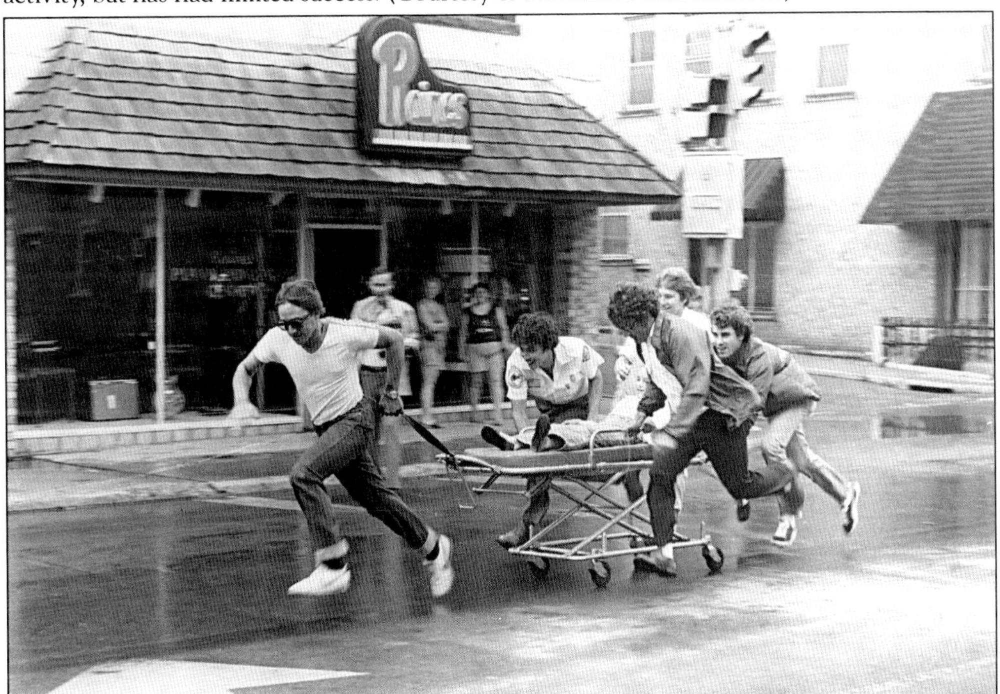

ER SHUFFLE. A team of competitors is shown on Mercer Street in a fun competition from June 1981. Fairs and festivals have long been exciting in Princeton. (Courtesy of *Princeton Times* archives.)

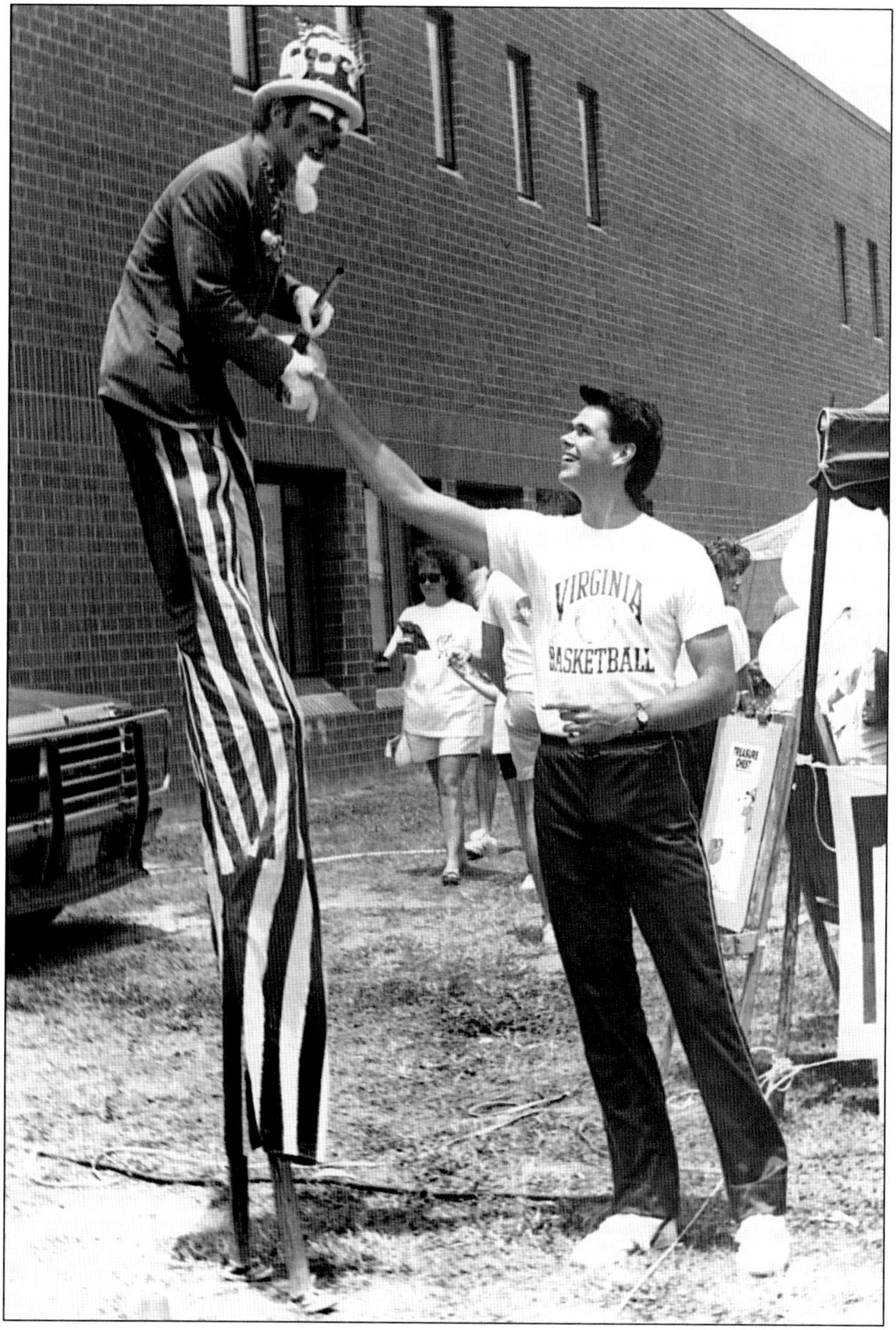

THE MAGICIAN. Jimmy Miller scorched the nets for the Princeton Tigers basketball team in the late 1970s and was sought after by several major colleges. He finally decided on the University of Virginia, where he had a stellar career and eventually went into coaching after trying his hand as a professional slight-of-hand magician. Miller is shown here at the July 1990 SummerFest. (Photograph by the author.)

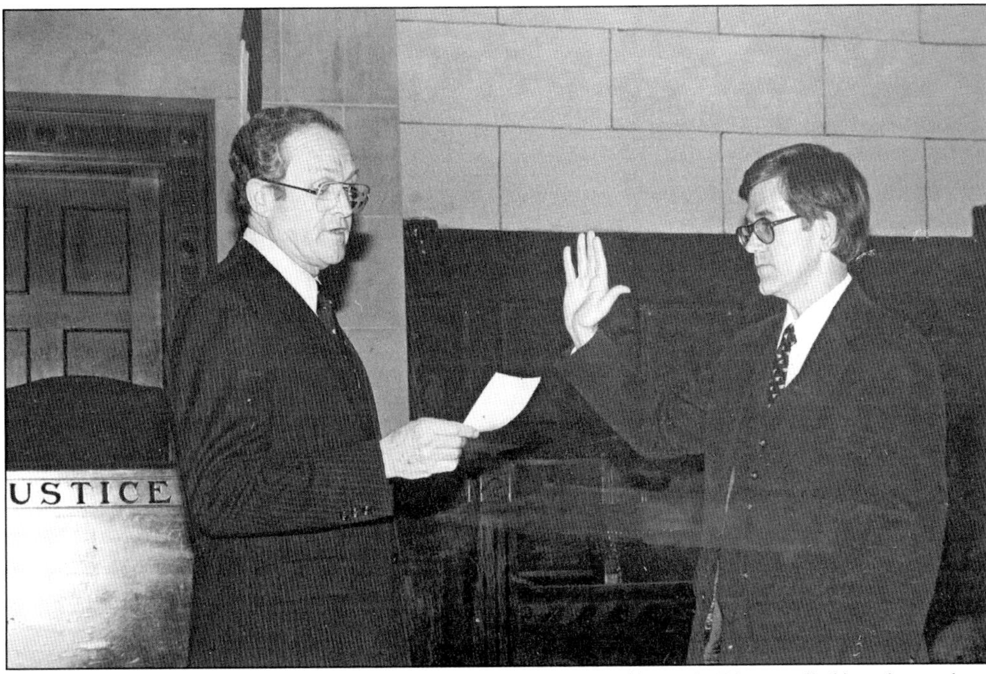

Taking the Oath. Mercer County Circuit Court judge William O. Blevins (left) is shown here administering the oath of office to Circuit Court judge John R. Frazier in this December 3, 1981, photograph. (Courtesy of *Princeton Times* archives.)

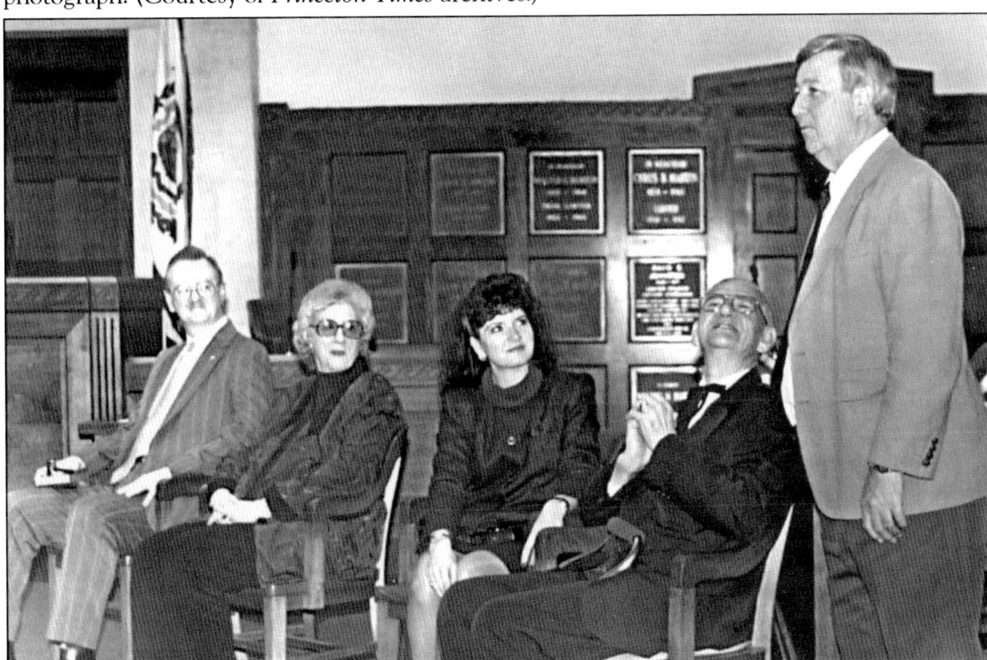

Here Comes the Judge. Mercer County Circuit Court judge David Knight is shown here in February 1991 about to receive the oath of office. Judge Knight served several years as Mercer County prosecuting attorney until ascending to the bench. Shown here from left to right are Jim Dent, Jean Giampacaro, Aleta Linkous, Luther Byrd, and Judge Knight. (Photograph by the author.)

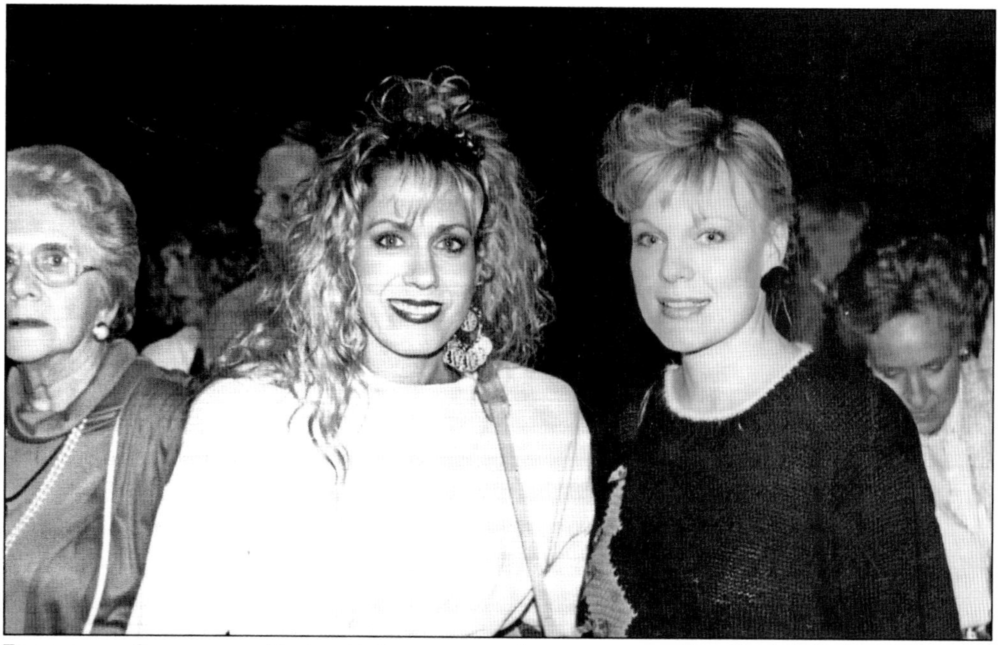

PRINCETON SONGBIRDS. Nationally-known recording artist Suzi Carr (left), who had a number-one single as the female lead singer with Will to Power in their remake of "Freebird/Baby I love Your Ways," was honored in December 1989 with Suzi Carr Day in Princeton. Carr is shown with her longtime friend Donna Charles (right), also a popular singer. (Photograph by the author.)

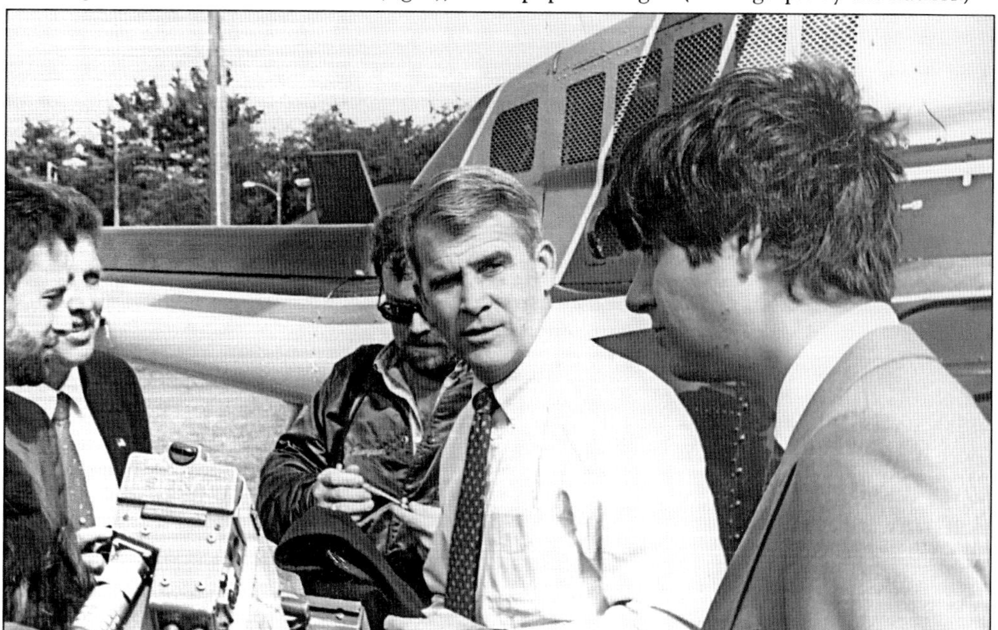

SILENT OLLIE. Oliver North, a key figure in the Iran-Contra arms-for-hostages crisis during the Reagan administration, emerged from a withering barrage of congressional questioning to campaign for Republican candidates. He came to Princeton in September 1992 to campaign for Ben Waldman, who ran unsuccessfully for the third district seat in Congress. (Photograph by the author.)

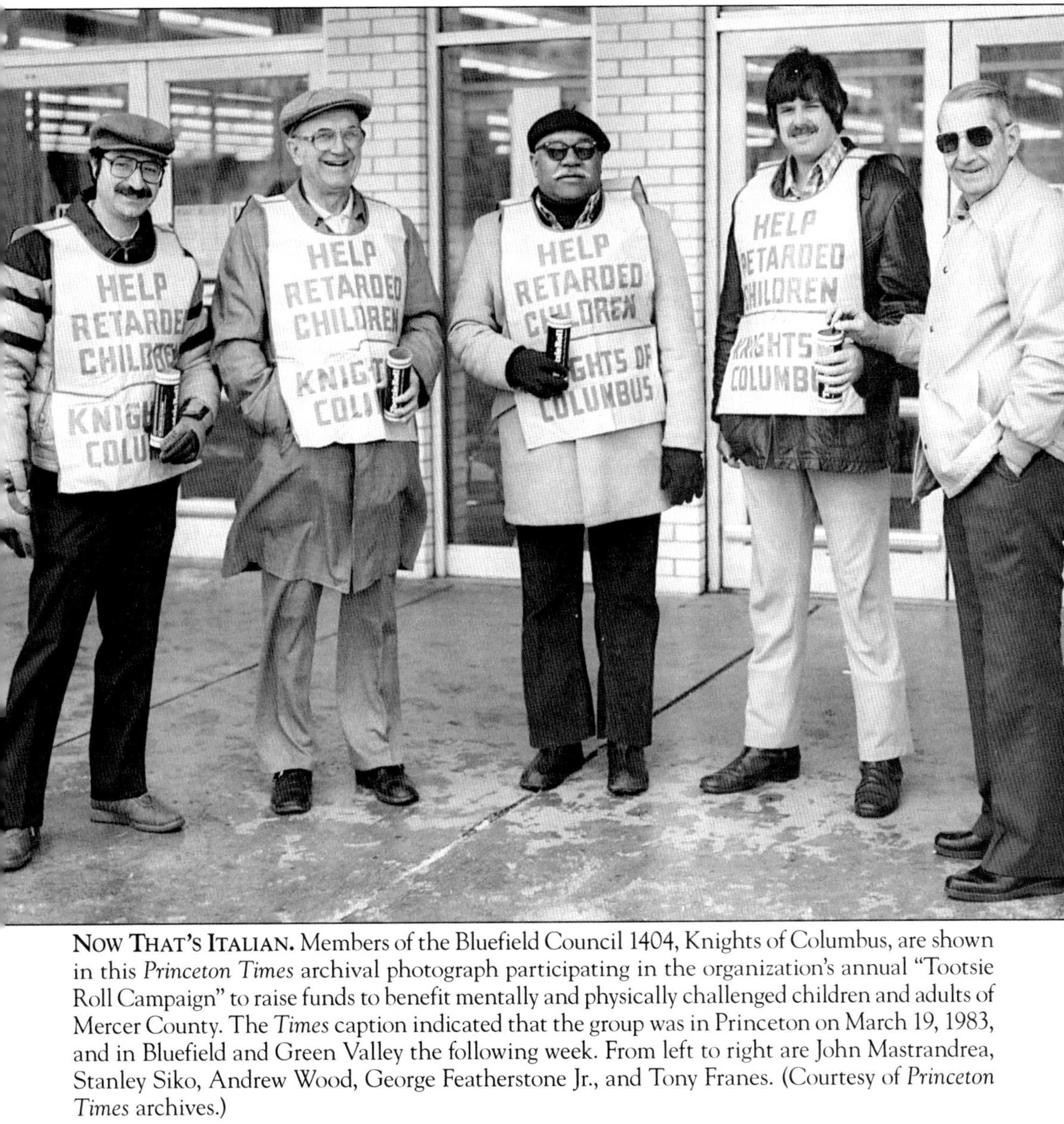

Now That's Italian. Members of the Bluefield Council 1404, Knights of Columbus, are shown in this *Princeton Times* archival photograph participating in the organization's annual "Tootsie Roll Campaign" to raise funds to benefit mentally and physically challenged children and adults of Mercer County. The *Times* caption indicated that the group was in Princeton on March 19, 1983, and in Bluefield and Green Valley the following week. From left to right are John Mastrandrea, Stanley Siko, Andrew Wood, George Featherstone Jr., and Tony Franes. (Courtesy of *Princeton Times* archives.)

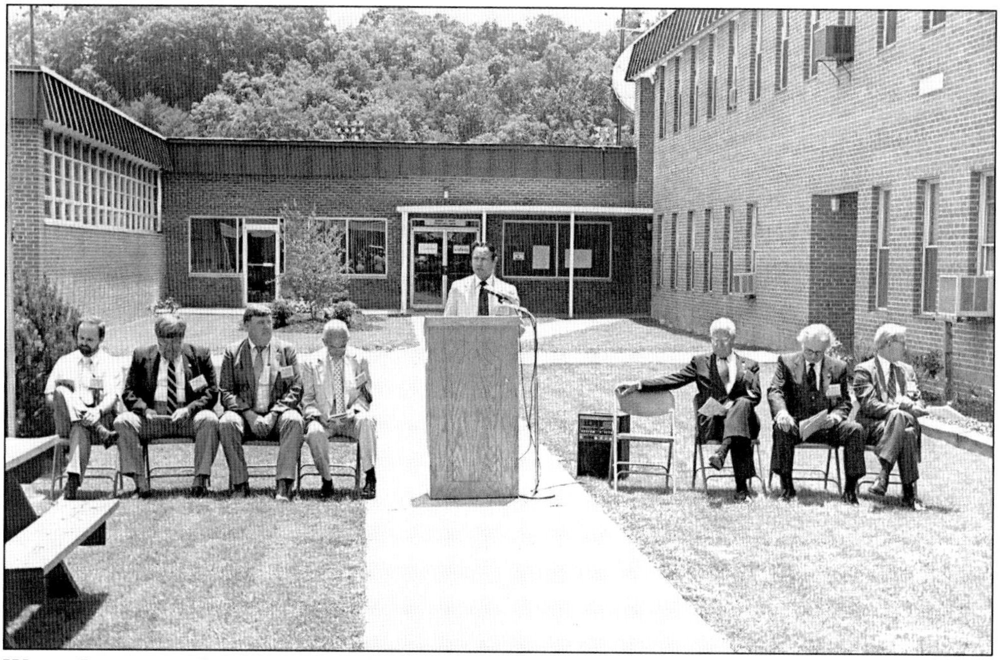

WOOD INDUSTRY CHAMPIONS. Robert Bailey, former director of the Mercer County Technical Education Center (MCTEC), is shown addressing the opening of the Appalachian Hardwood Expo in June 1992. MCTEC has been at the forefront of industry leadership for many years. (Photograph by the author.)

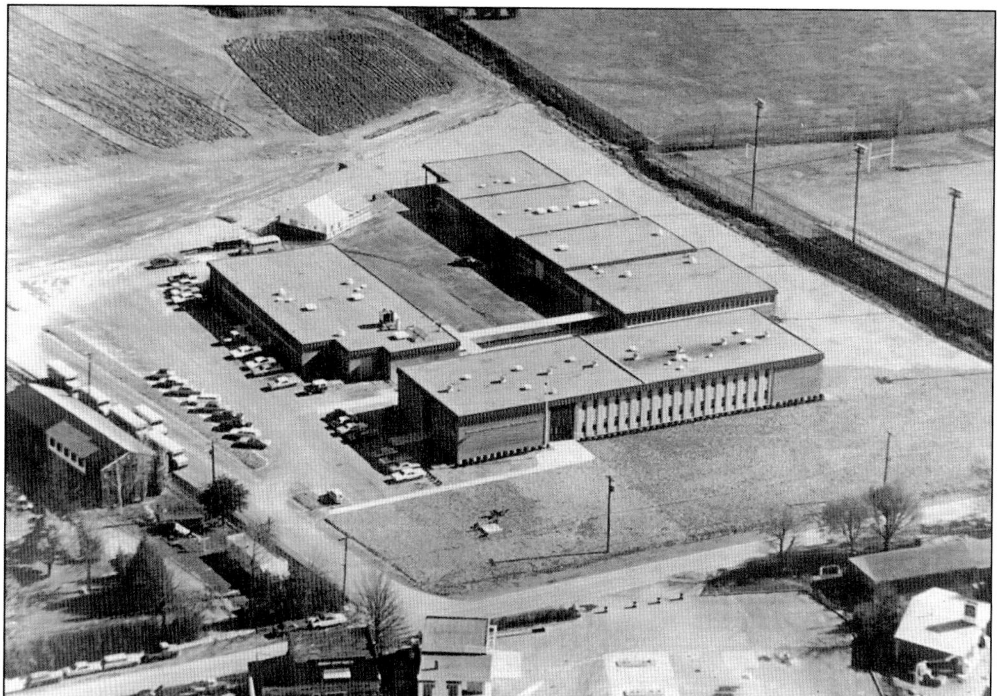

SCHOOL ZONE. The Mercer County Technical Education Center is shown here when it was one of the first buildings in that section of town. (Courtesy of Huber Bailey and Bill Sherwood.)

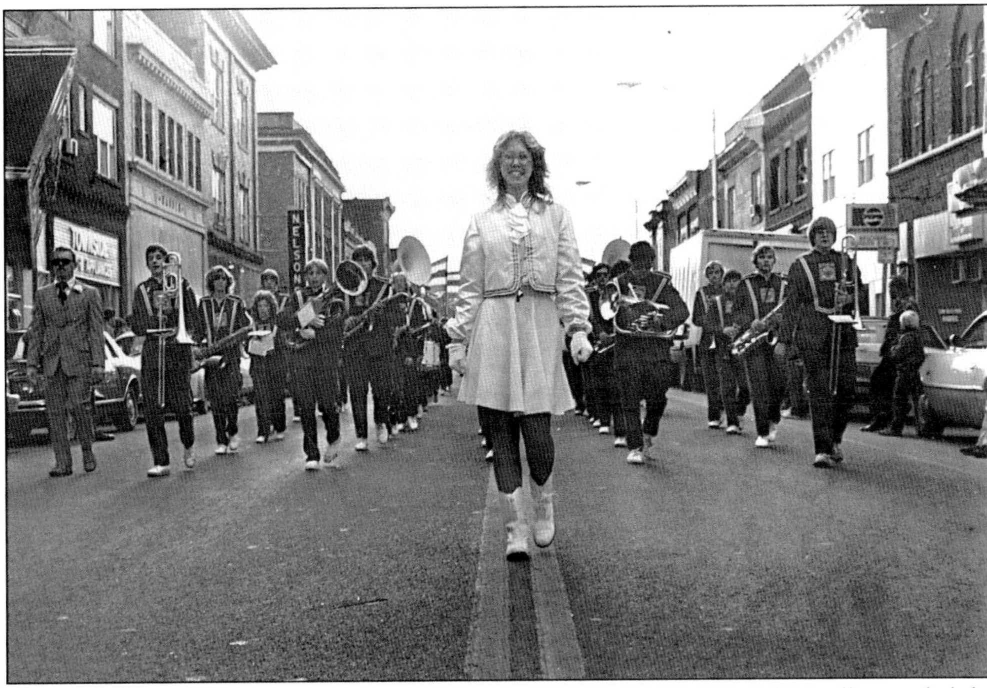

THE BIG PARADE. The annual Christmas parade down Mercer Street traditionally signaled the start of the Christmas season. (Courtesy of *Princeton Times* archives.)

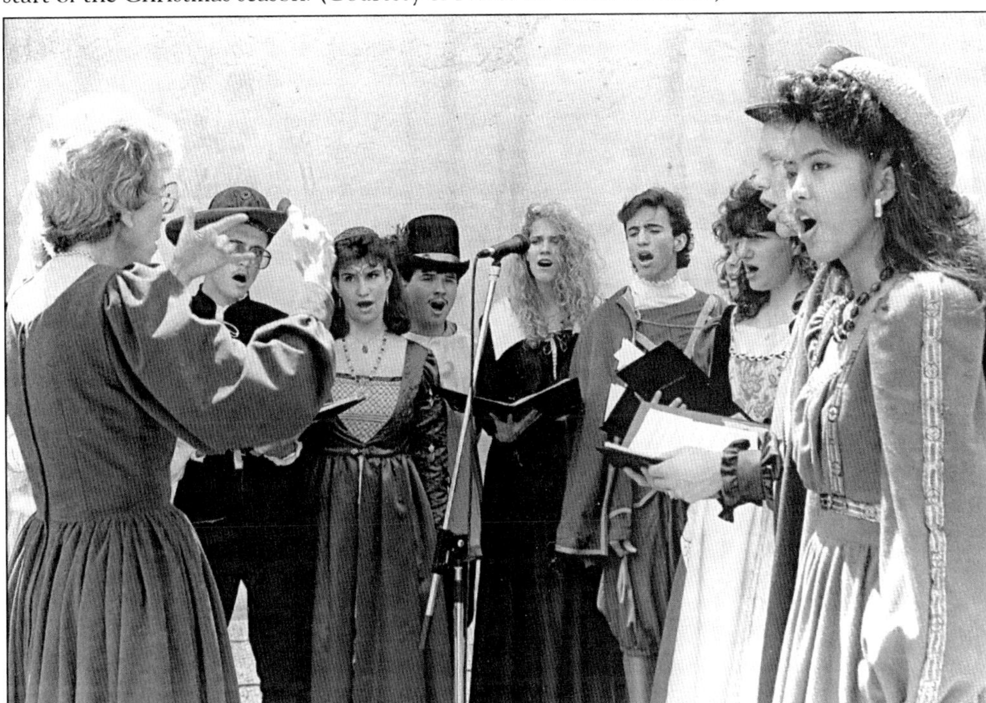

TRAVELING MADRIGALS. The Princeton Senior High School Madrigals remain one of the premier vocal ensembles of the region, regardless of the season. The group is shown under the direction of Linda Hawkins. (Courtesy of *Princeton Times* archives.)

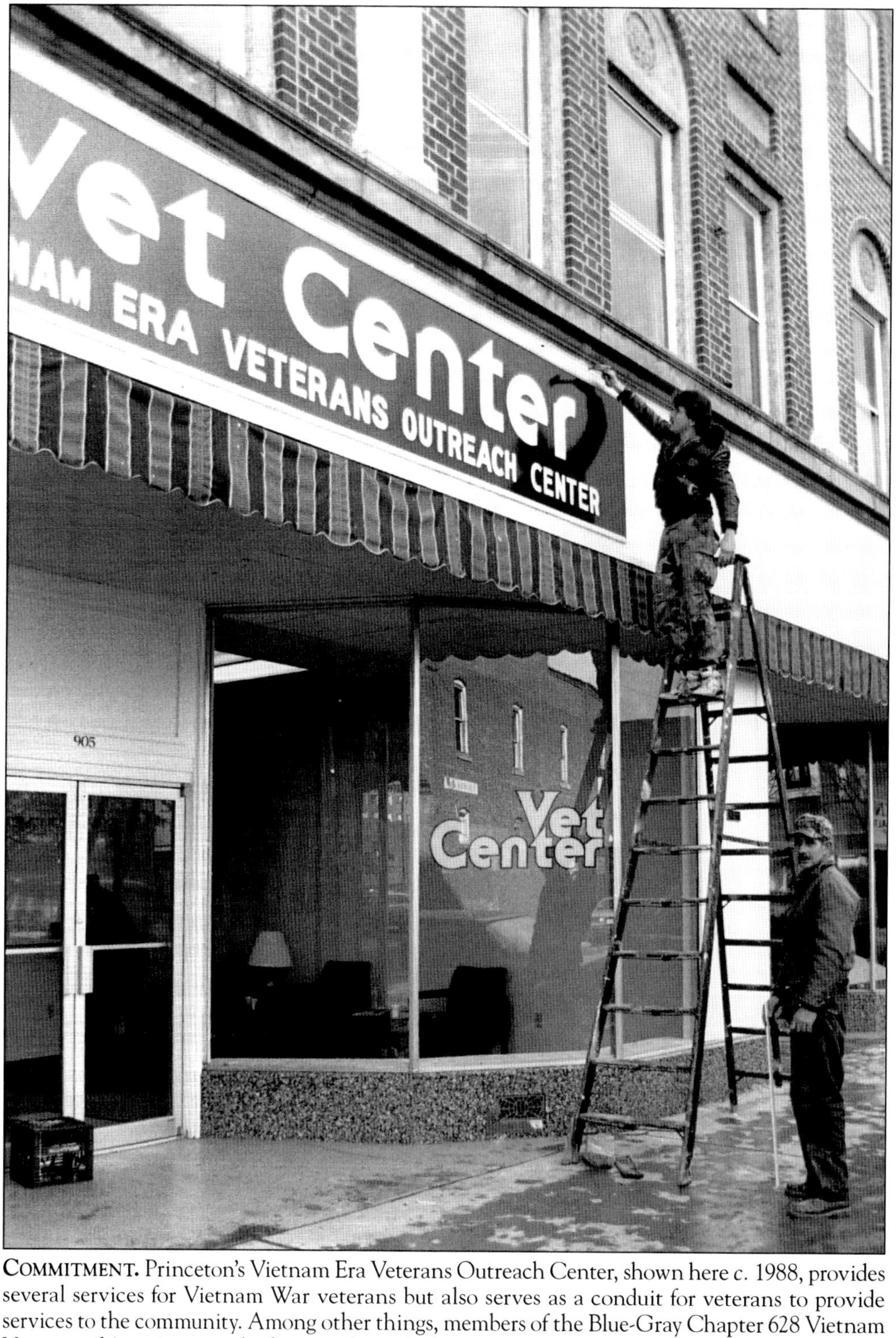

COMMITMENT. Princeton's Vietnam Era Veterans Outreach Center, shown here *c.* 1988, provides several services for Vietnam War veterans but also serves as a conduit for veterans to provide services to the community. Among other things, members of the Blue-Gray Chapter 628 Vietnam Veterans of America were the first people on the lines to give a sincere "Welcome home" to veterans of the Gulf War and, more recently, Operation Iraqi Freedom. (Photograph by Phil Farmer.)

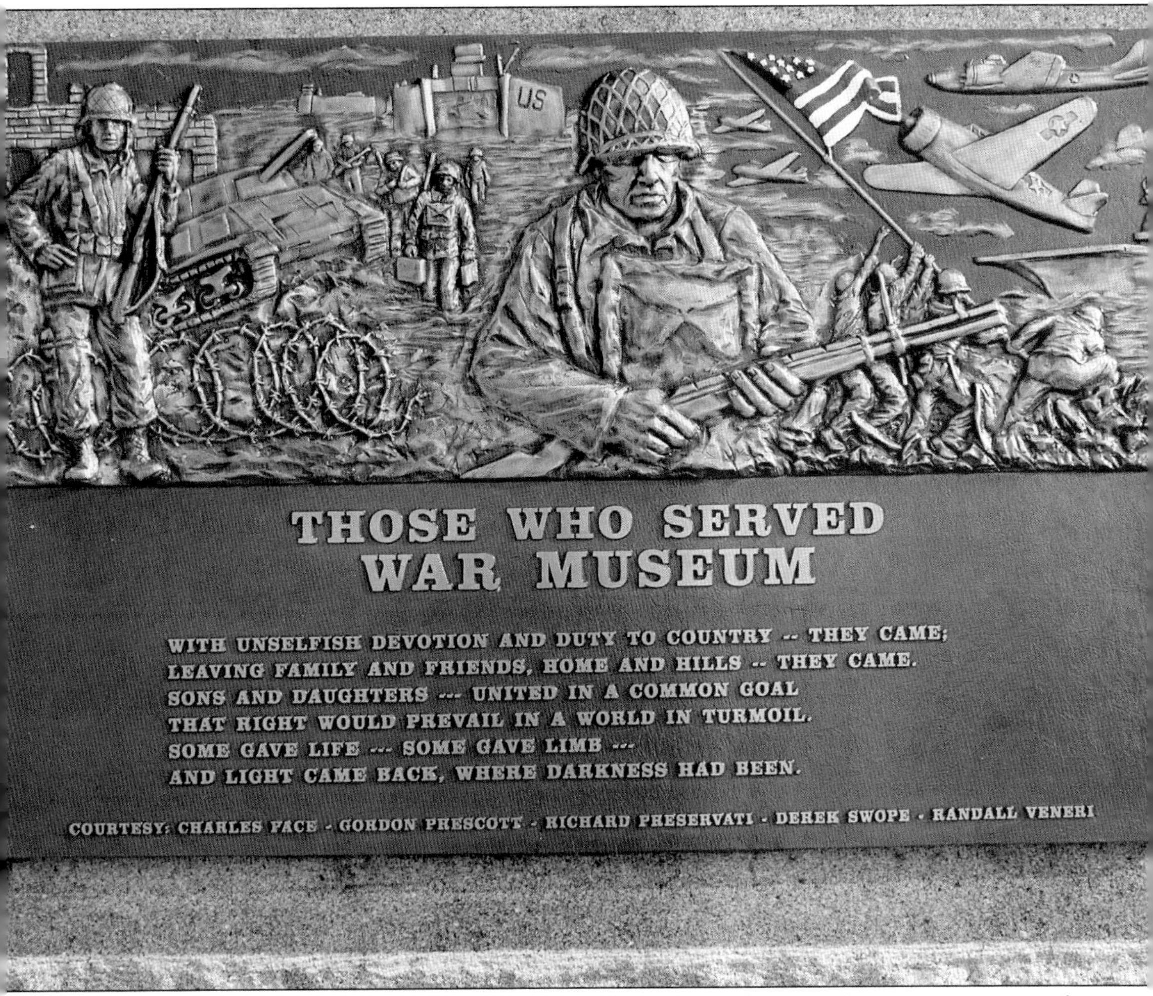

SERVICE AND SACRIFICE. Tony Whitlow, a former state senator and Mercer County assessor, started collecting some military equipment when he was serving as assessor and received permission from the Mercer County Commission to open a small museum in a small office in the old courthouse. He opened the museum in May 1999, and when others learned what Whitlow was doing, they started donating old uniforms, weapons, photographs, and other materials to his effort. The effort was so successful that the local veterans moved the museum to the Memorial Building, where this plaque is located. (Photograph courtesy of the Mercer County War Museum.)

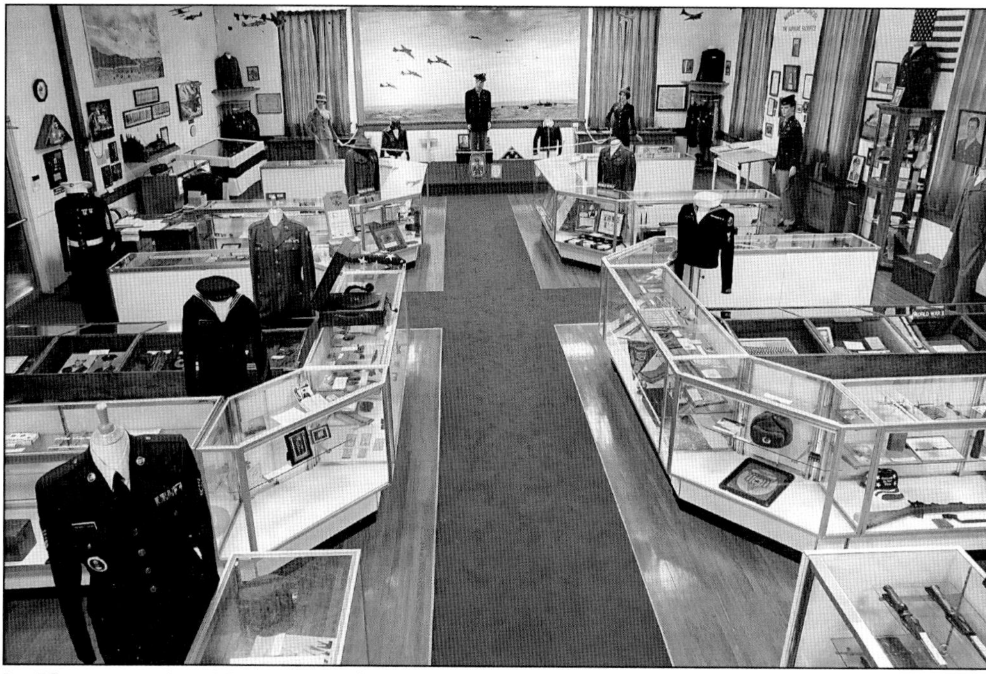

In Honor of All Veterans. The Mercer County veterans started building their collection to be more than a look at the men and women who served but also to show items from their personal lives, including letters to sweethearts, reading glasses, and other items that tend to make each story unique and personal. Tony Whitlow served in the Korean War, and a small display commemorating his service includes packaging of brand-name products he carried with him when he went to war. Volunteer veterans staff the museum from 10:00 a.m. to 4:00 p.m. Monday through Friday. (Courtesy of Mercer County War Museum.)

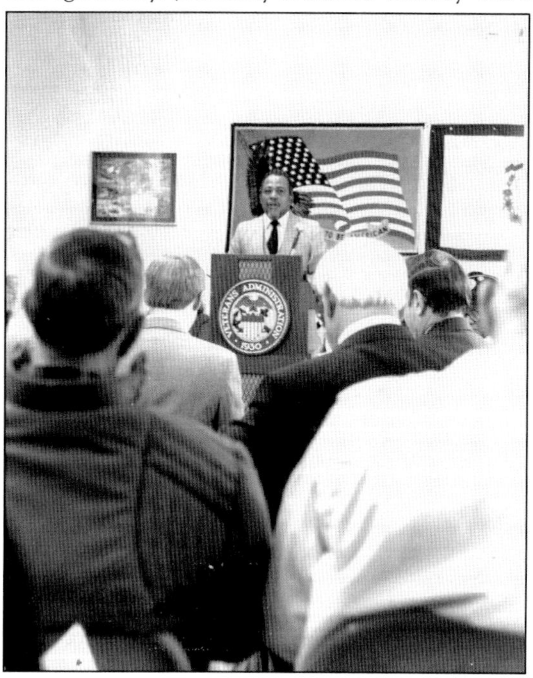

Man on a Mission. Sam Heflin came to Princeton when the veterans center was established in the late 1980s and has been serving veterans ever since. The center provides counseling to veterans but also offers a wide variety of outreach services that gives those who served opportunities to continue to serve the community. The Annual Veterans Dinner each Veteran's Day routinely attracts 700 to 800 people and includes the presentation of combat medals to soldiers, sailors, and marines who did not receive them when awarded due to uncontrollable circumstances. (Courtesy of *Princeton Times* archives.)

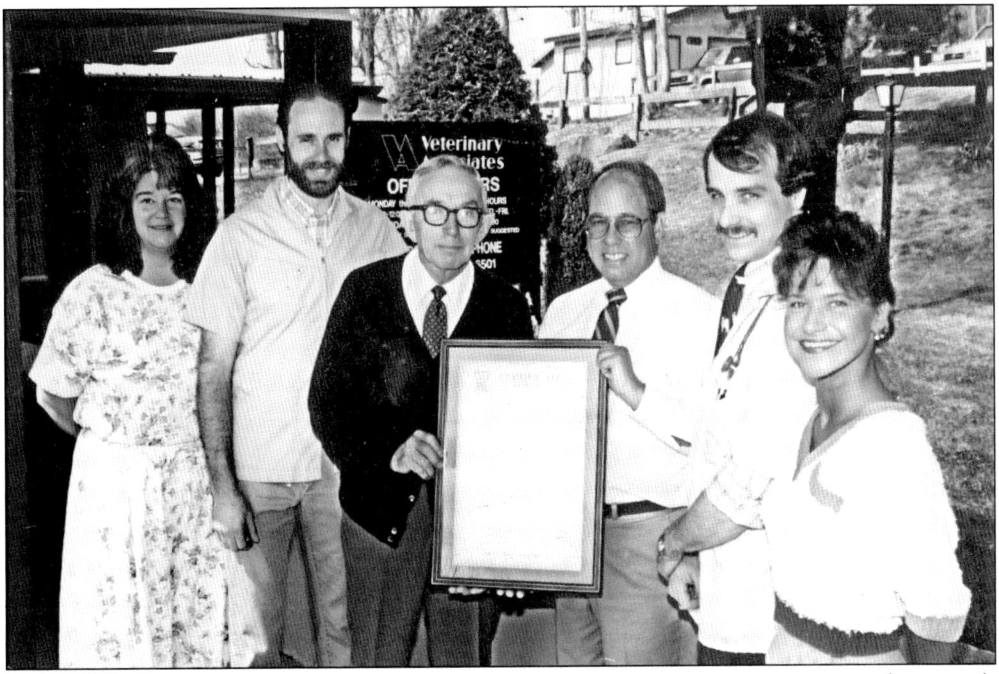

A SMALL WORLD AFTER ALL. Dr. James Bailey founded Veterinary Associates to serve the animals of the region and continued in that endeavor through a big part of the 20th century. From left to right are Sharon Welch, Dr. Gary S. Brown, Dr. Bailey, Dr. Bill Reynolds, Dr. William C. Streit, and Cricket Johnson. (Courtesy of *Princeton Times* archives.)

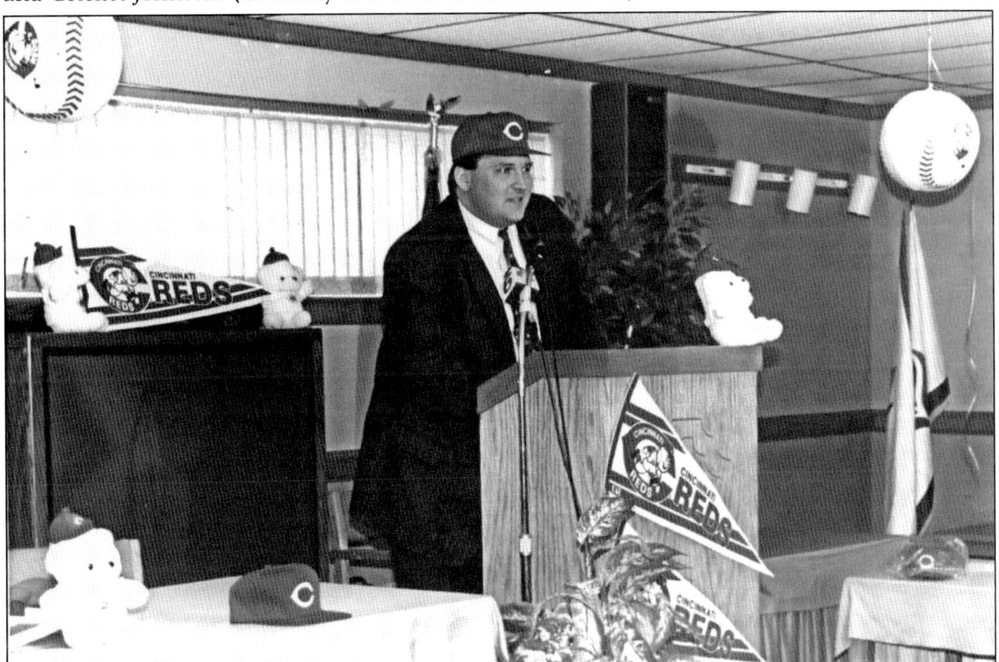

BIG RED MACHINE. Steve Schott of the Cincinnati Reds is shown here at a February 1991 press conference at the Mercer County Technical Education Center, when the Reds announced they would be joining forces with the Princeton Rookie League team. (Photograph by the author.)

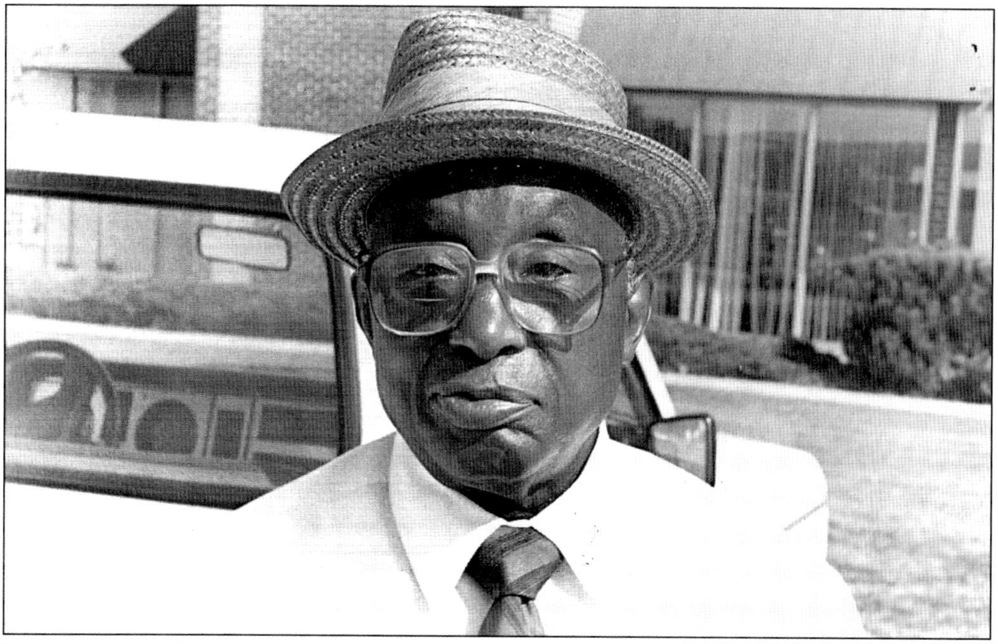

MAYOR MOON. Earlie Moon served many years on Princeton Town Council and served as the city's mayor. He was born in the Arista coal camp but attended school at Princeton's Dunbar Elementary–High School, a school that served African American students of Princeton from 1913 to 1967 but remained open as a gifted school from 1967 to 1971. During segregation, black students in Princeton attended elementary grades at Dunbar, then went to Genoa and Park Central High Schools in Bluefield to complete their secondary education. (Photograph by the author.)

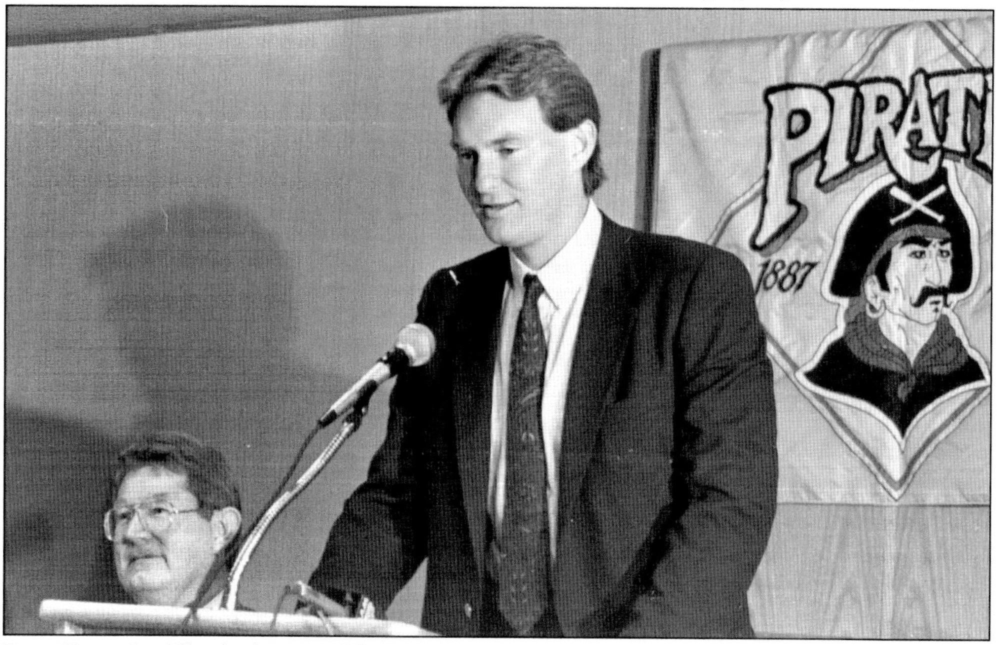

PLAY BALL. Jim Thrift, skipper of the Princeton Pirates, is shown here. For the past several years, the Princeton Appalachian League franchise has been affiliated with the Tampa Bay Devil Rays and are now the Princeton P-Rays. (Photograph by the author.)

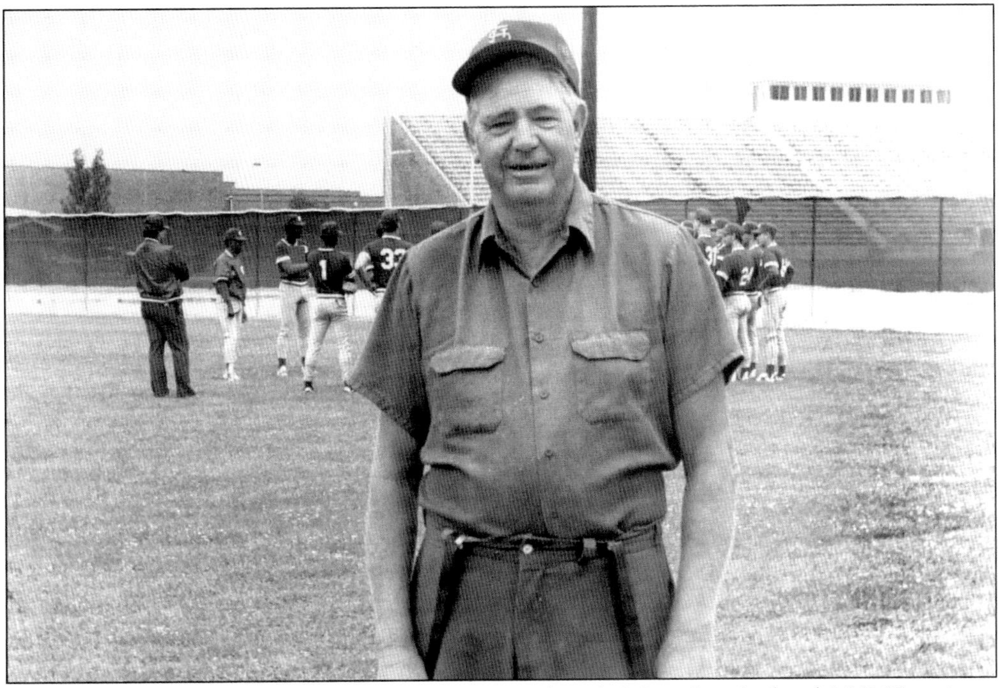

TRUE LOVE OF THE GAME. Princeton native Raymond "Lefty" Guard worked with H. P. Hunnicutt, Jim Thompson, Charlie Pace, and others to transform Hunnicutt Stadium into a first-class baseball park. Guard, a southpaw pitcher with a 93-mile-per-hour fastball, signed with the Boston Braves in 1941, served in World War II, where he was awarded the Bronze Star, and was traded to the St. Louis Cardinals in 1946, where he played with former Mountain State League star Stan Musial. Guard donated his time to bring baseball to the city in 1988 and continues to help P-Rays general manager Jim Holland. (Photograph by the author.)

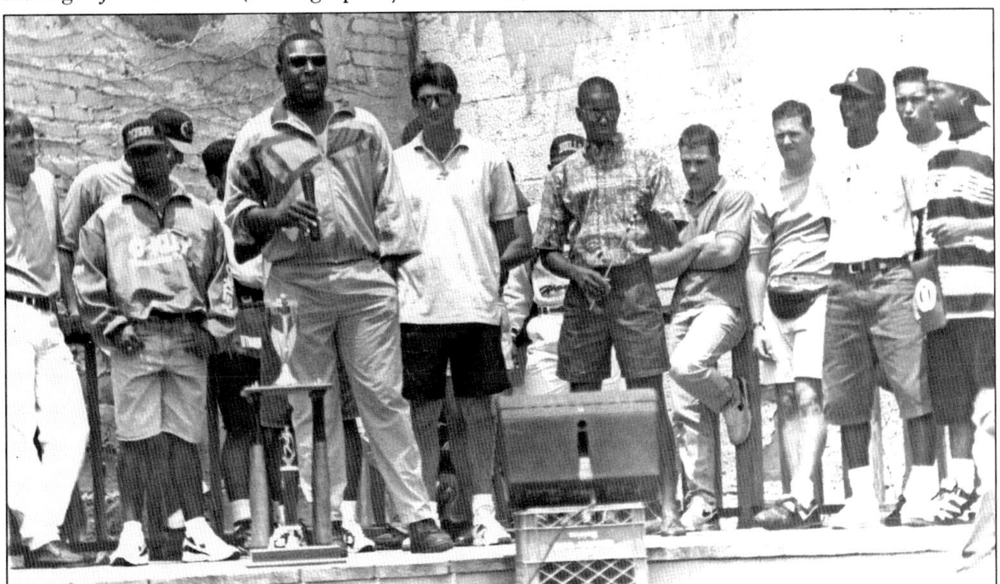

TEAM SPORT. Members of the Princeton Reds are shown here introducing themselves as part of the 1993 SummerFest activities. (Photograph by Evonda Archer.)

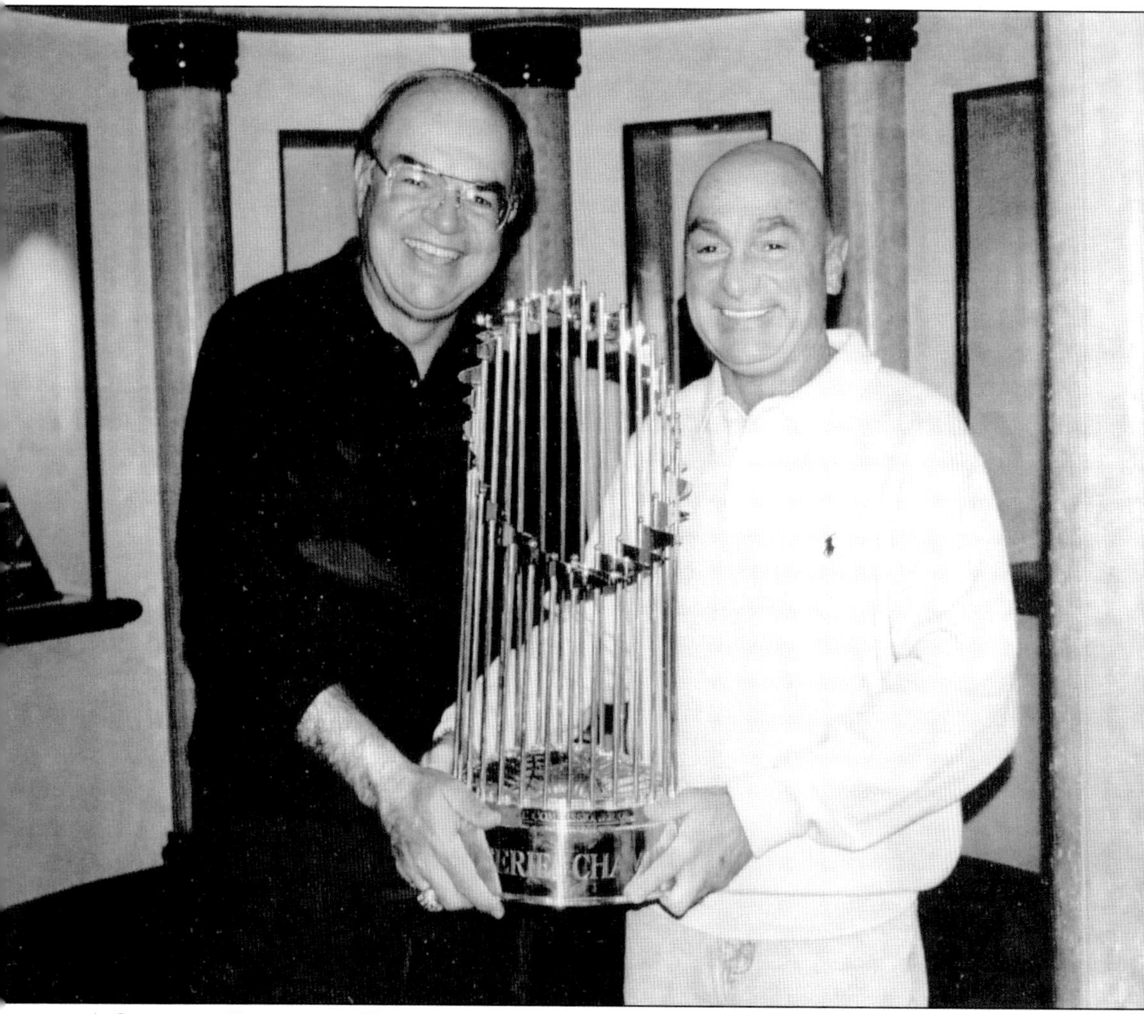

A COUPLE OF PRINCETON KIDS. Princeton brothers Ken (left) and Rick Kendrick are shown here holding the 2001 World Series trophy that the Arizona Diamondbacks earned with a series win over the New York Yankees. Ken Kendrick graduated from West Virginia University in 1965, started his career with IBM, and founded Datatel Inc. in 1968. He became a partner in the Diamondbacks in 1995, and he and his brother, Rick, both travel extensively to assess talented athletes. Rick maintains a base in Princeton and remains active in the community through his efforts with the Douglas Center, a popular activity center in the city. (Courtesy of Rick Kendrick.)

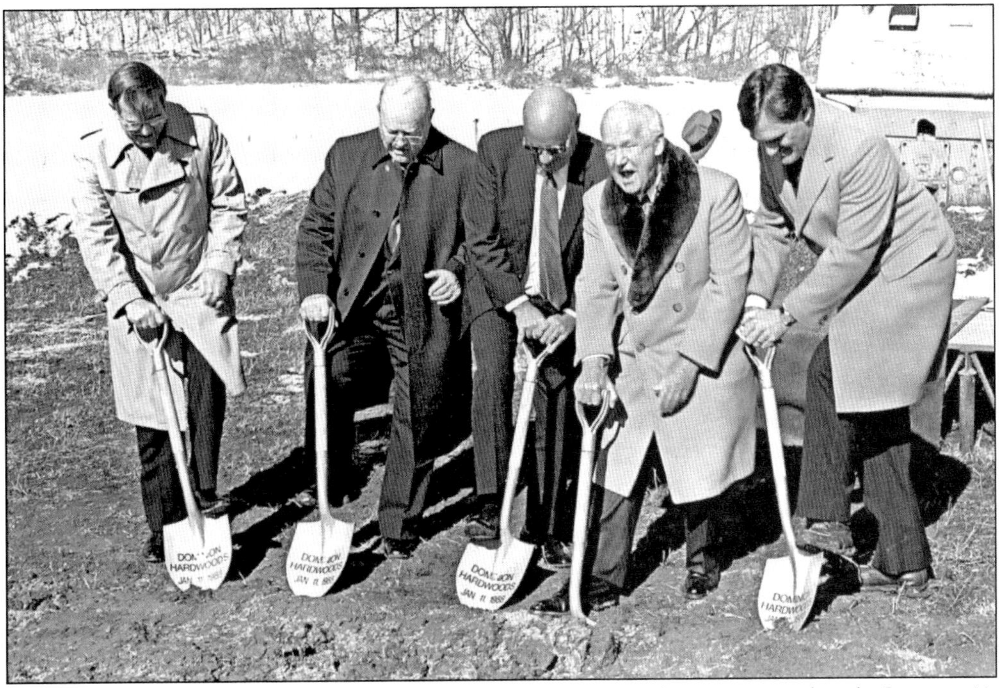

New Dominion. Former governor Arch Moore, second from right, participated in the January 11, 1988, groundbreaking ceremony for Dominion Hardwoods in Princeton. (Courtesy of *Princeton Times* archives.)

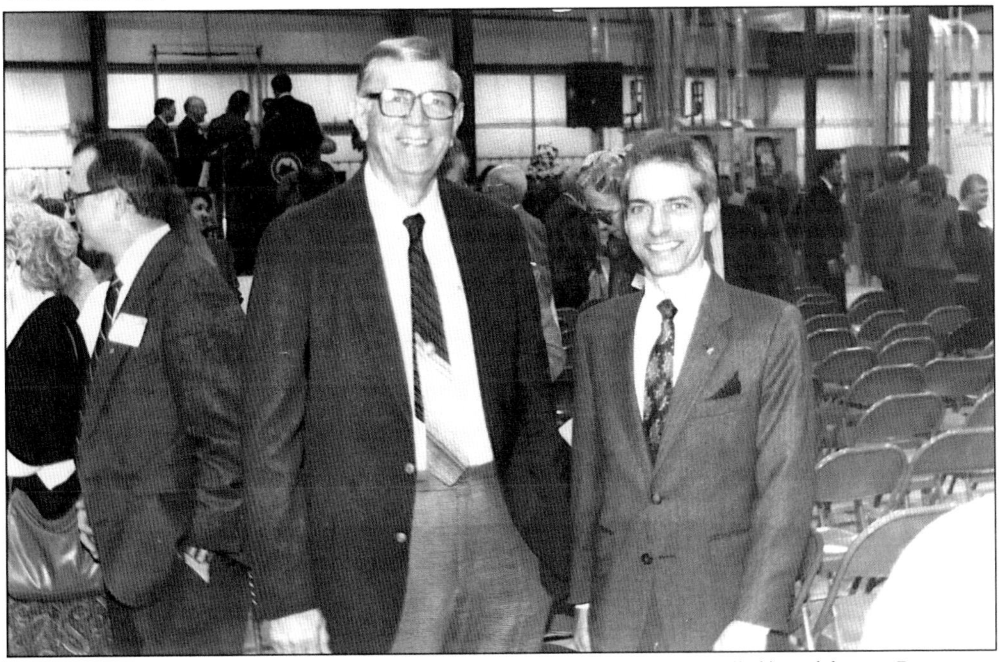

Two for the Show. Former Mercer County administrator Fred Parker (left) and former Princeton city manager Gary Christie are shown here at the Dominion Hardwoods grand opening. The plant was later acquired by California-based Pacific Encore and is now headquarters for Smith Services Inc. (Photograph by the author.)

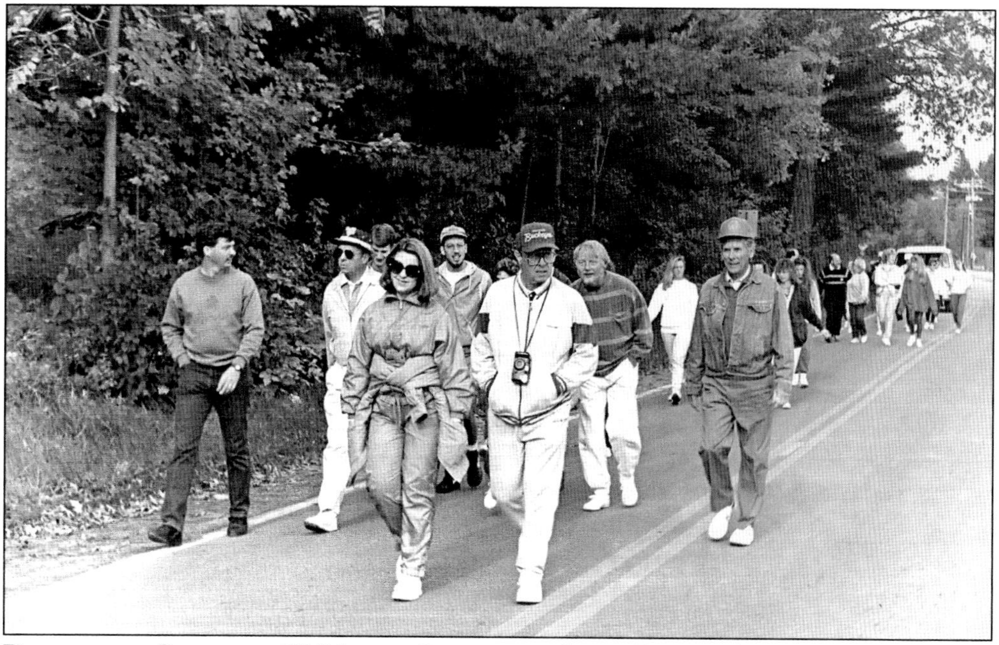

DOLLARS FOR SCHOLARS. Well-known Princeton architect E. T. "Ted" Boggess is shown here with a camera strapped around his neck as he participates in the October 21, 1992, Pam Hawkins/ Chuck Mathena Scholarship Walk-a-Thon. The annual event has raised many thousands of dollars in scholarship funds since 1989. Pam Hawkins was a victim of domestic violence in 1986, and Chuck Mathena died as a result of injuries he received in a car wreck in 1992. (Photograph by the author.)

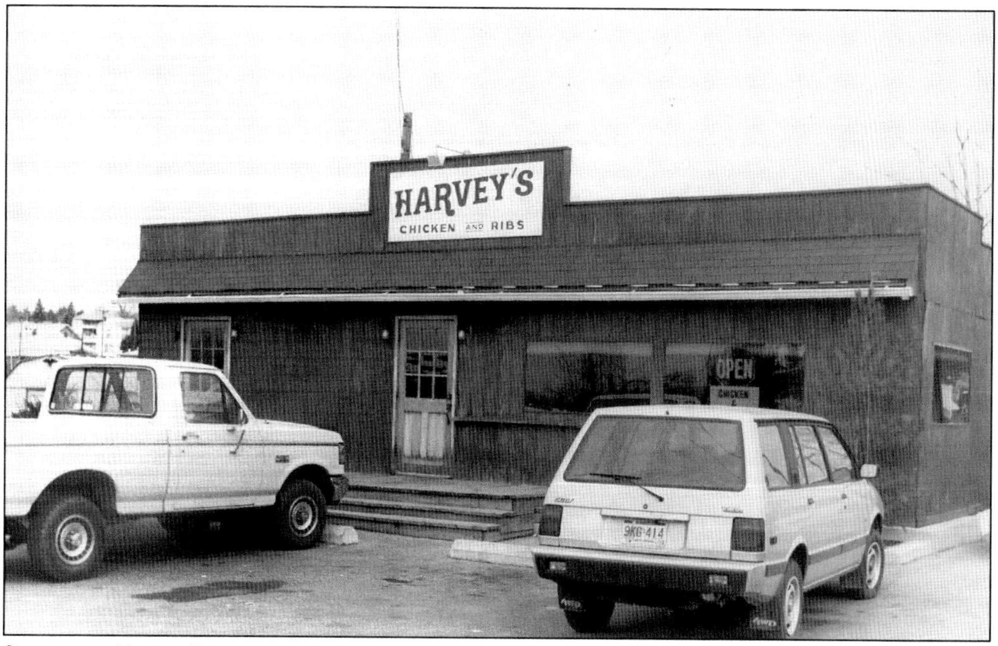

STAFFORD DRIVE INSTITUTION. Harvey's Chicken and Ribs was a popular Stafford Drive eatery. Harvey Phlegar, the business owner, was an advocate of his customers' right to have a cigarette before, during, and after their meals. (Photograph by Evonda Archer.)

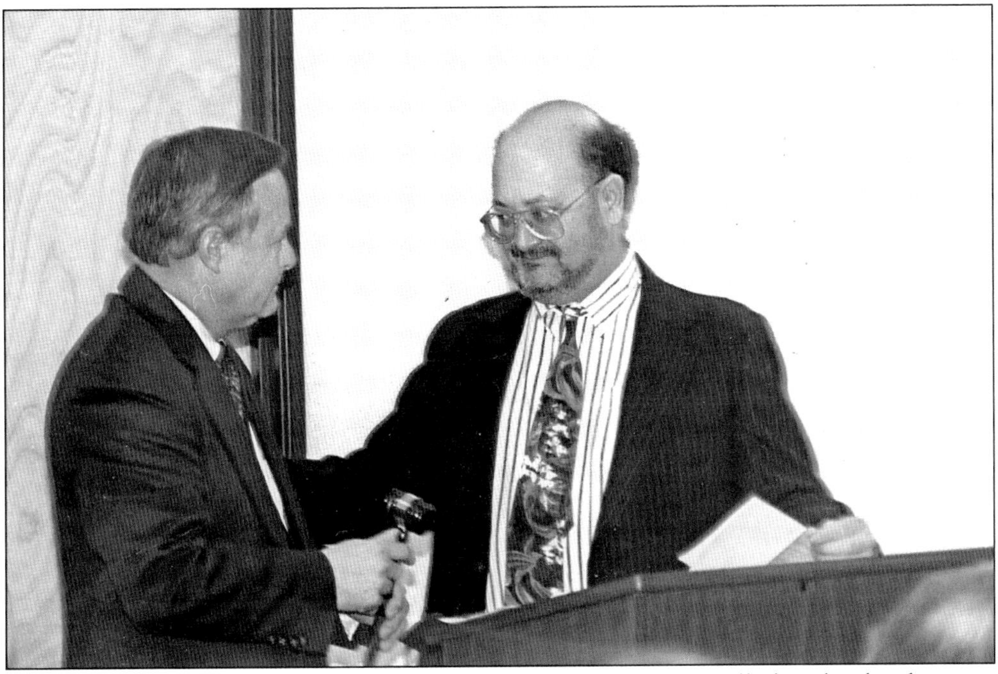

BY GEORGE. Former Princeton Community Hospital administrator Bill Shepphard is shown in this January 14, 1993, photograph with George Santon, then-executive director of the Princeton-Mercer County Chamber of Commerce. (Photograph by Evonda Archer.)

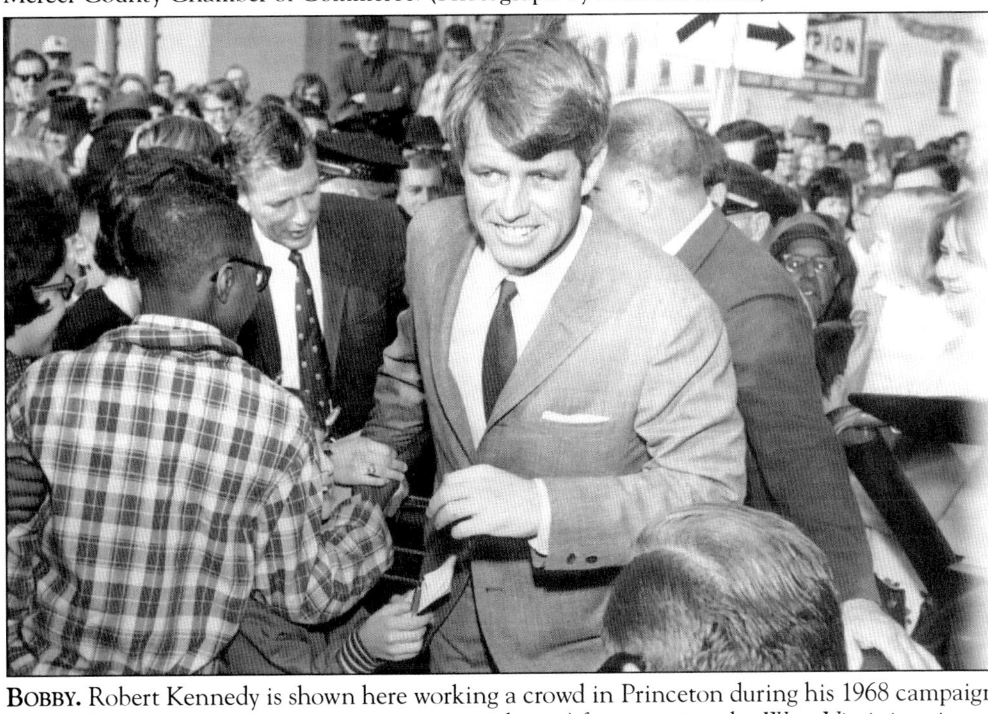

BOBBY. Robert Kennedy is shown here working a crowd in Princeton during his 1968 campaign for the Democratic party's nomination as president. After winning the West Virginia primary in May, Kennedy's life was cut short by an assassin's gun following his victory in the California primary. (Photograph by Vernon Fields.)

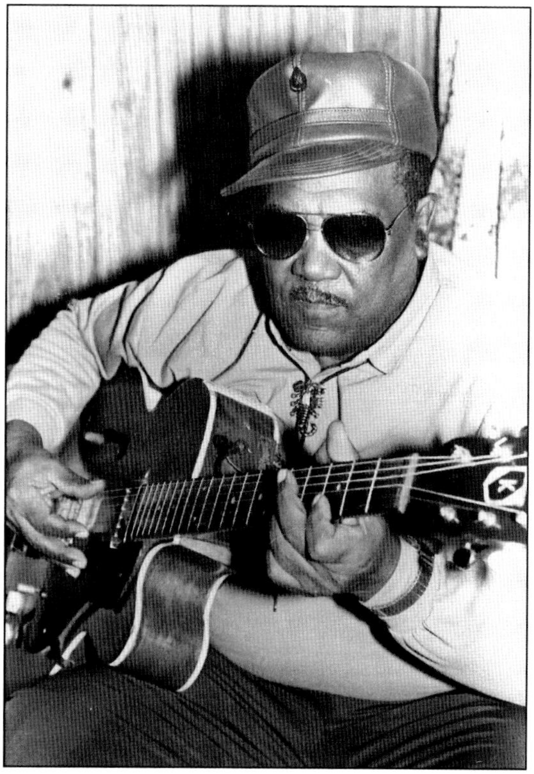

BLUES MAN. The incomparable Nat Reese has become nearly legendary in blues circles and still plays out a little. He came to Princeton in 1927 when his father got a job at the Virginian car shops and has stayed ever since. (Courtesy of *Princeton Times* archives.)

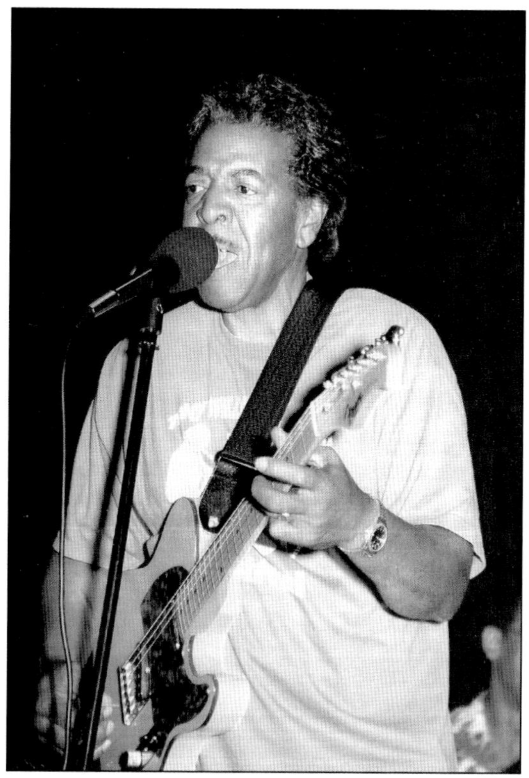

STILL JAMMIN'. Arnold "A. J." Palmer continues to thrill audiences with his smooth electric blues style, a style that he started perfecting as a high school student in the 1960s. Princeton's Palmer family has a long legacy of musical talent as well as a reputation for service to the city's faith-based community. (Photograph by Eric DiNovo.)

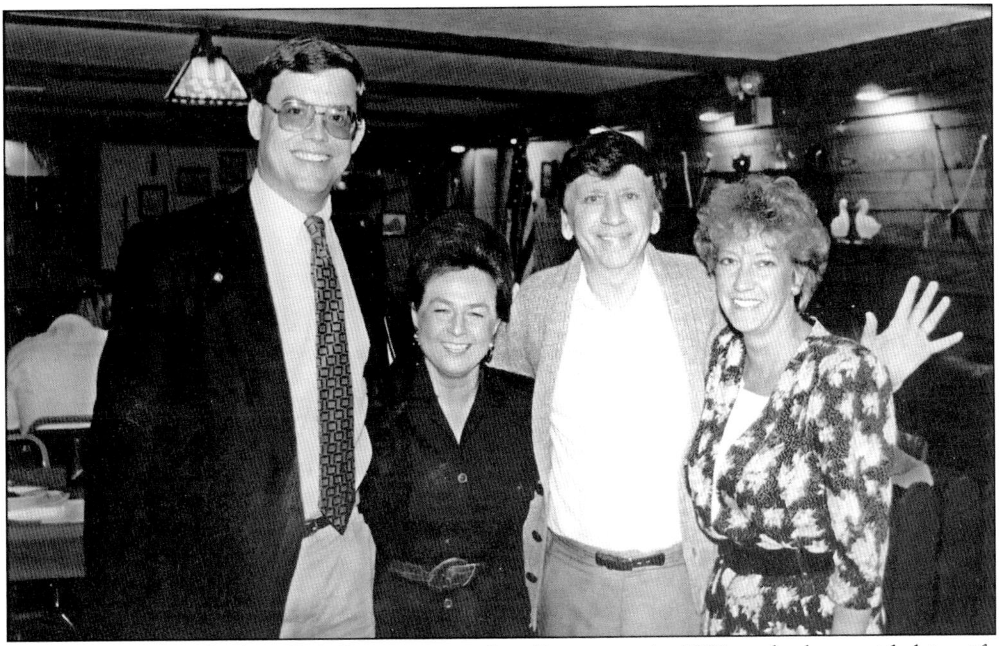

Ahoy Friends. The late Bob Denver moved to Princeton in 1991 and, along with his wife Dreama, became involved in community service. Denver is shown at a 1992 SummerFest event with Kirk Story, Elizabeth Osborne (on the left) Lynette Maxhimer (on the right). The Denver Foundation and Little Buddy Radio continues to serve the community following Denver's death on September 2, 2005. (Photograph by the author.)

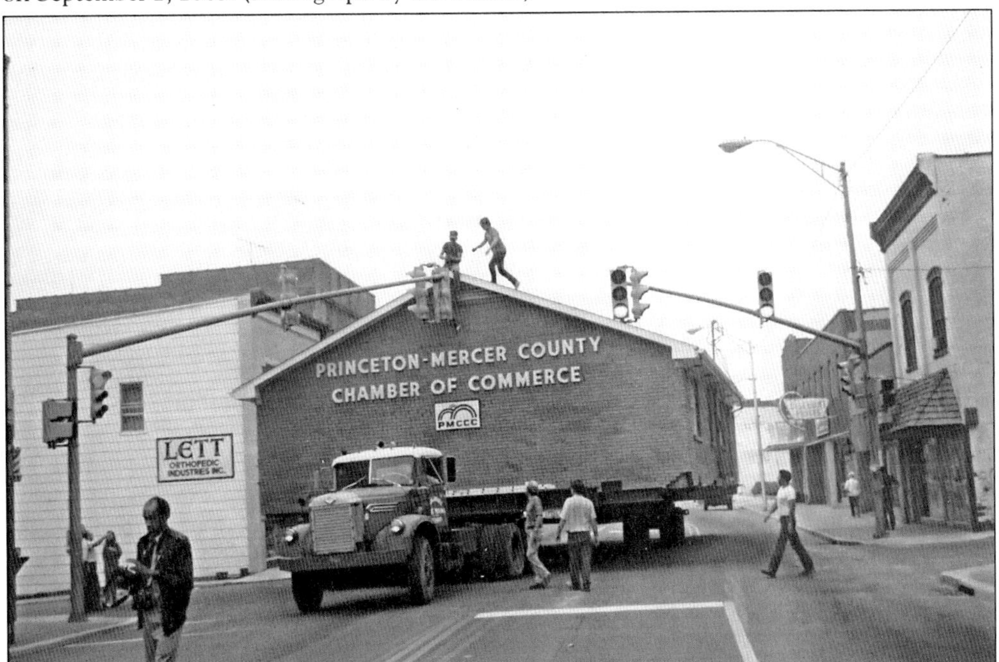

Around Town. The Princeton–Mercer County Chamber of Commerce is shown during the late 1980s on a move to a location near Interstate 77. The chamber returned to the city's oldest building, the McNutt house, in 2005. (Courtesy of *Princeton Times* archives.)

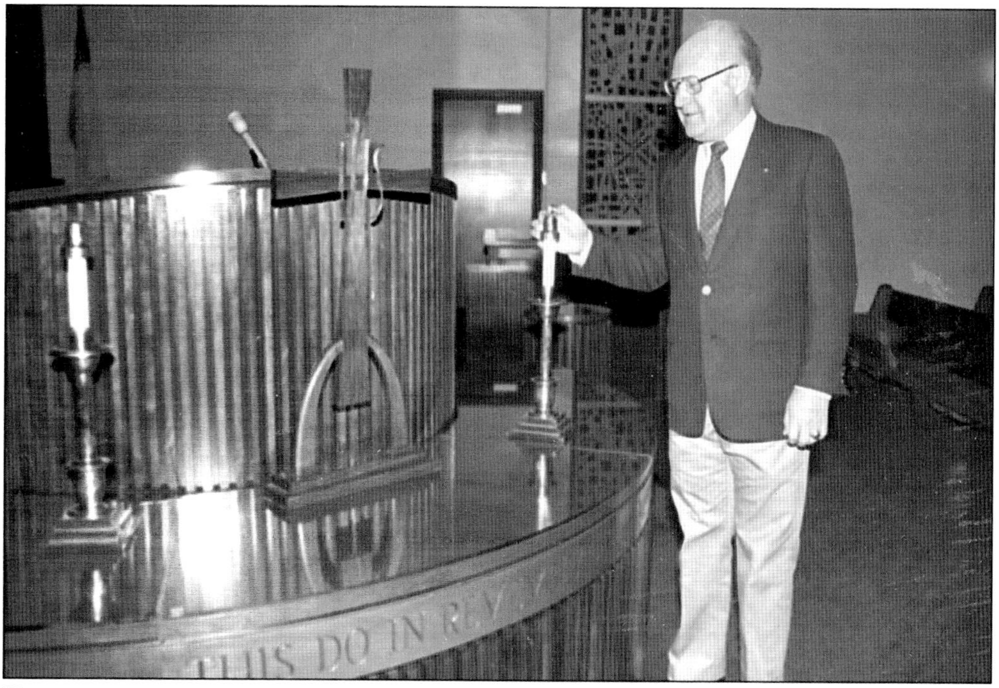

KEEPING THE FAITH. Rev. Harry Christie is shown here at the altar of the Princeton Presbyterian Church on Main Street. Christie and his wife, Ruth, served as both religious leaders and community leaders for many years. (Courtesy of *Princeton Times* archives.)

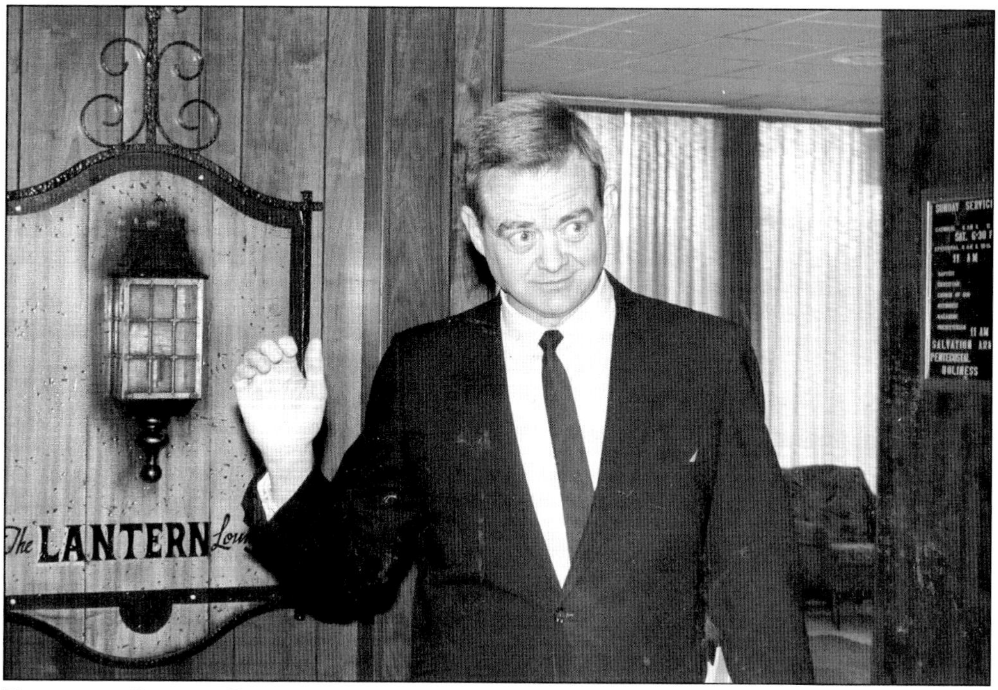

DEDICATED SERVICE. Former state senator Odell Huffman was a longtime advocate for Princeton throughout his career as a lawyer and through his commitment to public service. (Courtesy of *Princeton Times* archives.)

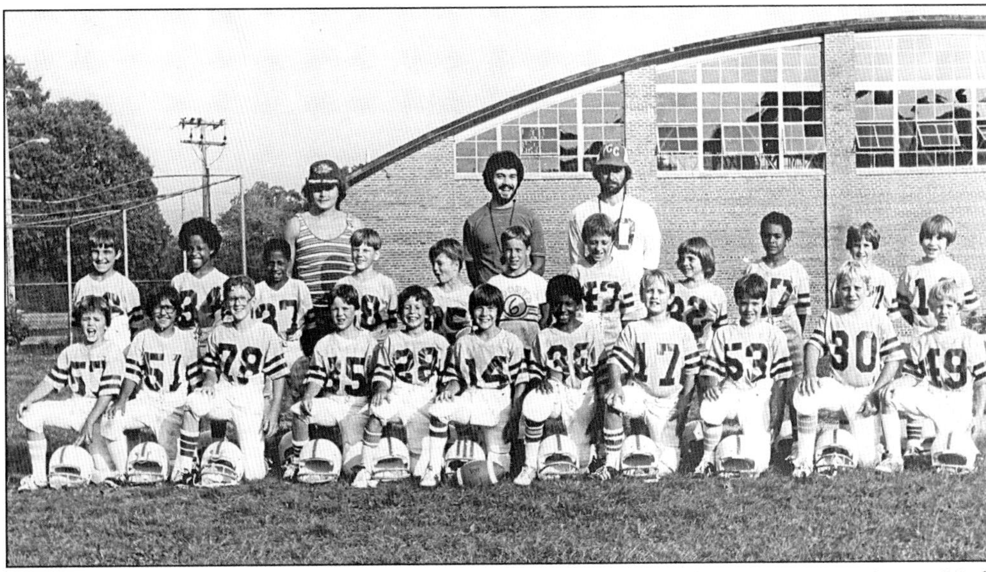

THE MOOSE TEAM. A youth football team is shown on their field near Princeton Junior High School. Pictured from left to right are (first row) Sarge Vines, Brent Logan, Brian Ridenour, Roy Catron, Douglas Csanyi, Kevin Graham, Troy Palmer, Troy Price, Kenny Tennant, Willy Greene, and Bill Reed; (second row) Frank Smith, Bobby Lindsay, Winky Hill Jr., Barry Tilley, John Keatley, Mark Rathell, Scott Greene, Billy Harmon, John Harmon, Erick Clark, and Kelly Joe Barker. Coaches from left to right are (standing) Gary Woodring, David Marquis, and Wayne Davidson. (Courtesy of *Princeton Times* archives.)

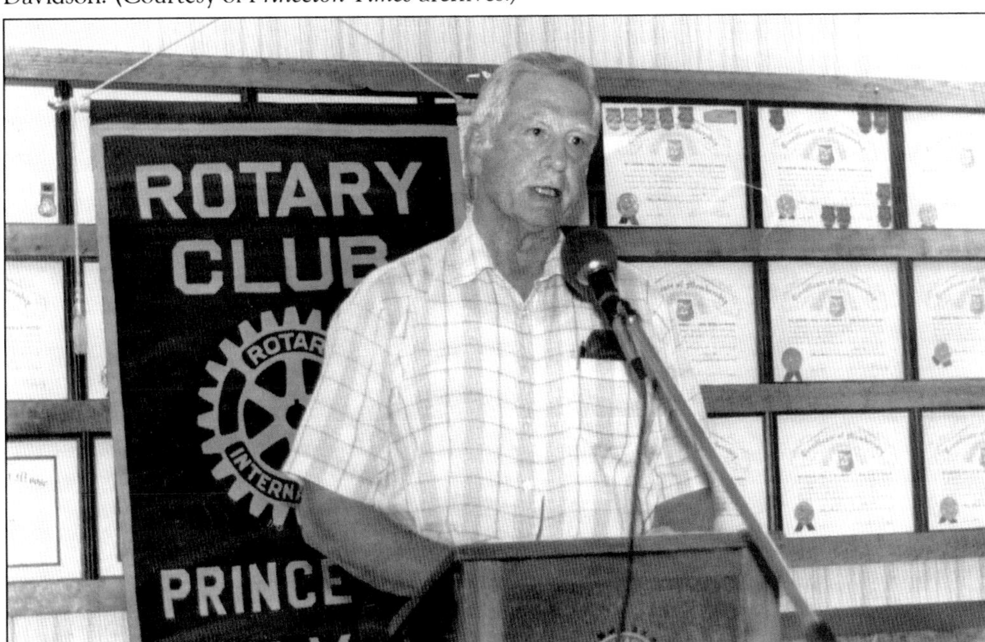

I LIKE IKE. Ira "Ike" Southern is shown speaking to the Princeton Rotary Club. Southern, a Princeton native, was in the U.S. Army and survived the Japanese attack on Pearl Harbor on December 7, 1941. He built a successful career in the radio communications industry and plays a pretty good banjo upon request. (Photograph by the author.)

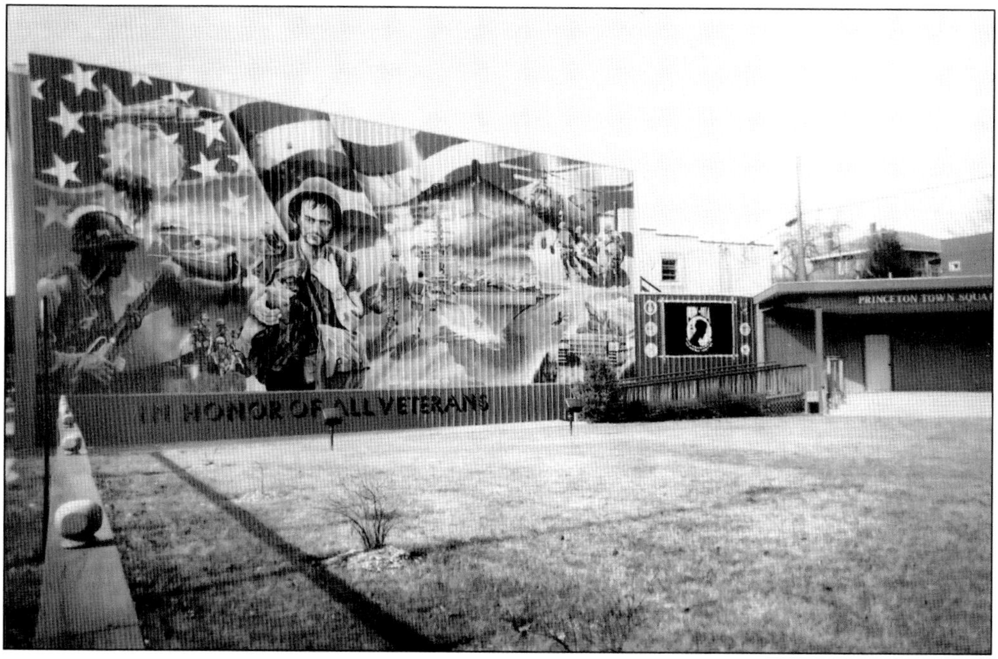

HONORING SERVICE. Tom Acosta and Elden Justice completed this mural "in honor of all veterans" in 2002 to complete the ambitious Princeton Town Square project. The lot was made vacant by an early-1980s fire that destroyed a popular nightclub, but volunteers transformed the site into a park that hosts concerts each Friday through the summer. (Photograph by the author.)

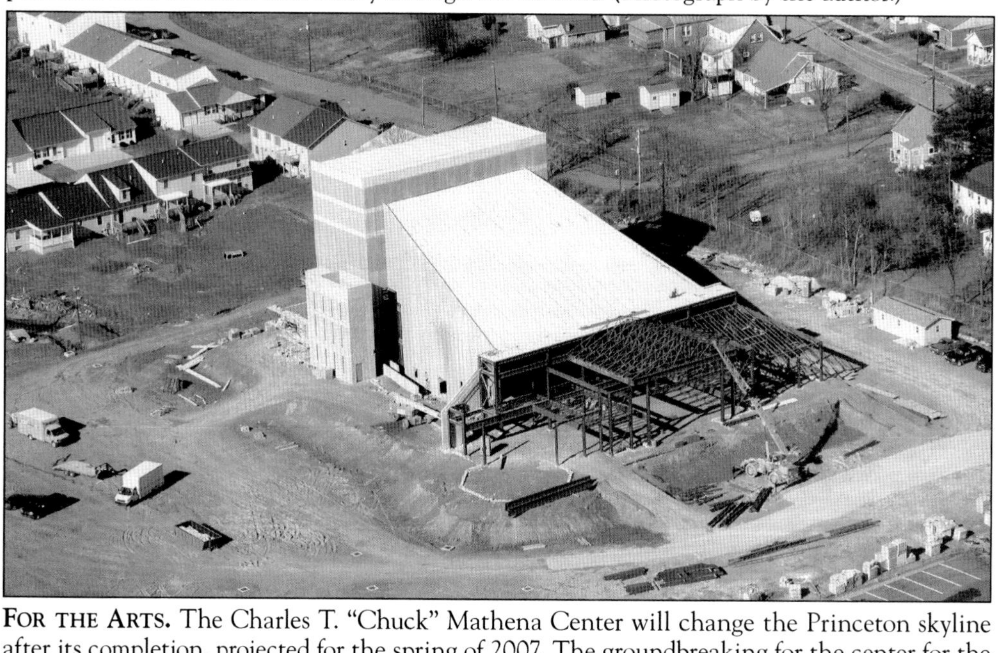

FOR THE ARTS. The Charles T. "Chuck" Mathena Center will change the Princeton skyline after its completion, projected for the spring of 2007. The groundbreaking for the center for the performing arts was on March 2, 2005. Chuck Mathena died in an automobile accident on March 11, 1992. From 1992 to 2005, his parents, Charlie and Marquita, and their family and friends raised $129,050 in scholarship funds given to local students and spearheaded the Mathena Center drive. (Aerial photograph by Mel Grubb.)

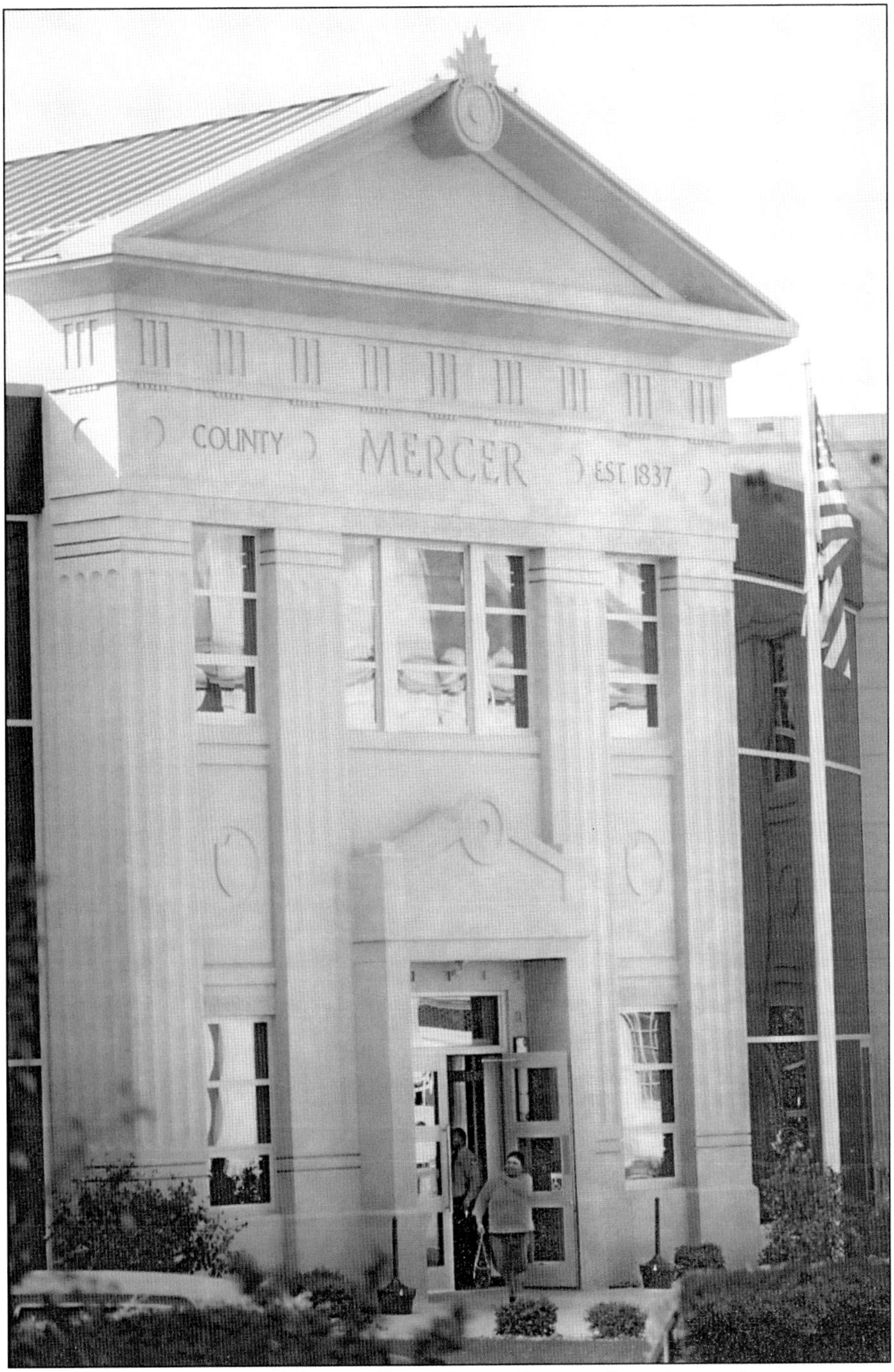

NEW LOOK. The long-awaited $5.5-million Mercer County Courthouse Annex project was dedicated on August 11, 2005, to provide much-needed space to accommodate the growth of county government. Architectural designers E. T. Boggess and Associates of Princeton worked to remain true to the work of Alex B. Mahood, who designed the existing courthouse that was dedicated on August 8, 1931. (Photograph by the author.)

ACKNOWLEDGMENTS

This is my fourth book in Arcadia Publishing's Images of America series, and each project gives me the opportunity to meet wonderful friends who know the history of their community and are willing to help others understand. My wife, Evonda Archer, has worked with me every step of the way through this project, and I appreciate her steadfast and unwavering support. These books are truly our joint projects.

Many people helped by providing images and insights about Princeton. My friends R. A. "Randolph" Belcher and his wife, Betty, not only gave me access to an incredible collection of E. R. Belcher's award-presentation photographs, but Betty also gave me a delicious spaghetti dinner. I spent several productive hours with John G. Waldron and got to know Bernard and Sheila Shorter. My friend Bill Carper helped me improve my understanding of Princeton, as did my friends Jo Anna and Ott Fredeking.

Many more friends, like Reed Wheby, Eileen Mooney, Billie Blankenship, Beulah Shrewsbury, Mel Grubb, David McNeil, Deb Griffith, Jim Wolfe, Darrell Bailey, Winfrey Shrewsbury, Rod Thorn, Ted Gillespie, Lynn Whitteker, Rick Kendrick, Judith B. Collins, Dick Copeland, Vernon Fields, Bill Looney, Huber Bailey, Bill Sherwood, Shirley Smith, Greg Morton, Eric Cole and the Pocahontas Land mapping department, Tony Whitlow, Bob Holroyd, Kim Scott, Todd Boggess, Eric DiNovo, Tammie Toler of the *Princeton Times*, Randy Deason and Tom Colley of the *Bluefield Daily Telegraph*, Elizabeth Osborne, and the Mercer County Historical Society, all contributed to the creation of this book.

I dedicated my last book to my wife, and I would like to dedicate this book to our children and their spouses, Dannie and Ann Morgan, Oscar and Coleen Martinez, and Tim and Adrienne Bickers.